James Sime, Edward Augustus Freeman

**History of Germany**

James Sime, Edward Augustus Freeman

**History of Germany**

ISBN/EAN: 9783337339029

Printed in Europe, USA, Canada, Australia, Japan

Cover: Foto ©ninafisch / pixelio.de

More available books at **www.hansebooks.com**

*Historical Course for Schools.*

# HISTORY

OF

# GERMANY.

By JAMES SIME, M.A.

London:
MACMILLAN AND CO.
1874.

[*The Right of Translation and Reproduction is reserved.*]

# PREFACE.

It is right for me to say that this volume of the series has been carefully revised by Mr. A. W. Ward, than whom England can supply no one better fitted to deal with matters of German History of all dates. Mr. Ward must be understood as guaranteeing only the general accuracy of the narrative. In other respects the volume falls under the same rules as its fellows. As I have already said in the Preface to the History of England, this volume, like the others, is strictly the work of its own author, subject only to the requirement of a general agreement in form and treatment with the other volumes of the series.

EDWARD A. FREEMAN.

Somerleaze, Wells,
 *February 11th, 1874.*

# CONTENTS.

## CHAPTER I.
ANCIENT GERMANY . . . . . . . . . . . . . . 1

## CHAPTER II.
THE GERMANS AND THE ROMANS . . . . . . . . 11

## CHAPTER III.
THE FRANKS . . . . . . . . . . . . . . . . 16

## CHAPTER IV.
THE MAYORS OF THE PALACE, AND DUKES OF THE FRANKS . . . . . . . . . . . . . . . . 27

## CHAPTER V.
CHARLES THE GREAT . . . . . . . . . . . . 32

## CHAPTER VI.
THE LATER KARLINGS . . . . . . . . . . . 37

## CHAPTER VII.
THE SAXON EMPERORS . . . . . . . . . . . 43

## CHAPTER VIII.
THE FRANCONIAN EMPERORS . . . . . . . . . 58

## CHAPTER IX.
THE HOHENSTAUFEN EMPERORS . . . . . . . . . 72

## CHAPTER X.
SOVEREIGNS OF DIFFERENT HOUSES . . . . . . . 94

## CHAPTER XI.
THE LUXEMBURG EMPERORS . . . . . . . . . . 104

## CHAPTER XII.
EMPERORS OF THE HOUSE OF AUSTRIA . . . . . 113

## CHAPTER XIII.
CHARLES V.—THE REFORMATION . . . . . . . . 128

## CHAPTER XIV.
THE THIRTY YEARS' WAR . . . . . . . . . . . 146

## CHAPTER XV.
WARS WITH FRANCE . . . . . . . . . . . . . 162

## CHAPTER XVI.
FREDERICK THE GREAT . . . . . . . . . . . . 172

## CHAPTER XVII.
THE FALL OF THE EMPIRE AND OF THE KINGDOM
OF GERMANY . . . . . . . . . . . . . . 193

## CHAPTER XVIII.
THE STRUGGLE WITH BUONAPARTE. . . . . . . 204

## CHAPTER XIX.
REVOLUTIONARY MOVEMENTS . . . . . . . . . 223

## CHAPTER XX.
RECENT EVENTS. . . . . . . . . . . . . . . 243

# CHRONOLOGICAL TABLE.

|  | B.C. |
|---|---|
| Cæsar defeats Ariovistus | 58 |
| Drusus in Germany | 12-9 |

|  | A.D. |
|---|---|
| Defeat of Varus | 9 |
| Arminius and Germanicus | 14-16 |
| The Marcomannic War | 167-180 |
| Confederations of tribes formed | 200-300 |
| Chlodwig | 482-511 |
| Battle of Testri | 687 |
| Charles Martel defeats the Arabs | 731 |
| Winfrith appointed to the See of Mainz | 745 |
| Pippin the Short crowned King | 753 |
| Charles the Great | 768-814 |
| Charles is crowned Emperor | 800 |
| Lewis the Pious | 814-840 |
| Treaty of Verdun | 843 |
| The later Karlings | 843-911 |
| Conrad I. | 911-918 |
| The Saxon Emperors | 919-1024 |
| Henry I. | 919-936 |
| Henry I. defeats the Hungarians | 933 |
| Otto I. | 936-973 |
| Otto I. defeats the Hungarians | 955 |

# CHRONOLOGICAL TABLE.

|  | A.D. |
|---|---|
| Otto I. is crowned Emperor | 962 |
| Otto II. and Otto III. | 973-1002 |
| Henry II. | 1003-1024 |
| The Franconian Emperors | 1024-1125 |
| Conrad II. | 1024-1039 |
| Conrad II. is crowned King of Burgundy | 1032 |
| Henry III. | 1039-1056 |
| General Peace proclaimed | 1043 |
| Henry IV. | 1056-1106 |
| Henry IV. at Canossa | 1077 |
| Henry V. | 1106-1125 |
| The Concordat of Worms | 1122 |
| Lothar of Saxony | 1125-1137 |
| The Hohenstaufen Emperors | 1137-1254 |
| Conrad III. | 1137-1152 |
| Frederick Barbarossa | 1153-1190 |
| Humiliation of Henry the Lion | 1180 |
| Henry VI. | 1190-1197 |
| Kings Philip and Otto | 1197-1215 |
| Frederick II. | 1215-1250 |
| The Teutonic Order conquers Prussia | 1230-1260 |
| Conrad IV. and William of Holland | 1250-1256 |
| The Interregnum | 1256-1273 |
| Rudolf of Habsburg | 1273-1291 |
| King Adolf | 1292-1298 |
| Albert of Austria | 1298-1308 |
| Henry VII. | 1308-1313 |
| Lewis IV. | 1314-1347 |
| Frederick the Fair | 1314-1330 |
| Battle of Morgarten Pass | 1315 |
| The First Electoral League | 1338 |
| The Luxemburg Emperors | 1347-1437 |
| Charles IV. | 1347-1378 |

# CHRONOLOGICAL TABLE.

|  | A.D. |
|---|---|
| The Golden Bull | 1356 |
| Wenceslaus | 1378-1400 |
| Battle of Sempach | 1386 |
| Rupert of the Palatinate | 1400-1410 |
| Sigmund | 1410-1437 |
| The Council of Constanz | 1414-1418 |
| John Huss burned | 1415 |
| Frederick of Hohenzollern receives the Mark of Brandenburg | 1415 |
| The Council of Basel | 1431-1443 |
| Albert II. | 1438-1439 |
| Frederick III. | 1440-1493 |
| Peace of Thorn | 1466 |
| The Archduke Maximilian marries Mary of Burgundy | 1477 |
| Maximilian I. | 1493-1519 |
| Perpetual Public Peace proclaimed | 1495 |
| The Imperial Chamber established | 1495 |
| Maximilian I. takes the title of "Emperor Elect" | 1508 |
| Germany divided into Circles | 1512 |
| Charles V. | 1520-1556 |
| Beginning of the Reformation | 1517 |
| Luther before the Diet of Worms | 1521 |
| Albert of Brandenburg becomes Duke of Prussia | 1525 |
| The Archduke Ferdinand becomes King of Bohemia and Hungary | 1526 |
| The Augsburg Confession | 1530 |
| Religious Peace of Nürnberg | 1532 |
| The Schmalkaldic War | 1546 |
| Battle of Mühlberg | 1547 |
| The Interim | 1548 |
| The Elector Maurice marches against Charles V. | 1552 |
| Henry II. of France seizes Metz, Verdun, and Toul | 1552 |

## CHRONOLOGICAL TABLE.

|  | A.D. |
|---|---|
| Religious Peace of Augsburg | 1555 |
| Abdication of Charles V. | 1556 |
| Ferdinand I. | 1556-1564 |
| Maximilian II. | 1564-1576 |
| Rudolf II. | 1576-1612 |
| The Letter of Majesty | 1609 |
| The Elector of Brandenburg becomes Duke of Prussia | 1611 |
| Matthias | 1612-1619 |
| Beginning of the Thirty Years' War | 1618 |
| The Winter King | 1619 |
| Defeat of the Bohemians | 1620 |
| The Danish War | 1624-1629 |
| Wallenstein raises an army | 1626 |
| Gustavus Adolphus in Germany | 1630-1632 |
| Battle of Lützen | 1632 |
| Murder of Wallenstein | 1634 |
| Ferdinand III. | 1637-1657 |
| Peace of Westphalia | 1648 |
| Leopold I. | 1658-1705 |
| Treaty of Welau | 1657 |
| Battle of Fehrbellin | 1675 |
| Peace of Nimwegen | 1679 |
| Strassburg seized by Lewis XIV. | 1681 |
| The Turks besiege Vienna | 1683 |
| Peace of Ryswick | 1697 |
| Frederick I., King of Prussia | 1701-1713 |
| The War of the Spanish Succession | 1701-1714 |
| Battle of Blenheim. | 1704 |
| Joseph I. | 1705-1711 |
| Charles VI. | 1711-1740 |
| Peace of Rastatt | 1714 |
| Peace of Baden | 1714 |

# CHRONOLOGICAL TABLE.

|  | A.D. |
|---|---|
| Frederick William I. of Prussia | 1714-1740 |
| Maria Theresa | 1740-1780 |
| Frederick II. of Prussia | 1740-1786 |
| The First Silesian War | 1740-1742 |
| Charles VII. | 1742-1745 |
| The Second Silesian War | 1744-1745 |
| Francis I. | 1745-1765 |
| The Seven Years' War | 1756-1763 |
| Treaty of Hubertusburg | 1763 |
| Joseph II. | 1765-1790 |
| The First Partition of Poland | 1773 |
| League formed by Frederick II. | 1785 |
| Frederick William II. of Prussia | 1786-1797 |
| Leopold II. | 1790-1792 |
| First War of the Revolution | 1792 |
| Francis II. | 1792-1806 |
| The Second Partition of Poland | 1793 |
| The Third Partition of Poland | 1795 |
| Peace of Basel | 1795 |
| Peace of Campo Formio | 1797 |
| Frederick William III. of Prussia | 1797-1840 |
| Congress at Rastatt | 1798 |
| War with France | 1799 |
| Battle of Hohenlinden | 1800 |
| Peace of Lunéville | 1801 |
| Buonaparte seizes Hanover | 1803 |
| Battle of Austerlitz | 1805 |
| Peace of Pressburg | 1805 |
| The Confederation of the Rhine | 1806 |
| Francis II. resigns the Imperial Crown | 1806 |
| Battle of Jena | 1806 |
| Peace of Tilsit | 1807 |
| Battle of Wagram | 1809 |

|  | A.D. |
|---|---|
| Peace of Schönbrunn | 1809 |
| Prussia and Russia declare war against France | 1813 |
| Austria and Sweden join the Allies | 1813 |
| Battle of the Katzbach | 1813 |
| Battle of Leipzig | 1813 |
| First Peace of Paris | 1814 |
| The Congress of Vienna | 1814 |
| Battle of Waterloo | 1815 |
| Second Peace of Paris | 1815 |
| The German Confederation | 1815 |
| A Customs Union proposed | 1828 |
| Death of Francis I. of Austria | 1835 |
| Ferdinand I. of Austria | 1835-1848 |
| Frederick William IV. of Prussia | 1840-1861 |
| Popular risings in Vienna and Berlin | 1848 |
| The National Assembly in Frankfurt | 1848 |
| War with Denmark | 1848-1850 |
| The Imperial title offered to Frederick William IV. | 1849 |
| Constitutional government set up in Prussia | 1850 |
| The Frankfurt Diet restored | 1851 |
| William I. of Prussia | 1861 |
| War with Denmark | 1863 |
| Alliance between Prussia and Italy | 1866 |
| Battle of Königgrätz | 1866 |
| Peace of Prague | 1866 |
| The North German Confederation | 1866 |
| Customs Parliament meets in Berlin | 1868 |
| France declares war against Prussia | 1870 |
| Battle of Sedan | 1870 |
| Surrender of Metz | 1870 |
| William I. of Prussia declared Emperor in Germany | 1871 |
| Surrender of Paris | 1871 |
| Peace of Frankfurt | 1871 |

# HISTORY OF GERMANY.

## CHAPTER I.

### ANCIENT GERMANY.

*Geographical character of Germany* (1)—*central position; relations of the Germans to their neighbours* (2)—*the words "Deutsch" or "Dutch," and "German"* (3)—*High and Low Dutch* (4)—*the country in the time of Tacitus* (5)—*ancient German Tribes* (6)—*the Ingaevones, Istaevones, and Herminones* (7)—*character of the people* (8)—*Nobles, Freemen, Slaves, and Liti* (9)—*the Wergeld* (10)—*Marriage; position of the wife; authority of the father; uncles; quarrels of freemen adopted by relatives* (11)—*Villages; the land; Hundreds* (12)—*Chiefs; the Comitatus* (13)—*meetings of the Village, the Hundred, and the Tribe* (14)—*all freemen armed; their armour; the Herzog; mode of attack* (15)—*the German religion* (16).

1. **Geographical character of Germany.**—Germany, or *Deutschland*, occupies a large part of central Europe. Speaking roughly, it now reaches from the *Alps* to the *Baltic* and the *North Sea*, and from the valleys of the *Rhine* and the *Maes* to the *Danube* as far as the *March* and the *Mur*, and to the *Prosna* and the *Lower Niemen*. The country is mountainous in the south, hilly in the centre, and flat in the north, where it forms part of the great plain which takes in the whole of north-eastern

Europe. The western part of this plain takes in the country between the *Teutoburg Wood* and the *North Sea*. As it passes eastwards it widens till it reaches from the *Erz* and *Riesen mountains* to the *Baltic*. A part of South Germany slopes towards the east, and is watered by the *Danube;* but the general slope of the country is towards the north. Among the rivers flowing northwards are the *Rhine*, the *Ems*, the *Weser*, the *Elbe*, the *Oder*, and the *Vistula*.

2. **Central position of Germany.**—Germany has varied very much in extent at different times. This is due partly to the fact that it has no clearly-marked natural boundaries on the east and west, but chiefly to the peculiarity of its position. It is the central country of Europe. Being surrounded by most of the leading nations of the Continent, the Germans have been involved, more than any other people, in the general history of Europe. Of all their neighbours, the Scandinavians are most nearly allied to the Germans. Both are branches of the *Teutonic* race. But the Germans are also connected, although not so closely, with the other surrounding peoples. All, if we except the *Magyars* or *Hungarians*, who are *Turanians*, belong to the great *Aryan* family.

3. **Names of the people.**—The Germans call themselves *Deutschen*. We formerly used the word *Dutch* in the same wide sense, but now usually confine it to the people of *Holland*. *Deutsch* or *Dutch* is the modern form of *Theotisc* (*Theod, people*), which first came into use in the ninth century. The word *German* is probably of *Celtic* origin. It is believed to have been first applied to a particular tribe, and then to the race to which the tribe belonged.

4. **High and Low Dutch.**—The Germans or *Dutch* are divided into two great groups, the *High* and the *Low*. The *Low Dutch* live by the mouths of the rivers flowing into

the North Sea, the *High Dutch* in the inland and mountainous parts of Germany. They are branches of the same people; but they differ a good deal in character and customs, and, above all, in language. On the Continent the only Low-Dutch language which remains the organ of an important living literature is spoken in *Holland.* The educated classes of the country, or group of countries, which we now call Germany, speak and write High-Dutch.

5. **Ancient Germany.**—Our chief authority for the condition of ancient Germany is the "*Germania*" of *Tacitus*, written in the year 98 A.D. At that time the greater part of the country was covered by forests, in which were bears, wolves, buffaloes, elks, and other wild animals. The climate was damp and foggy; and in winter the cold seems to have been keener, and to have lasted longer than at present. The soil was in many places marshy; but much of it was very fertile. There were many flocks and herds, generally of a small breed.

6. **German Tribes.**—The ancient Germans were divided into many different tribes. These sometimes united among themselves for purposes of attack or defence; but they were politically independent, each being separated from the others by tolerably well-marked boundaries. On the right bank of the Rhine, beginning with the country now called *Hessen* and passing northwards, there were, besides various others, the *Chatti*, the *Tencteri* and *Usipetes*, the *Sicambri*, the *Marsi*, and the *Bructeri*. The *Frisians*, *Chauci*, and *Saxons* occupied the coasts from the Rhine to the Elbe. The territory of the *Cherusci*, one of the bravest of German tribes, took in the *Harz mountains* and the country around as far as the *Aller*, the *Weser*, the *Werra*, the *Elbe*, and the *Saal*. The country from the Danube and the Middle Rhine northwards to the Baltic was held by tribes

connected closely enough to be known by the common name of the *Suevi*. First among the Suevi were the *Semnones*, stretching from the southern part of what is now *Brandenburg* to the *Riesen mountains*. The *Longobardi*, or, as they were afterwards called, the *Lombards*, were settled on the banks of the *Lower Elbe*. The *Marcomanni* were neighbours of the Chatti, between the *Rhine*, the *Main*, and the *Danube*; and further to the south-east were the *Quadi*. There were other Suevic tribes; but it is these with whom history has most to do. It was long believed that the *Goths* were the original stock from which all Germans had sprung; but they held to other Germans merely the relation of sister tribes, and their language is more nearly akin to the Low than to the High German. They occupied the banks of the *Lower Vistula*. The *Vandals*, *Burgundians*, and *Rugii*, all kindred tribes, were scattered to the west of the Vistula, along the shores of the Baltic. The Gothic tribes soon passed altogether out of German history, and had probably begun even in Tacitus' time to separate from their kinsmen. It must not be forgotten that at an early period various German tribes crossed the Rhine in search of new settlements. At the time of *C. Julius Cæsar* a large part of the left bank was held by Germans, among whom the *Ubii* were distinguished. The *Batavians*, who are said to have sprung from the Chatti, held the island formed by the two branches of the Lower Rhine.

7. **Groups of Tribes.**—These tribes did not call themselves by any common name; but, according to Tacitus, three great groups were recognised—the *Ingaevones*, the *Istaevones*, and the *Herminones*. The first took in all the tribes on the coasts of the North Sea, the second those holding the Rhine country, and the third those in the centre of Germany. These groups were believed to have

sprung from the three sons of *Mannus*, the first man, the son of the god *Thuisto*. The division had no political importance; but it had probably some real meaning, for it reappears in another form in later history.

**8. Character of the people.**—The Germans were generally tall and strong. They could be fierce and cruel; but they were brave, truthful, simple in their manners, and hospitable. They celebrated in songs the great deeds of their forefathers, and were usually ready to die rather than give up freedom. Although an agricultural people, the occupations they most delighted in were war and hunting. Their chief faults were indolence, drunkenness, and excessive gambling. They left the tilling of the fields and all other peaceful work as much as possible to women and to men incapable of bearing arms.

**9. Classes of men.**—The ancient Germans, like other Aryan peoples, were divided into two great classes, the *nobles*, and the *common freemen*. The former were the *Eorls*, the latter the *Ceorls* of the ancient *English*. The nobles were usually richer than the freemen, but their position did not altogether depend on their wealth. What their special rights and privileges were, we do not know; but they were held in high esteem, and took a foremost place in public life. The freemen formed the great body of the people. Each was an independent member of the community, and enjoyed equal rights with his fellows. Both freemen and nobles had *slaves*. This class consisted for the most part of prisoners of war and their offspring, and of those condemned to slavery on account of some crime. They were usually well treated; but they were the absolute property of their masters, and had no redress against injustice. They were not allowed, under any circumstances, to bear arms. Between the freemen and the slaves was a peculiar class, consisting partly of freedmen, and called *Liti*.

The Liti were in no sense any one's property, and they had certain rights which they could enforce; but they had no share in the political life of the community. They could not possess land. They could only hold it of some master, with whom they were obliged to share the produce. They were thus neither freemen nor slaves, but a class apart.

10. **The Wergeld.**—If a noble, a freeman, or one of the Liti was killed, the murderer was not put to death. He had to pay a fine, which was in later times called the *Wergeld*. The amount of the Wergeld varied amongst different tribes; but the Wergeld of a noble was always greater than that of a freeman, as a freeman's was greater than that of one of the Liti.

11. **The Family.**—The ancient Germans did not marry till their physical and mental powers were fully developed. The bridegroom did not exactly purchase the bride; but on the day of their marriage he brought her a valuable gift, which she kept as her own property. The wife was subject to the husband; but her position was not a degraded one. She was her husband's companion and friend, and often went with him on distant warlike expeditions. She was expected to know the use of arms, and was usually brave and virtuous. The clan was not, in the time of Tacitus, the foundation of society; but family relations were of great importance. The father had supreme authority over his children. He had even the power, in extreme cases, of putting them to death. Uncles, especially on the mother's side, were looked up to with deep respect. When a freeman died, his children were protected by their relatives, until they were able to defend themselves. A freeman's quarrels were always taken up by his relatives; and if he was killed, it was their duty to see that the Wergeld, which was divided amongst the family, was paid.

**12. Villages and Hundreds.**—There were no cities in ancient Germany. In some parts of the country every freeman lived apart with his family on his own land; but the great majority lived in *villages*. These villages were made up of a number of huts, each hut standing apart from the rest, surrounded by a piece of ground. The land around a village originally belonged to the community, and much of it remained common property; but from an early period grants of land had been made to individuals, and the number of those who held land as their private property always tended to increase. An undefined number of villages formed what was called a *Hundred*. Whether the *Gau* was a name for the entire land of a tribe, or was merely a division taking in several Hundreds, is uncertain. Perhaps the name did not arise till a later period. At all events, the Hundred was the really important division, for traces of it are to be found among all German peoples.

**13. Chiefs. The Comitatus.**—Every village and Hundred had its own *Chief*, elected by the freemen. Higher than the chiefs of the Hundreds and villages was the chief of the tribe, appointed in the same way. Some tribes had *Kings;* but even Kings were elected, although always from some particular noble family believed to have sprung from the gods. The chiefs of the Hundreds formed what Tacitus calls the *princes* of a tribe, and acted as a *Council* to the King or other supreme chief. By far the most important right of a chief was the power to form a *Comitatus* or *Gefolge*—that is, to gather round him a body of men devoted to his service. The princes vied with each other in having large numbers of followers. The men swore to be always faithful to their lord; and to be untrue to this oath was thought the worst possible crime. In return for their services, the chief provided his men with war-horses, armour, and food; and if the tribe was not at war, he often gave them fresh opportunities of distinguishing themselves by taking part in the wars of other tribes.

14. **Meetings of the people.**—Important as was the position of the chiefs in ancient Germany, their power was comparatively limited. Above all chiefs were the *Meetings of the people.* Even the village had its Meeting; but the really important Meetings were those of the Hundred and of the tribe. These Meetings were not, like modern Parliaments, representative. All freemen had a right to attend them. The Meetings of the village and of the Hundred did not concern themselves with the affairs of the tribe. These came before the Meeting of the whole people. It was in this general Meeting that the chiefs were elected—not only the King or other chief of the tribe, but the chiefs of the various Hundreds. Here also the young freeman received from his father or some prince the arms which were the symbol that he had attained to a position of independence in the tribe. All difficult cases of justice were decided by the Meeting of the tribe; it also declared war and concluded peace, and sanctioned the occasional distant expeditions of the chiefs with their followers. When questions of unusual difficulty were to come before the Meeting, they were discussed beforehand by the King or other chief and the princes of the tribe; but the ultimate decision lay with the people themselves. The common freeman rarely took a leading part in the deliberations. The chiefs laid their proposals before the people in plain terms, stating the arguments on each side. If the freemen did not agree with their chiefs, they expressed their opinion by cries of dissent; they signified their approval of a proposal by clashing their armour.

**15. The Army.**—The army was not something different from the people; it was the people themselves. Every freeman bore arms, and might at any moment be called into active service. Spears were the weapons most commonly used. Each warrior had also a shield long enough to cover almost the whole body. The cavalry had no other armour; but those who fought on foot had missile weapons, which they could hurl to a great distance. They sometimes used battle-axes and clubs; swords were little known. The cavalry never used saddles. The different companies were not made up of men chosen at random; the freemen of each Hundred kept together, and the minor divisions were composed of kinsmen and friends. Each prince commanded his own Hundred. The supreme command was undertaken by the king or chief of the tribe, or by a *Herzog* elected by the freemen. If several tribes united to carry on a war, the Herzog, or commander-in-chief, was elected by the princes. The line of battle was arranged in the form of a wedge, the bravest and most experienced being put in front. Cavalry and infantry were so placed that they helped to protect each other. When about to make an attack, all joined in a sort of chant, putting their shields to their mouths to make the sound more terrible. To throw away their shields on the field of battle was in the highest degree disgraceful. Those guilty of this crime often killed themselves, being unable to bear the contempt of their kinsmen.

**16. Religion.**—The Germans, like their Scandinavian kinsmen, inherited the common Aryan religion, and gave it forms adapted to their own modes of thought and feeling. Their chief god was *Wodan.* *Donar,* or *Thor,* the god of thunder, was also very powerful. The gods were not worshipped in temples, but in sacred groves. Sacrifices were offered to them, sometimes even human sacrifices; and their will was found out by means of lots, the flight of birds, and the neighing of sacred horses. The Germans believed that the gods took a direct interest in human affairs, and that in a future life they rewarded brave men and punished cowards.

## CHAPTER II.

### THE GERMANS AND THE ROMANS.

*Ariovistus; C. Julius Cæsar; Germans in the Roman service* (1)
*—Drusus tries to conquer Germany* (2)*—Tiberius in Germany;
Arminius defeats Varus* (3)*—Germanicus and Arminius* (4)
*—Maroboduus; defeated by Arminius; death of Arminius;* (5)
*Claudius Civilis rebels against the Romans; encouraged by
Velleda; is defeated* (6)*—the Marcomannic War* (7).

1. **Ariovistus. C. Julius Cæsar.**—The first German name that appears in history is that of *Ariovistus*, a Suevic king whose fame had spread beyond the bounds of Germany. The *Sequani* and *Ædui*, two Gallic tribes, having fallen out, the former begged this great chief to come to their aid. He did so, but in the end, in 60 B.C., conquered both tribes. He thus made himself master of the whole territory between the Upper Rhine and the Loire. The Romans at first treated him as a friend; but, in the year 58 B.C., *C. Julius Cæsar*, to whom the Gauls had appealed for help, marched against him, and defeated him. Cæsar conquered the Germans on the left bank of the Rhine as completely as the Celtic inhabitants of Gaul. He twice crossed the Rhine; but he did not do much harm either time. He formed a high opinion of German bravery, and got many warriors to enter the Roman service. From this time it became common for Germans to serve as Roman soldiers; and in the end they formed by far the best part of the Roman army.

2. **Drusus.**—About the beginning of the Christian æra the Romans tried hard to make Germany a Roman province. The first general who made the attempt was *Drusus*, the step-son of the Emperor *Augustus*. He cut a canal between the *Rhine* and the *Yssel*, and in the year 12 B.C. sailed along the coasts of the North Sea. He defeated the *Bructeri*, who had collected a fleet in the Ems for the purpose of opposing him. Drusus afterwards made three different expeditions into the heart of Germany. In the year 9 B.C. he defeated the *Chatti* with their allies the *Marcomanni*, and advanced as far as the Elbe. On his way back he was killed by a fall from his horse. Had Drusus lived, he would probably have conquered a considerable part of Germany. He had built no fewer than fifty fortresses along the Rhine, besides others in different parts of the country.

3. **Tiberius. Varus. Arminius.**—The struggle begun by Drusus was carried on by *Tiberius*. In 8 B.C. the latter conquered the *Tencteri* and *Usipetes*. The *Sicambri* bravely opposed him; but having got their chiefs in his power by treachery, he easily overcame the people. In order to make them harmless for the future, he sent about 40,000 of them into Gaul, near the mouths of the Rhine, where they remained unwilling subjects of Rome. After this several tribes became allies of the Romans, and it seemed for a time as if Germany were soon, like Gaul, to form part of the Roman Empire. It was the foolish conduct of *Quinctilius Varus*, a Roman general, that kept this from coming about. Varus came to Germany in the year 6 A.D., and, fancying that the people were thoroughly subdued, began to rule as he had formerly done among the eastern subjects of Rome. He even claimed the right to put German freemen to death. The Germans were indignant at this treatment, and longed to throw off the foreign yoke. At last

a young Cheruscan chief, called *Arminius*, who had served in the Roman army, and had been made a Roman citizen and knight, resolved to win back the freedom of his people. He spoke in secret with the chiefs of his own and other tribes, and found them more than willing to support him. When everything was ready, Varus, who was in the land of the Cherusci, not far from the Weser, was told that a tribe in the north had revolted. At the head of a large army he at once set out to punish the rebels. He was led, with his legions, into the depths of the Teutoburg Wood. Heavy rains had been falling for some time, so that marching was difficult. Suddenly, when no one dreamed of danger, the Romans looked up, and saw that the wooded heights above and around them were covered by armed men. The Germans fiercely avenged the wrongs they had suffered. Of the whole Roman army scarcely a man escaped. Varus, severely wounded, fell upon his sword and killed himself.

4. **Germanicus.**—In consequence of this defeat, the Romans did not even enter Germany for some years. But when *Tiberius* became Emperor, *Germanicus*, the son of Drusus, tried to follow in the steps of his father. In the year 14 he suddenly attacked the *Marsi*, a tribe on the right bank of the Middle Rhine, and defeated them. The neighbouring tribes at once rose against him, and compelled him to withdraw. Next year he returned, and was joined by many Germans, the *Chauci* being especially useful allies. Arminius, whose wife *Thusnelda* had been sent by Germanicus as a prisoner to Rome, hurried through the land of the Cherusci and allied tribes, and roused the people against the Romans. He attacked the Roman cavalry in the Teutoburg Wood, where Germanicus halted to bury the remains of the warriors who had fallen five years before. The Germans gained no decided victory, but Germani

was weakened, and felt it necessary to retreat. In the year 16, he put forth all his strength against the Germans, and defeated them in a battle near *Minden.* The Romans claimed the victory in a second battle, but their losses were so great that they had to retreat to their ships. These were overtaken by a violent storm, and greater part of the fleet perished. After this the Romans did not again try to conquer Germany.

5. **Maroboduus. Death of Arminius.**—Meanwhile, a new danger had arisen within Germany itself. After being defeated by Drusus, the Marcomanni, headed by their chief *Maroboduus,* had wandered eastwards and taken possession of the country now called *Bohemia.* Maroboduus became a very powerful king, and conquered the leading Suevic tribes. He might have brought all Germany under his rule; but after the withdrawal of Germanicus, Arminius made war on him, and so utterly defeated him that his kingdom was broken up, and he himself had to seek refuge in Rome. Arminius thus probably saved the freedom of the Germans a second time. We know nothing of the last years of Arminius. In the year 21, at the age of thirty-seven, he was murdered. He was a true hero, to whom the whole Teutonic race owes a debt of gratitude.

6. **Claudius Civilis.**—In the year 69 the Batavians and the Germans on the left bank of the Rhine rebelled against the Romans. The rebellion was headed by *Claudius Civilis,* a Batavian who had for many years served in the Roman army, but had been harshly treated by the Emperor *Nero.* Some Gallic tribes joined him; and the Bructeri and other Germans on the right bank of the Rhine gladly sent him aid. A Bructerian maid, *Velleda,* who lived in a lonely tower in the forests near the *Lippe,* and was looked up to as a prophetess, encouraged him and his followers by high-sounding promises. For a time Civilis was successful; but

fortune soon turned. The Roman general *Cerealis* twice defeated him. Civilis still held out for a time; but in the end the Batavians had to return to their allegiance. They were not asked to pay tribute, but had to send men to the Roman army.

7. **The Marcomannic War.**—In the second century there were new wars between the Romans and the Germans, but now the latter, not the former, were the aggressors Of these wars the chief was *the Marcomannic war*, carried on by *Marcus Aurelius* for thirteen years against a vast body of Germans, headed by the *Marcomanni* and the *Quadi*, and joined by various non-German tribes. The invasion which led to this war may be looked on as the first of those which were afterwards to break up the Empire.

# CHAPTER III.

## THE FRANKS.

*German tribes leave the mother country (1).—the Alemanni; the Franks; the Saxons and Frisians; the Thuringians; the Bavarians (2)—the Franks the most important group of tribes; the Ripuarians (3)—the Salian Franks (4)—King Chlodio; state of Society among the Salians about Chlodio's time (5)— Merowig; Childeric (6)—Chlodwig; conquers Gaul (7)—becomes Christian (8)—conquers the Alemanni; unites all Frankish tribes (9)—lands seized by Chlodwig; allodial and fiscal lands (10)—Chlodwig's successors (11)—power of the Merowingian Kings (12)—Gaus and Duchies; Dukes and Counts (13)— Benefices (14)—Officers of the royal household (15).*

1. **Wanderings of German Tribes.**—Between the third and the sixth centuries great changes took place in Germany. Whole tribes and confederations of tribes left the mother country and founded powerful kingdoms elsewhere. The *Goths* were the first to set the example. They pushed towards the south-east. In the fourth century their great King *Eormenric* ruled over a kingdom reaching from the *Baltic* to the *Black Sea*. This kingdom was broken up by the *Huns*, to whom the *East Goths* became for a time subject, while the *West Goths* crossed the Danube and settled within Roman territory. Early in ·the fifth century the *Vandals*, the *Burgundians*, and various *Suevic* peoples wandered westwards into *Gaul*. The Suevi and the Vandals entered *Spain*, and conquered it. The Vandals

afterwards founded a kingdom in *Africa*, the capital of which was *Carthage*. The Burgundians remained in Gaul, and founded a kingdom which in the end took in the valley of the *Rhone* and the *Saône*, and the western half of *Helvetia*. These tribes were followed by the West Goths, who conquered Spain and the southern part of Gaul. The East Goths, under their King *Theodoric*, established a great kingdom in *Italy*. Some years after they were driven from Italy, in the sixth century, their place was taken by the *Lombards*, whose power proved firmer and more enduring. In the fifth century our own forefathers began to leave their seats on the shores of the North Sea, and to settle in Britain. Many of the lands which these tribes had held fell into the hands of the Sclaves, so that the *Elbe* and the *Saal* became the eastern boundary of Germany.

2. **Groups of Tribes.**—We hear very little, after the third century, of the many tribes formerly scattered over Germany. They still existed, but they were joined together in groups or confederations. How these were formed, we do not know. The tie which united the members of a confederation was very loose. Still, the members of each confederation had a certain sense of kinship, and this prepared the way for a closer political connexion. The *Alemanni*, who took in a number of Suevic tribes, were one of the most powerful of the confederations. In the third century they held the country between the Danube and the Main, and from thence made many incursions into Roman territory. They gradually advanced southwards and westwards as far as the *Upper Rhine*, the *Aar*, and the *Vosges mountains*. To the north of the Alemanni, from the Main to the mouths of the Rhine, were the *Franks*. The land to the east of the Franks was held by the *Saxons* and *Frisians*. The latter held the whole line of coast from the Rhine to the Elbe; the former,

the basins of the Lower Elbe, the Weser, and the Ems. The centre of what is now Germany was in the hands of the *Thuringians*. They held the wooded mountains which are still called by their name, and some part of the country to the north and south. These various confederations may probably be identified with the groups into which the Germans, in the time of Tacitus, divided themselves. If so, the Saxons and Frisians would represent the ancient *Ingaevones;* the Franks the *Istaevones*, and the Alemanni and Thuringians the *Herminones*. Another confederation was gradually formed by the *Goths* who remained in Germany, the *Marcomanni*, and others. These were the *Bojoarii* or *Bavarians*, whose country took in greater part of the basin of the *Inn*, and who became subject in turn to *Odoacer* and to *Theodoric the Great*.

3. **The Franks. The Ripuarians.**—Of these groups of tribes, the *Franks* were by far the most important. The history of the Franks is for several centuries the history of Germany. They conquered the Gauls and their own kinsmen, and laid the foundation of the future kingdoms of *Germany* and *France*. From the third century the Franks on the right bank of the Middle Rhine often broke into Gaul, and attacked the Romans. They several times conquered *Köln, Mainz*, and *Trier*, and harried the neighbouring lands. In the fourth century they were driven back by *Constantine* and *Julian*, and in the fifth by the great general *Aëtius;* but in the latter half of the fifth century they were masters of the whole country between the Middle Rhine and the Maes. They held also part of the banks of the Moselle, and had lands as far south as the northern boundaries of the Alemanni and Burgundians. At this time their chief town was *Köln;* and they were called' (probably from *Ripa, a bank*) *Riparii* or *Ripuarii*.

4. **The Salian Franks.**—The Franks who held the

banks of the Lower Rhine were called by the Romans *Salians*. The Ripuarians were more numerous than the Salians; but it was the Salians who founded the great Frankish kingdom. They sprang for the most part from those Sicambri whom Tiberius settled near the mouths of the Rhine, and were probably called Salians from a tribe which wandered westwards from the *Yssel* or *Isala*, and united to form one people with the Sicambri. The Salians were nominally subject to the Romans, and served in the Roman army; but they kept their native institutions, and always tried, when they had a chance, to become independent. At the time of Julian they held the country from the Lower Rhine to the west of the Maes. Julian advanced against them, and defeated them; but he allowed them to keep the land they had seized. About the beginning of the fifth century they still served in the Roman army, but no longer recognised Roman supremacy. They probably then held the whole country between the Lower Rhine and the Schelde.

5. **King Chlodio. The Salic code.**—The Salians were governed by Kings. Probably their first King—at all events, the first of whom we know anything—was *Chlodio*. He reigned about the middle of the fifth century. He was defeated by the Romans under Aëtius; but he succeeded in pushing his boundaries as far west as the *Somme*. He became a faithful ally of the Romans, who often afterwards—especially in the great battle fought in 451 against *Attila*—received important aid from the Salians. The famous *Salic Code* was probably drawn up about the time of Chlodio. The state of society which it represents is in many respects the same as that described by Tacitus. The people, like all their kinsmen who had not left Germany, are still heathens. The tribe is divided into Hundreds, and these again into villages; and the

occupation of the people, when they are not engaged in war, continues mainly agricultural. But the position of the King has changed. He no longer receives his authority from the people; he inherits it, and exercises it as a right. He appoints the chiefs, who are called *Grafs* or *Counts*, and decides cases of justice which the Meeting of the Hundred—the largest that seems now to be held—cannot settle. There is no trace of the old noble class; what raises men above their fellows is connexion with the King. Those whom he appoints to an office, and the members of his "Gefolge" or "Comitatus," hold a very high position. The "Wergeld" of a Graf and of a follower of the King is three times as large as that of a common freeman. The King has thus already become the central element in the constitution. He exercises supreme authority, and is the fountain of honour. This great increase of the royal power was perhaps partly due to the influence of Roman ideas, for the Salians in the Roman army would naturally learn habits of strict obedience.

6. **Merowig. Childeric.**—The successor of Chlodio is said to have been *Merowig*. We know nothing certainly of this King. If he really existed, he must have made a deep impression on the men of his time, for the future Kings of the Franks were called after him *Merowingians*. *Childeric*, whose capital was *Tournay*, was a great Salian King in the latter half of the fifth century. He aided the Romans against the West Goths, and is said also to have opposed the Alemanni, who were threatening Italy. The close connexion of the Salians with the Romans at this time prepared the way for the great career on which they were about to enter.

7. **Chlodwig. Conquest of Gaul.**—Childeric was succeeded, in 481, by his son, *Chlodovech* or *Chlodwig*.

Chlodwig was a mere boy when he became King, but he was destined to become one of the greatest conquerors in the history of the world. He began his career by attacking *Syagrius*, the governor of the part of Gaul which was still directly subject to Rome. Having defeated Syagrius near *Soissons*, Chlodwig took possession of the country as far as the *Seine*. He afterwards became master of the land between the *Seine* and the *Loire*, where the Armorican Republic is said to have been established. He also defeated the Burgundians, and made their King pay him tribute. Crossing the Loire, he defeated the West Goths in a battle near *Poitiers*. Chlodwig was unable to conquer the southern part of Gaul; but after the defeat of the West Goths his kingdom reached as far south as the *Garonne*. Thus, within a short time, he had conquered nearly the whole of Gaul.

8. **Causes of Chlodwig's success.**—At first sight it appears strange that a petty King with comparatively few followers should do such great things; and that, having conquered such vast territories, he should afterwards be able to hold the people in subjection. The chief cause of Chlodwig's success was that he had become a Christian. On Christmas day of 496 he was baptized with great pomp, with 3,000 of his warriors, at *Rheims*. The story is that his baptism was the result of a vow made in the heat of a battle with the Alemanni near *Zülpich*, that if the God of the Christians gave him the victory he would give up his gods and accept Christianity. The Franks in the old settlements in the neighbourhood of the Schelde were not converted for some time; but from the time of his baptism Chlodwig's kingdom was at least nominally Christian. This fact did more for him than all the bravery of his troops. The Germans already settled in Gaul were Christians; but they

were not members of the Catholic Church. They were *Arians.* The Catholic clergy, therefore, were their enemies, and longed for some ruler who should uphold the true faith. From the beginning they looked to Chlodwig with hope. When he entered the Church they warmly supported him; and their friendship meant the good-will of the great body of the people. Another circumstance aided Chlodwig. The Emperor *Anastasius,* anxious that the barbarian conqueror should have some formal connexion with the Roman Empire, sent him, after his victory over the West Goths, the titles of *Consul* and *Patrician.* This seemed to make Chlodwig the lawful ruler of Gaul, and probably won over some whom even the Church might have failed to influence.

9. **Conquest of the Alemanni. Union of all Frankish Tribes.**—Chlodwig was far more than the conqueror of Gaul. The Saxons, Thuringians, and Bavarians, did not fall under his power; but he subdued the Alemanni, and seems to have colonized the part of their territory between the Neckar and the Main with a Frankish population. He also united all the Frankish tribes under his rule. When he began his reign there was no political connexion between the Salians and the Ripuarians; and the Salians themselves had other Kings besides Chlodwig. Chlodwig slew these Kings, and the King of the Ripuarians, together with their heirs. He appears to have taken possession of Salian territory as a right; the Ripuarians elected him to be their King. The Franks of every tribe thus acknowledged one lord, and began to feel themselves bound together by many common interests. As the centre of a great kingdom, destined to be the most enduring of all the States founded by the Germans in foreign countries, they could not but learn to be proud of the common Frankish name.

10. **Lands seized by Chlodwig.**—Chlodwig was not

followed into the heart of Gaul by the Salians as a people. He was accompanied only by his "Gefolge" and an army of freemen. He did not, therefore, like other German conquerors demand any particular proportion of the conquered territory. But he took possession of all public lands and of lands which had no certain owner. These were divided between himself and those who accompanied him. Land allotted to, or seized by, a freeman, was called *allodial*. Allodial land was the absolute property of the possessor, held by him subject to no condition except that of aiding, when necessary, in the defence of the State. The lands kept for the King must have been very extensive. They were called *fiscal* lands, and became the chief source of the royal revenue.

11. **Chlodwig's successors.**—Chlodwig died in 511 in *Paris*. His kingdom was divided among his four sons. This division did not break up the unity of the kingdom. The subjects of the four brothers continued to look on themselves as members of one State. The East or Rhenish Franks, and those Germans to the east of the Rhine whom Chlodwig had conquered, were placed under Chlodwig's eldest son, *Theodoric*. His was by far the most powerful of the four divisions. He made the bulk of Thuringia tributary; and his son and successor, *Theudebert*, subdued the *Bavarians*, and completed the subjection of the *Alemanni*. Thus the greater part of Germany was brought under the rule of the Franks. The Saxons and Frisians alone remained independent. Theodoric's brothers, who, after the death of *Theodoric the Great* in 526, found little hindrance to their schemes of conquest, thoroughly mastered *Burgundy*, and gained possession of the southern part of Gaul. *Chlotachar*, or *Clothair I.*, Chlodwig's youngest son, joined together again the whole Frankish kingdom. Under him the kingdom was almost as extensive as at any

time for more than two centuries afterwards. Like his father, he was succeeded by his four sons; but when one of these died, the kingdom was again divided. After this the different parts of the kingdom were several times brought together under one King; but more usually there were three kingdoms—*Austrasia*, the kingdom of the East Franks, *Neustria*, the kingdom of the West Franks, and *Burgundy*. Neustria and Burgundy often went together, but Austrasia always tried to have a King of its own, and became more and more separated from the other kingdoms.

12. **The Merowingian Kings.**—The Merowingian Kings were usually very bad rulers, but at first they had great power. There was for a time a yearly gathering of Frankish freemen, called, from the fact that it met in March, the *Marchfield.* This was soon given up in Neustria, because the Franks lived at great distances from one another, and could not easily go to Meetings far away from their homes. In Austrasia the Marchfield was probably only a military assembly. Thus the power which had once belonged to all freemen gradually passed into the hands of the King. The position of the Kings was further raised by their Roman subjects readily conceding to them some of the powers which had belonged to the Emperors.

13. **Dukes and Counts.**—The Frankish kingdoms were divided into *Gaus* or *Districts*, each of which was governed by a Count. A number of Gaus made a *Duchy*, over which was a *Herzog* or *Duke*. Each of the great groups or confederations of tribes in Germany formed a separate Duchy. The Dukes and Counts in Gaul were appointed solely by the King, and were looked on as his officers. The Bavarians elected their own Dukes; and they always chose them from one noble family, the *Agilolfings*. The Alemanni and Thuringians had also some share in the

appointment of their Dukes. The freemen of each German Duchy met their Duke once in the year, and consulted with him on affairs of importance. Thus the Germans to the east of the Rhine kept more of the old freedom than their Frankish conquerors.

14. **Benefices.**—The Merowingian Kings soon adopted the Roman custom of granting lands on condition of military service. Such grants were called at first *benefices*, but afterwards *fiefs*. They were made from the royal lands, and were usually given to the King's *men* or *vassals*—that is, to the Dukes, Counts, and members of the "Gefolge." Thus the service required by a Merowingian King from the holder of a benefice was not, like that required for lands granted by the Roman Government, service to the State; it was the service of a vassal to his lord. The relation between the two was wholly personal in its character. Those who did not already hold this personal relation to the King, on receiving a benefice, became his men, and swore to be faithful to him and to give him service in war. From this combination of Roman and Teutonic ideas sprang the system of *feudal tenures*. [See the *General Sketch of European History* in this Series.] When benefices became hereditary, the holders usually granted pieces of land to others, who entered into the same relation to them that they held to the King. And in times of confusion, freemen very often gave up their lands to some powerful lord, and received them back as *fiefs*, thus binding themselves to serve him in war while he undertook to protect them against their enemies. In the end, the Dukes and Counts came to hold their Duchies and Counties *in fief*, and thus looked on all fief-holders within their districts as their vassals. But this was not for some time yet.

15. **The Royal household.**—The Merowingian Kings,

having become rich and great, lived in a style of which the early German Kings and chiefs had never dreamed. The duties of their household were divided among a large number of officers, among whom were the *Seneschal*, the *Marshal*, and the *Chancellor*. Over all officers of the court was the *Major Domus*, or *Mayor of the Palace*. An officer of less importance, at this time, was the *Palsgrave*, or *Count of the Palace*, whose duties had to do with the royal tribunal. These, and all other great officers, were taken chiefly from the members of the " Gefolge." They formed a Council which aided the King in administering justice and in carrying on the affairs of the State.

## CHAPTER IV.

### THE MAYORS OF THE PALACE, AND DUKES OF THE FRANKS.

*A new aristocracy arises; the power of the Kings lessened* (1)—*the Mayors of the Palace the real rulers of the Frankish kingdoms* (2)—*Pippin of Herstall rules the East Franks; defeats the West Franks at Testri* (3)—*Charles Martel; victory over the Arabs* (4)—*Pippin the Short becomes King* (5)—*conversion of German tribes through the preaching of English missionaries; Winfrith; the See of Mainz the head Church of Germany* (6).

1. **The rise of a new aristocracy.**—The holders of benefices tried from the beginning to make their lands hereditary; and many of them soon succeeded in doing so. Thus a great new aristocracy arose which took the place among the Franks of the old noble class. This aristocracy soon lessened the kingly power. Its leading members often met, and not only shared the government with the King, but sometimes forced him to confirm them in rights which they had seized. Such gatherings took the place, to some extent, of the old national Meetings. The various Kings had given away so many lands as benefices that they were soon too poor to defend themselves. They were also weakened by carrying on many cruel wars with each other. Thus it came about that by the middle of the seventh century the Merowingian Kings, who had for a time been so great, had lost nearly all their power. The

Dukes, Counts, and other rich men, acted as if they were independent princes. The great German Duchies, although still nominally subject to the Franks, were practically free.

2. **Mayors of the Palace.**—During this time of confusion the Mayors of the Palace rose to great power. They had long ceased to be mere household officers. They had at first been appointed by the King; but, as they became more powerful, the aristocracy took the right of appointing them into its own hands. For a long time they were the real rulers of the Frankish kingdoms. They sometimes tried to keep the aristocracy in check; but they were usually its representatives and leaders. One of the most famous Mayors of the Palace was *Pippin* of *Landen*, who, with *Arnulf*, Bishop of *Metz*, ruled Austrasia in the early part of the seventh century. A little later, *Ebroin* was a great Mayor in Neustria and Burgundy. He made war on the East Franks, and was for some time successful; but in the end he was killed.

3. **Pippin of Herstall.**—While Ebroin ruled the West Franks, *Pippin* of *Herstall*, grandson of Arnulf by the father's, and of Pippin of Landen by the mother's side, and his cousin *Martin*, became leaders of the East Franks. They were called Dukes, and their position was very much the same as that of Dukes among the German kinsmen of the Franks. After Martin's death, the whole power fell into Pippin's hands. Although the East and West Franks had often been at war, neither had hitherto thoroughly overcome the other. In 687, Pippin utterly defeated the West Franks in the *Battle of Testri*. This battle marks an epoch in Frankish history, for after it the first place in the kingdom openly belonged to the East Franks. Pippin did not dethrone the reigning Merowingian King; but he kept all real power in his own hands. In Neustria, he took the title of Mayor of the Palace; but in Austrasia, he

ruled, as before, as *Duke of the Franks*. He was by far the best ruler the Frankish kingdom had yet had. He fought hard to make the German Dukes return to their allegiance; and he was to some extent successful. He also made most of the Dukes and Counts in Gaul acknowledge his authority, and restored the Marchfield and other institutions that had been allowed to die away. Thus Pippin brought back something like order to the Frankish kingdom, and tried to make it once more a great and united State. He died in 714.

4. **Charles Martel.**—After Pippin's death the Neustrians made war on the East Franks; but his son *Charles* defeated them, first at *Cambrai*, and afterwards at *Soissons*. Charles thus rose like his father to supreme power. He also nominally ruled as a subject of the Merowingians. In order to have the means of rewarding his men, he "resumed" many of the lands held by the Church in Gaul. This roused the opposition of the clergy, but it enabled Charles to surround himself by a large number of faithful followers. The task of joining together again the Roman and German provinces, which Pippin had begun, Charles carried on; and he extended the kingdom by overcoming the *Frisians*. In 731 he gained a famous victory over the *Arabs*, who, having conquered Spain, tried also to conquer Gaul. From this victory, Charles was called *Martel*, or the *Hammer*. It won him great renown as the protector of Christendom. During the last few years of his life he was strong enough to rule without the appointment of a nominal King; but he never took the royal title. He died in 741, and was succeeded by his two sons, *Pippin the Short* and *Carlman*.

5. **Pippin the Short.**—One of the first acts of the two brothers was to appoint a successor to the last Merowingian King. They also tried to make the Church friendly to

them. In 747 Carlman went into a monastery, and thus left the whole power to Pippin. The latter then began to think of making himself King. Even yet the people looked on the Merowingians as their lawful rulers; but in 751 Pippin got Pope *Zacharias* to decide that one who had the power of a King had a better right to the crown than one who was merely a King in name. Pippin held an Assembly at Soissons in 753, where *Childeric III.* was dethroned, and he himself was elected and crowned King. Thus the Merowingians were altogether thrust aside, and a new and stronger dynasty reigned in their stead.

6. **Conversion of German Tribes.**—During this period many German tribes became Christian. So early as the sixth and the beginning of the seventh century, Irish and Frankish missionaries had tried to convert the Germans. In the latter half of the seventh century the task was taken up by countrymen of our own; and they were the first to labour with the sanction of the Pope. *Wilfrith*, who was accidentally driven, in 677, on the shores of Friesland, preached there with great success. His work was carried on by *Willibrord*, who lived among the Frisians about fifty years. Greater than either of these was *Winfrith*, afterwards called *Saint Boniface* and the *Apostle of the Germans*. He helped Willibrord for some time, but spent the greater part of his life in Southern and Central Germany. In 723 he was made "*Episcopus Regionarius*" of Germany—that is, Bishop without any special diocese. After this he brought tribe after tribe within the Church, and founded various bishopricks and monasteries. In 732 he received the archiepiscopal *pallium*, and in 742 presided over the first *German Synod*. In 745 he was appointed, as Metropolitan of Germany, to the *See of Mainz*, which from this time occupied in the German Church the position held by the See of Canterbury in

the Church of England. Ten years afterwards he was killed in Friesland while on his way to confirm some converts. At the time of Winfrith's death, and chiefly owing to his efforts, all Germany, with the exception of Saxony, was nominally Christian. The old pagan ideas still influenced to some extent the minds of the people; but the good seed had been sown, and soon began to spring up and to bear fruit.

# CHAPTER V.

## CHARLES THE GREAT.

*King Pippin; defeats the Lombards; is made Patrician; his wars* (1) —*Charles the Great; conquers the Saxons* (2)—*conquers the Lombards* (3)—*conquers part of Spain* (4)—*deprives the Duke of Bavaria of his Duchy; conquers the Avars* (5)—*lessens the power of the provincial governors; Margraves; Missi Dominici; National Assemblies; protection of the Church; encouragement of learning; Alcuin* (6)—*is crowned Roman Emperor* (7) —*conquest of Bohemia; boundaries of the Empire; capitals of the Empire* (8)—*Charles's son Lewis crowned; death of Charles* (9) —*Lewis the Pious; divides the Empire among his sons; their rebellions* (10)—*battle of Fontenay; Treaty of Verdun* (11).

1. **King Pippin.**—At this time the Lombards had possession of *Ravenna*, and were threatening Rome. Pope Zacharias, in aiding Pippin to become King, had hoped that he would come to the help of the Church. For some time he did not do so; but in the end he made two expeditions into Italy, and defeated the Lombards. He thus became lord of Rome. Probably in return for his services, he received from the Pope the title of *Patrician*. The Pope had no legal right to give this title, and the duties connected with it were very vague; but it made Pippin still more friendly to the Church, and added considerably to his dignity. The rest of Pippin's life was chiefly spent in wars, which he carried on with great vigour. After a struggle which lasted for seven years, he finally

wrested the south of Gaul from the Arabs; and he forced the Aquitanians to submit, really as well as nominally, to Frankish authority. He died in 768.

2. **Charles the Great. Conquest of the Saxons.**—The kingdom was divided between Pippin's two sons, *Charles* and *Carlman*. The latter died in 771, and Charles became sole King. Charles was a man of great strength both of mind and body, and soon became one of the greatest Kings that have ever lived. When he began his reign, the only German people who had never been subject to the Franks were the Saxons. They were still heathens, and kept almost all the old German institutions. Their land reached from the mouths of the Elbe southwards to Thuringia and westwards nearly to the Rhine. Charles resolved to conquer them, and in 772 set out against them with a large army. He took their chief fortress, *Eresburg*, and destroyed *Irminsûl*, a mysterious column which they held in great awe. As the people seemed to submit, he thought he had already conquered them; but in reality he had begun a war which was to last thirty years. The Saxons loved freedom, and again and again, when they had seemed utterly worn out, arose and threw off the Frankish yoke. A chief called *Widukind* especially distinguished himself by his resistance to Charles. Charles was so irritated by the trouble the people gave him that in 782 he caused no fewer than 4,500 prisoners to be put to death; but even this did not crush them. In the end, however, he overcame them, and forced them to accept Christianity.

3. **Conquest of the Lombards.**—When Charles was engaged in his first expedition into Saxony, the Lombards again threatened Rome. He at once hastened to the help of the Pope and the Roman people, and in 774 thoroughly conquered the Lombards. He allowed Lombardy to remain a separate kingdom, but deposed the Lombard

King, and himself took the crown. From this time Charles's full title was *King of the Franks and Lombards and Patrician of the Romans*.

**4. Expedition into Spain.**—While Charles was in Saxony, in 777, holding an Assembly at *Paderborn*, ambassadors from the governors of *Zaragoza* and *Huesca* came and asked him for help against *Abderrhaman*, the Caliph of *Cordova*. He promised to aid them, and in 778 made an expedition into *Spain*, the result of which was that he extended the boundary of his kingdom across the *Pyrenees* as far as the *Ebro*. When coming back he sustained a heavy loss. He himself, with the greater part of his army, reached the northern side of the Pyrenees in safety; but a large body bringing up the rear was suddenly attacked by the *Basques* in the pass of *Roncesvalles*, and almost wholly cut down.

**5. The Duke of Bavaria. Conquest of the Avars.**—At this time there was a very powerful Duke in Bavaria, called *Thassilo*, of the native house of the Agilolfings. He had been defeated by Pippin the Short, but had soon thrown off his allegiance. In 785, Charles marched against him. He at once submitted, but as he rebelled in the following year he was condemned to death by an Assembly which met at *Ingelheim*. Charles spared his life, but deposed him, and in future governed Bavaria by means of Counts. He also made the bishoprick of *Salzburg* into an archbishoprick, which took in the whole of Bavaria. Some years afterwards Charles conquered the *Avars*, a Turanian people who had a great kingdom to the east of Bavaria in ancient *Pannonia* and the neighbouring lands on the left bank of the Danube.

**6. Government of Charles.**—Charles was not less great as a ruler than as a conqueror. One of his chief objects during his whole reign was to lessen the power of the

Dukes and Counts. In Germany he did away altogether with the title of Duke. The border districts of the kingdom were made into *Marks*, and placed under *Margraves* or *Marquesses*, whose chief duty was to drive back or conquer neighbouring tribes. Of these Marks *Carinthia*, which reached from the Adriatic to the Danube, was one of the chief. Another, to the east of Bavaria, intended at first for the defence of Bavaria against the Avars, was afterwards called *Oesterreich* or *Austria*, and became one of the most important lands in Germany. All parts of Charles's dominions were visited four times in the year by a peculiar class of officers called *Missi Dominici*. They reported to him the state of the country, and heard appeals from the lower tribunals. An appeal might be made from them to the royal tribunal, which was now presided over by the *Palsgrave*. Two Assemblies met Charles in the course of the year—one in May, and another in autumn. They were attended by the Dukes, Counts, Prelates, and other leading men of the State. These gatherings could only discuss and advise; Charles himself decided what should become law. Meetings of the people were also held in different parts of the kingdom, at which new laws were made known by the *Missi*. Charles acted always as a protector of the Church. He founded many bishopricks and monasteries, and gave them rich lands. He also made the payment of tithes compulsory throughout his dominions. Everywhere, but especially in Germany, he gave the prelates a much higher position than they had yet had, that they might act as a check on the secular governors. Charles also encouraged learning, and got many scholars to come and stay at his court. Of these the chief was *Ealhwine* or *Alcuin*, a countryman of our own. He was Charles's most honoured friend and counsellor for about twenty years. By his advice Charles set up schools in connexion with monasteries. Some of these schools became very famous, and helped during several centuries to keep learning from altogether dying out.

7. **Charles crowned Roman Emperor.**—By the end of the eighth century Charles ruled so many lands that he was crowned *Emperor of the Romans* by Pope *Leo III.* in St. Peter's on Christmas Day of 800. [See the *General Sketch of European History.*] Soon after his coronation he made his subjects renew their oath of allegiance to him. They had to swear allegiance to him as Emperor, for as Emperor he claimed far more thorough submission than was due to a mere King, perfect obedience to the Emperor being in those days looked on as one with perfect obedience to God.

8. **Extent of Charles's Empire.** — Even after his coronation as Emperor, Charles had some trouble with the Saxons ; but they were worn out by their long struggle, and had at last to submit. Thus all Germany was brought for the first time under the rule of one man. Charles also carried on wars with the *Danes,* and with the *Czechs* or *Bohemians* and the other Slavonic tribes on the eastern borders of Germany. All these submitted to him. When at its height, Charles's Empire reached from the *Baltic* to the *Ebro,* from the *North Sea* and the *Eider* to *Central Italy,* and from the *Atlantic* to the *Save,* the *Theiss,* the *Oder,* and the *Lower Vistula.* Of this great Empire the Rhineland, the home of the East Franks, was looked on as the centre. Its capitals were *Rome* and *Aachen;* and Charles had also palaces at *Engilenheim* or *Ingelheim, Worms,* and *Herstall.* Aachen was his favourite city. He built there not only a palace, but a fine basilica, from which the town has received its French name of *Aix-la-Chapelle.*

**9. Death of Charles.**—Charles wished to divide his Empire between his three sons, *Charles, Pippin*, and *Lewis;* but the two first died before him. Lewis, therefore, was crowned as his father's successor at an Assembly in Aachen in 813. Early in the following year (814), Charles died, and was buried under the dome of the basilica which he had built in Aachen.

**10. Lewis the Pious.**—Lewis—called *Lewis the Pious*—proved altogether unfit for his great duties. He was well-meaning, but had no strength of character. Although crowned in his father's lifetime, he allowed the ceremony to be repeated by Pope *Stephen III.* at *Rheims*. In 817 he summoned an Assembly at Aachen, and divided the Empire between his three sons, *Lothar, Pippin*, and *Lewis*. Lothar, who was associated with his father in the Empire, received the *Rhineland* and *Italy;* Pippin, *Aquitania;* and Lewis, *Bavaria* and the adjoining districts. Afterwards Lewis had a fourth son, *Charles*, by a second marriage. In 829, he made a separate kingdom for this son. The three older sons, thinking themselves wronged, rebelled, and got the better of Lewis, who for a time lost all power. In 833 the same sons again rebelled. This time Lewis's troops went over almost in a body to the rebels; and Lothar not only proclaimed himself Emperor, but put his father in a monastery, and afterwards made him appear before a public Assembly and confess a long list of crimes. Lewis was again placed on the throne; but he soon brought new troubles on himself. After Pippin's death, in 838, he agreed to an arrangement by which the greater part of the Empire was divided between Lothar and Charles (afterwards called *The Bald*), while Bavaria alone was left subject to Lewis. The latter at once took up arms. While the Emperor was trying to put down this new rebellion, he was overtaken by illness.

He retired to an islet on the Rhine near Ingelheim, and there, in 840, died.

11. **The Treaty of Verdun.**—Lothar took the Imperial title, but war at once broke out between him and his brothers Lewis and Charles, who united against him. A great battle was fought at *Fontenay* in 841, in which, after fearful slaughter, the allied brothers gained the victory. At last, in 843, the war was brought to an end by the *Treaty of Verdun*. Lothar, who kept the title of Emperor, received Italy and a long narrow strip of territory reaching from the Mediterranean to the North Sea. This kingdom was called, after Lothar, *Lotharingia*—a name which was afterwards confined to the country to the north of Burgundy. The territory to the west of Lothar's country was given to Charles. It was called *Karolingia*. Lewis received Germany, or the *Teutonic Kingdom*. It reached from the Rhine eastwards to the Elbe, the Saal, and the Bohemian Forest, and from the North Sea southwards to the Alps. Lewis also received the three towns, *Mainz*, *Speyer*, and *Worms;* and he claimed supremacy over the Slavonic tribes which Charles the Great had conquered. All three brothers were called Kings of the Franks. The two younger brothers allowed a certain pre-eminence to the elder as Emperor; but in reality they were quite independent of him. From this time is usually dated the existence of Germany as a separate kingdom.

# CHAPTER VI.

### THE LATER KARLINGS.

*Wars of Lewis the German with the Northmen and the Slaves* (1)—
*Charles the Fat becomes King of Germany and Emperor; dethroned* (2)—*the East and West Franks separate* (3)—*Arnulf defeats the Northmen; becomes Emperor* (4)—*invasions of the Magyars; Lewis the Child defeated* (5)—*feudal tenures in Germany* (6)—*power of the feudal lords; private wars* (7)—*wealth of the Church; good influence of the clergy* (8)—*source of the King's revenue* (9)—*the Diet; attended by the nobles* (10)—
*"Heliand"* (11).

1. **Lewis the German.**—King Lewis—called *Lewis the German*—had enemies who taxed his strength to the utmost. Even in the days of Charles the Great, Scandinavian pirates, or *Northmen*, as they were called, threatened the northern coasts of Europe. The fame of Charles kept them in check; but after his death they became more bold, and spread alarm through a great part of Europe. Their plan was to enter the larger rivers in shallow boats, attack the towns they passed, and seize all the booty on which they could lay their hands. They even carried their skiffs sometimes to inland streams, and appeared suddenly where they were not in the least expected. They were not only heathens, but appear to have hated Christianity, for they never spared churches and monasteries. During the reign of Charles the Bald alone they twice sailed to *Paris*, where they gave themselves up to every excess. Lewis the German also

had to resist them. He did his utmost to protect his kingdom; but all his efforts could not prevent the invaders from doing much harm. About 847 a large body of them sailed up the Elbe to *Hamburg*, and burned greater part of the town. The Emperor Lewis had founded an archiepiscopal See in Hamburg, which was to be the centre of the northern missions. The Archbishop now fled to *Bremen*, which henceforth became the seat of the northern archbishoprick of Germany. Besides resisting the Northmen, King Lewis was often at war with the Slaves; he also had quarrels with Charles the Bald, who was always trying to add to his kingdom, and got himself crowned Emperor in 875. Lewis died suddenly in *Frankfurt* in 876.

2. **Charles the Fat.**—Lewis's son, *Charles the Fat*, at first reigned in Germany along with his elder brothers, *Carlman* and *Lewis;* but after their death he became sole German King. He also became King of Italy, and received from the Pope the Imperial crown. In 884 the West Franks, who were never in greater need of a powerful ruler, elected him to their vacant throne. If we except the kingdom of Burgundy, which had passed into the hands of Charles the Bald's brother-in-law, *Duke Boso*, almost the whole of the Empire of Charles the Great was now re-united under Charles the Fat. The Northmen poured into his dominions at many points, and in 885 appeared a third time before Paris. They were bravely resisted; but the Emperor, instead of helping Paris, was mean enough to buy off the enemy by paying a large sum. Charles was so weak a ruler that, at an Assembly held at *Tribur* in 887, he was dethroned. He then retired to a monastery, and died in 888.

3. **Separation of the East and West Franks.** — The Karolingian Empire now fell to pieces. The Eastern and Western kingdoms were never again joined together; and

for a time Italy and Burgundy were also separated from Germany. The King of Germany was still called *King of the East Franks;* but *East Francia,* or *Franconia,* was only one part, although at this time the leading part, of the German kingdom. It took in the basins of the Main, the Neckar, and the Lahn. To the north were *Saxony* and *Thuringia,* and to the south and south-east *Alemannia* or *Swabia,* and *Bojoaria* or *Bavaria.* As yet *Lotharingia* did not belong decidedly either to the Eastern or Western kingdom.

4. **Arnulf.**—The successor of Charles the Fat in Germany was his brother Carlmans's illegitimate son, *Arnulf.* This brave King won great fame by defeating the Northmen at *Löwen* in 891. After this Germany was comparatively little troubled by the Scandinavian sea-robbers. In 894, Arnulf went to Italy, and, having taken Rome, was crowned Emperor. He had, however, no real power in Italy, and soon returned to Germany, where he died in 899.

5. **Lewis the Child. The Hungarians.**—Arnulf was succeeded by his son, *Lewis the Child.* The short reign of Lewis was one of the most unhappy in the history of Germany. A Turanian race, called *Magyars* or *Hungarians,* had now begun to settle in the country formerly held by the Avars. They had helped Arnulf in a war he carried on with the Moravians; but almost immediately after his death they invaded Germany, and year after year they came back during the whole of Lewis's reign. As they fought on horseback, while the Germans for the most part fought on foot, the latter were defeated in nearly every battle. The people had almost no means of sheltering themselves, for as yet there were few towns in Germany, so that multitudes were slain, and others were driven into Hungary as captives. The Hungarians were a fierce people, and always made a desert of the country they

passed through. In 910 Lewis made a great effort to drive them back, but he was defeated and compelled to pay tribute. He died in the following year; and with him ended in Germany the Karolingian dynasty.

6. **Feudalism in Germany.**—The old constitution of Germany had now almost altogether died out. We have seen that Charles the Great did away with the ducal title in Germany. After his time strong local governors were so much needed that Dukes began again to be appointed. Thus at the time we have now reached, or soon afterwards, each of the great groups or confederations of tribes had its own Duke. The Dukes generally sprang from the old ducal families; but they now held their Duchies in fief of the King. That is, they were his men, and swore to be faithful to him; and in return he undertook to protect them in their lands and offices. Beneath the Dukes were the Margraves, Counts, and other great fief-holders within the Duchies. These held the same relation to the Dukes that the Dukes held to the King, and had, or might have, many vassals under them. The great feudal lords were looked on as *noble*, and had quite taken the place of the old noble class spoken of by Tacitus. There were now very few powerful freemen in Germany. During the reign of Charles the Great many had become vassals of great lords, because the service they had to render as vassals was not so hard as that which Charles required of freemen in order to carry on his many wars. In the time of confusion which followed his reign, some were forced by powerful neighbours to change the free tenure of their lands into a feudal tenure; others made the change of their own will, in order to obtain protection against great nobles or foreign invaders. Many freemen who did not become feudal tenants, but who were unable to protect themselves, lost their freedom altogether. Thus the class which had once formed the chief strength

of the State became less and less important, till at last free communities no longer existed except in towns and in districts where they could not easily be subdued, as among the valleys of the Alps and along the shores of the North Sea. The lowest class in the State was made up of tributary and dependant peasants, and of serfs who usually passed with the land from one master to another.

7. **Position of the King. Private War.**—Feudalism having thus taken the place of the old constitution in Germany, the King was now much more the head of a great aristocracy than the sovereign of a nation. There was still a royal tribunal, presided over by the Palsgrave; but each great feudal lord had his own court, in which he administered justice according to local customs. When his vassals were faithful to him, the King was still very powerful; but the Dukes usually gave him service unwillingly, unless they had some end of their own to gain. On the other hand, the Margraves, Counts, and others treated the Dukes in this respect exactly as the Dukes treated the King. When any of the nobles fell out, they rarely settled their quarrel peacefully. Every good King tried to put down private war; and some succeeded, or nearly succeeded, for a time. But the nobles always returned to the custom when the weakness of the Government gave them a chance of doing so, and in the end it became one of their chief rights.

8. **The Church.**—As Germany had now been for some time nominally Christian, there were bishopricks and monasteries in all parts of the land. Among the chief monasteries were those of *St. Gallen*, *Fulda*, and *Corvey*. The See of Mainz remained the head Church. Many lands had been given to the Church by Kings, Emperors, and rich nobles. These lands were not taxed. When held, however, by a feudal tenure, the holder had usually to aid

his superior in war. Sometimes the Archbishops, Bishops, and Abbots even appeared in the field at the head of their vassals. The ecclesiastical lords were more numerous, and had more secular power, in Germany than in any other country. Some of the clergy were as rude and ignorant as the laity, but this was not usually the case. For centuries they were the only class that made any pretensions to learning, and as a rule they tried to soften the manners of the nobles, and to shield the weak and oppressed against the tyranny of the strong.

9. **The revenue of the King.**—The King drew his revenue from the crown lands, which lay chiefly along the Rhine, and from customs, tolls, the right of coining, and other royal dues. He was not allowed to keep fiefs which he had held before being made King, nor could he add vacant fiefs to the crown lands.

10. **The Diet.**—There were now very few meetings of the people in Germany. An Assembly or Diet, however, met the King at certain times to consult with him on the affairs of the State. Ordinary freemen no longer attended it. It was made up of the leading nobles, secular and spiritual. This Diet existed, in one form or another, till the German Kingdom was broken up.

11. **Literature.**—The old heathen poetry treating of the famous deeds of heroes did not die out for a long time after Germany became Christian; but poems on Christian subjects began also to be written. Of these the best was "Heliand," a poem telling the story of the Gospels in a clear and forcible style. It is in a Low-Dutch dialect, and is said to have been written by a Saxon poet at the request of Lewis the Pious.

# CHAPTER VII.

## THE SAXON EMPERORS.

*Conrad of Franconia elected King; his army defeated by Henry of Saxony; his death (1)—Henry I. elected (2)—Henry I. defeats the Hungarians; seizes Lotharingia; his wars with the Duke of Bohemia, the Wends, and the Danes (3)—Henry I. builds towns and fortresses (4)—death of Henry I. (5)—election of Otto I.; he puts down a rebellion; gives Duchies to members of his family (6)—wars with the Danes and Slaves (7)—first expedition into Italy; Otto I. puts down a second rebellion (8)—defeat of the Hungarians (9)—Otto I. becomes King of Lombardy, and Emperor (10)—effects of the connexion of Germany with the Empire (11)—Otto II. crowned as Co-Imperator; death of Otto I. (12)—Provincial Palsgraves (13)—rebellion of Henry the Wrangler; wars of Otto II.; his death (14)—wise rule of Theophanô; Austria given to Leopold I. (15)—Otto III.; his schemes; death (16)—war of Henry II. with the Duke of Poland; his friendliness to the Church (17)—the title of "King of the Romans" (18)—Fürsten or Princes; castles of the nobles; private war (19)—growing power of the Church (20)—towns increase; the Patricians; the Gilds (21)—Literature and Art (22).*

1. **Conrad I.**—After the death of Lewis the Child the leading nobles met and elected *Conrad* of *Franconia* as King. Conrad was in every way well fitted for the throne; but during nearly the whole of his reign he had to carry on wars with his great vassals, who disliked his attempts to

increase the royal authority. *Henry*, Duke of *Saxony*, was his chief opponent. He defeated an army sent against him by Conrad. Conrad was more successful against two Counts who tried to become Dukes in Swabia; he defeated them, and put them to death. He also defeated the Duke of Bavaria, and made him for a time seek refuge among the Hungarians. In 918, however, whilst carrying on war with the Bavarians, Conrad received a wound of which he soon afterwards died. Before his death he advised that the crown should be offered to his old enemy, Henry of Saxony, whom, of all living men, he saw to be the best fitted to succeed him.

2. **Henry I.**—The nobles of Franconia met at *Fritzlar*, and, carrying out the wishes of Conrad, elected Henry as his successor. Henry is usually called *Henry the Fowler*, from a tradition that the messengers who brought him the news of his election found him among the Harz mountains with his falcons. The Saxons were of course very willing that their Duke should become King; but the Dukes of Bavaria and Swabia opposed him. Within a short time, however, he was acknowledged by all; and he soon proved himself the wisest and strongest King who had yet reigned in Germany.

3. **Wars of Henry I.**—In Henry's time the Hungarians, who had made incursions under Conrad, began again to invade Germany. In 924 one of their princes fell into his hands. In return for this prisoner they granted him a truce for nine years, on condition that he should pay them tribute. When the truce was at an end, the Hungarians came back to Germany; but Henry was now so well prepared for them that he thoroughly defeated them in a great battle, said to have been fought near *Merseburg*. After this the Hungarians kept in their own country while Henry lived. The Germans were so grateful to their King

for the victory he had gained that they greeted him as
"Imperator" and "Father of the Fatherland." Before this
battle Henry, taking advantage of the confusion in the
Western kingdom, had seized *Lotharingia*, and given it to
a Duke who held it as a fief of the German crown. For
centuries after his time Lotharingia remained part of the
German kingdom. Henry had also had much fighting
with the Slaves. He had forced the Duke of *Bohemia* to
do homage for his Duchy, and had overthrown the *Wends*,
whose country lay to the north-east of Germany. After the
battle of Merseburg, Henry made war on the *Danes*, who
had invaded Saxony and Friesland. He not only drove
them back, but took possession of the lands between the
*Eider* and the *Schlei*.

4. **Government of Henry I. The Growth of Towns.**—
Henry was a wise ruler as well as a brave defender of his
kingdom. He introduced more orderly methods of fighting
than the Germans had yet known, and, that they might be
the better able to meet the Hungarians, trained the nobles
and their vassals to fight on horseback. But he is chiefly
famous as the founder of the *burgher class*. He saw how
necessary it was, if the Germans were to be safe against
such an enemy as the Hungarians, that there should be
strong places in which they could take refuge if they were
defeated. He therefore built walls round the towns which
already existed, and founded new towns. He also built
many fortresses, around which towns gradually grew up.
Every ninth freeman was compelled to live in the nearest
town or fortress as a defender and builder, while the remaining eight maintained him, and laid up stores against
time of need by giving a third of their produce. Henry
decreed that all public meetings and festivities should take
place in towns, and provided for the administration of
justice among the inhabitants. Thus encouraged, towns

grew quickly both during and after Henry's time; and many freemen came and lived in them. A new class, that of *burghers*, thus gradually arose in Germany. They were the great trading class of the country, and soon became the best friends of the Kings in their quarrels with the nobles.

5. **Death of Henry I.**—When Henry had defeated all his enemies, he thought of going to Rome to claim the Imperial crown; but he was never able to do so. In 935 he fell sick, and next year he died at *Memleben*. Before his death he had summoned a Diet at *Erfurt*, and got the nobles to promise that they would recognize his son *Otto* as his successor.

6. **Otto I.**—In accordance with the promise given to Henry by the nobles, Otto was elected and crowned King at Aachen in 936. He was twenty-four years of age when he began to reign, and had been married during his father's life-time to *Eadgyth* or *Edith*, daughter of the English King *Edward*, and granddaughter of *Alfred*. Henry had added so much to the kingly power that at Otto's coronation the Dukes for the first time performed the nominally menial offices of the royal household. The Duke of *Lotharingia* acted as *chamberlain;* the Duke of *Franconia* as *carver;* the Duke of *Swabia* as *cup-bearer;* and the Duke of *Bavaria* as *master of the horse*. In a short time, however, the Dukes of Franconia and Lotharingia joined *Thankmar*, Otto's half-brother, in a rebellion against the young King. Thankmar was soon slain; but his place was taken by the King's full brother *Henry*, who had always hankered after the crown. Otto fought bravely in defence of his rights, and he was at last victorious. The Dukes of Franconia and Lotharingia both fell, and Henry, after being several times forgiven, submitted. He received the Duchy of Bavaria, which fell vacant in 945; and he

garians. Otto kept the Duchy of Franconia in his own hands, and gave that of Lotharingia to *Count Conrad*, who afterwards married *Luitgard*, Otto's only daughter. When, in 949, Duke *Hermann* of Swabia died, Otto's son *Ludolf*, who had married Hermann's daughter, was appointed his successor. All the great Duchies were thus brought into the hands either of Otto himself or of members of his family, so that he became very powerful. He was by no means content to be a mere nominal King. The Dukes, although nearly related to him, knew, when doing homage for their Duchies, that he would insist on his rights to the uttermost, and that he had sufficient power to enforce them.

7. **Wars of Otto I.**—Otto was not only strong at home; he early made himself feared in other countries. He several times took part in the quarrels of the West Frankish Kingdom, and helped his brother-in-law, King *Lewis*, against the Dukes of France and Normandy. The Danes won back for a time the territory which Henry the Fowler had conquered; but Otto made war on them, compelled *Harold Blue Tooth* to become his man, and set up the Mark of *Schleswig* for the defence of the German border. The Duke of Poland had also to do homage for his Duchy. From this time, till the thirteenth century, Denmark and Poland were always looked on as fiefs of the German crown. Otto's Margraves, *Hermann Billung* and *Gero*, long fought bravely against the Slaves, and won Slavonic land—the former along the shores of the Baltic, the latter between the Middle Elbe and the Oder. In all lands conquered by him, Otto was careful to plant German colonies. He also founded bishopricks, and used every means to make the people Christian. In 968 he founded the archbishoprick of *Magdeburg*.

8. **Otto I. in Italy. Rebellion in Germany.**—In 951 an appeal was made to Otto on behalf of the beautiful

Queen *Adelheid*, whom *Berengar*, the Lombard King, wished to marry his son *Adalbert*. Otto went to Italy, and as his wife Edith had died six years before, he married Queen Adelheid. He took the title of *King of the Lombards*, but afterwards confirmed Berengar in the possession of Lombardy as his vassal. Soon after this Otto's son Ludolf, Duke of Swabia, rebelled; and he was joined by Conrad of Lotharingia, the Archbishop of Mainz, and other nobles. After much fighting the rebellion was at last put down. Otto gave the Duchy of Lotharingia to his brother, *Bruno*, Archbishop of Köln, and Swabia to *Burchard*, the son-in-law of Henry of Bavaria. *William*, Otto's eldest son, having entered the Church, was made Archbishop of Mainz.

9. **Defeat of the Hungarians.**—Taking advantage of the troubled state of Germany, the Hungarians had again begun to invade the country. In 955 they entered Bavaria in vast numbers. Otto had now put down Ludolf's rebellion, and was able to turn his whole strength against the enemy. A great battle was fought on the banks of the Lech, near *Augsburg*. Otto encouraged his troops by taking direct part in the battle, and he was bravely seconded by Conrad, who wished to wipe out the memory of his rebellion against his father-in-law. At last the Hungarians had to fly, and many thousands of them were slain. The victory was dearly bought, for Conrad and many other nobles fell. But the end was worth the sacrifice. By this victory Otto completed the work which his father had begun. The Hungarians now ceased to invade Germany, and till the thirteenth century their Kings were usually, at least in name, subject to the German Kings.

10. **Otto I. becomes Emperor.**—In 961 Otto's young son *Otto* was crowned King in Aachen. The elder Otto then went to Italy, which had again fallen into confusion.

During this second visit he caused himself to be crowned King of Lombardy, and on February 2, 962, he was crowned Roman Emperor by the Pope. His three immediate predecessors on the German throne had been neither Kings of Lombardy nor Emperors; but from this time the German Kings claimed as their right both the Lombard and the Imperial crowns. Otto and his successors thought very little of their royal as compared with their Imperial title. They still remained German Kings; but after their coronation at Rome they were usually thought and spoken of only as Emperors. An Emperor held a much higher position than a mere feudal Sovereign, and claimed from his subjects a more thorough submission.

11. **Effects of the connexion of Germany with the Empire.**—The connexion of the German kingdom with the Empire had many important results in Germany. Up to Otto's time there had been very little truly national feeling among the Germans. They thought of themselves as Franks, Saxons, Swabians, and so forth; hardly at all as a united people. But when their Kings acquired the right to be crowned Roman Emperors they themselves became the Imperial race. They began, therefore, to take pride in the common German name. A feeling of nationality was thus aroused, which never afterwards quite left the Germans even in their darkest periods. On the whole, however, Germany was not the better for its connexion with the Empire. By being Emperors the German Kings became involved in struggles with which their native kingdom had nothing to do. They thus wasted much German blood and treasure; and they lost almost all real power. Whilst they were absent, sometimes for years at a time, carrying on distant wars, their great vassals at home ruled as sovereign princes within their dominions. When the Emperors returned, and tried

to assert their right as feudal Kings, they too often found that they had spent nearly all their strength, and could do very little against a united and powerful aristocracy. Germany was thus kept from growing up, like France and England, into a firm monarchy, and was in the end divided into many practically independent small States.

12. **Coronation of Otto II. as Emperor. Death of Otto I.**—The last years of Otto's life were spent almost wholly in Italy, where he exercised to the full his Imperial rights. In 967 King Otto was crowned Emperor, and from that time reigned as "Co-Imperator" with his father. He was married in 972 to *Theophanô*, the daughter of the Eastern Emperor *Nicephorus*. In the same year the elder Otto returned to Germany, where he died in 973. During his lifetime he had been called Otto the Great, and he deserved the title, for he began an important epoch in history and raised his country to a great height of splendour.

13. **Provincial Palsgraves.**—One of the institutions of Otto which exercised considerable influence on the future of Germany was that of provincial Palsgraves. These officers managed the royal lands and dues, and dispensed justice in the name of the sovereign. They thus helped to deprive the Dukes of some of their importance. But they themselves were sometimes unfaithful servants. In the troubled periods through which Germany afterwards passed they often seized the royal lands and established themselves as independent feudal lords.

14. **Otto II.**—Otto II. was at the time of his father's death nineteen years old. He had much of his father's decision of character; but he did not live long enough to do all that he was capable of doing. He had not long reigned alone when *Henry the Wrangler*, of Bavaria, son of the Henry who had so often rebelled against Otto I., revolted. The rebellion was soon put down, and Henry

himself was imprisoned and deprived of his Duchy. King Harold of Denmark, and the Dukes of Bohemia and Poland, all tried to make themselves independent; but they were compelled, one after another, to submit. In 978, when Otto was in Aachen, *Lothar*, the West Frankish King, suddenly tried to seize Lotharingia. Aachen was taken; and Otto had just time to escape. A Diet was at once summoned, and the nobles willingly agreed to support Otto in winning back the Duchy. At the head of a considerable army he entered the West Frankish kingdom, and marched towards Paris. The Germans encamped on *Montmartre*, but as winter came on they had to return home without having taken the city. In the end, however, Lothar gave up all claim to Lotharingia. In 980, the Emperor, whose sympathies were always more Italian than German, went to Italy; and he never returned. Having tried to conquer Southern Italy, he was defeated in 982, and next year he died at Rome. Before his death he had summoned a Diet at *Verona*, where his infant son Otto had been elected his successor. The Wends had revolted during his absence, and destroyed several Episcopal Sees in the north.

15. **Regency of Theophanô.**—While *Otto III.* was a child, his mother Theophanô acted as Regent. Henry of Bavaria having been set free at once took the field, and for a time he got possession of the young King's person. He would perhaps have seized the throne, but the chief nobles remained loyal. *Willigis*, a wheelwright's son who had risen to the position of Archbishop of Mainz, and the Dukes of Swabia, Saxony, and Bavaria, all opposed Henry's claims. At last, in 984, he gave Otto back to Theophanô, and became so thoroughly reconciled to the dynasty that his Duchy was restored to him. During Theophanô's administration, the frontiers, except in the north, were well

defended. She gave the Mark of *Austria* to *Leopold I.* of the house of *Babenberg.* Leopold conquered a good deal of Hungarian territory, and peopled it with German colonists. From this time the house of Babenberg held the Austrian lands till the family died out in the thirteenth century.

16. **Otto III.**—Otto had various tutors, but by far the most distinguished was *Gerbert*, the profoundest scholar and most ambitious thinker of his age. Under him the youthful King made so much progress that he was called *The Wonder of the World.* In 996, when he was scarcely sixteen, he went to Rome with an army drawn from all parts of Germany, and was crowned Emperor. Three years afterwards he raised Gerbert to the Papal See. The young Emperor was very little of a German. He was dreamy and imaginative, and early formed the idea of making Rome once more the centre of the world, with Germany as a mere province of the Empire. His vague schemes, however, were suddenly cut short by his death near Rome in 1002. In the year 1000, when in Aachen, he had opened the tomb of Charles the Great, whose body, dressed in Imperial robes, still sat on its marble throne. Otto's body was, in accordance with his own request, carried to Aachen, and buried beside that of Charles.

17. **Henry II.**—*Henry*, Duke of Bavaria, son of Henry the Wrangler, was nearest of kin to the Saxon dynasty. His claim to the throne was for some time disputed, but in 1003 he was generally acknowledged King. During the reigns of Otto II. and Otto III. the great nobles had been making themselves more independent, so that Henry had much difficulty in getting his authority recognized. He had also to put down rebellions in the States subject to Germany. *Boleslaw Chrobry*, Duke of Poland, had conquered Bohemia and Silesia. For fourteen years war raged

between Henry and this powerful vassal. In the end, Boleslaw had to give up Bohemia and Meissen, and to do homage to Henry; but he was virtually independent, and after Henry's death he caused himself to be proclaimed King of Poland. In 1004 Henry had become King of Italy; and in 1014 he was crowned Emperor. He was a devoted friend of the Church, and treated it so generously that he was afterwards called "Saint." He died in 1024, and was buried in *Bamberg*, where he had founded a bishoprick.

18. **The Title of "King of the Romans."**—Up to the time of Henry II. the German Kings were called "Kings of the East Franks" or "Kings of the Franks and Saxons." They did not become Emperors till they had been crowned at Rome. Henry II. did not venture any more than his predecessors to call himself Emperor until he had received the Imperial crown from the Pope; but he was anxious to establish the principle that as German King he had the right of sovereignty over Rome. He therefore took the title of "King of the Romans." This afterwards became the recognized title of the German Kings before their coronation as Emperors.

19. **The Nobles.**—The highest class of nobles were now called *Fürsten* or *Princes*. Henry II. had done his utmost to make this class submissive; but he had only been partly successful. They were not for some time yet to become almost independent sovereigns; but during the reigns of the Ottos, whose duties as Emperors had taken them so much out of Germany, they had already done something towards gaining this end. At the head of the *secular* princes were the Dukes; after them came the Palsgraves and Margraves. Every prince and noble now lived in a castle or tower. These buildings were usually very cheerless; but they were strong, and it was chiefly to serve as

strongholds that they were built. They were commonly built on some high hill or other site where they could not be easily reached, and where they commanded a good view of the neighbouring country. The custom of private warfare was now very common; and for centuries after this time it was a source of great suffering to all classes.

20. **The Church.**—The connexion of Germany with the Empire had added very greatly to the power of the Church, for the Emperor was its secular head, and felt himself bound to support and strengthen it. It now possessed about half the land of Germany; and the great prelates held princely rank. There were six archbishopricks—those of *Mainz, Köln, Trier, Bremen, Magdeburg*, and *Salzburg*. The Archbishop of Mainz, as Primate of Germany, was the first *spiritual* prince; next in rank to him were the Archbishops of Köln and Trier. The Saxon Emperors, in adding to the power of the Church, doubtless wished, like Charles the Great, to lessen that of the aristocracy. But in the end the spiritual princes proved as dangerous as the secular princes. In the struggle which at a later time arose between the Empire and the Papacy, they rarely hesitated to side with the Papacy.

21. **The Towns.**—Many towns had been built since the time of Henry the Fowler. They grew up chiefly around cathedrals, monasteries, fortresses, and the castles of great nobles. They were divided into two classes—those which were immediately dependant on the crown, and those which were dependant on some mediate lord. In each town there was a *Burgrave* or *Bailiff*, who represented the King or other lord of the town, and administered justice. The old families of the towns kept themselves apart from the new-comers, and were afterwards called *Patricians*. In some towns this class was soon allowed to choose councillors who helped the Bailiffs in their duties; and in the

end they tried, especially in the immediate towns, to get rid of the Bailiffs altogether. The tradespeople formed themselves into *Gilds*, which at first had nothing to do with politics, but afterwards became of great political importance.

22. **Literature and Art.**—In the time of Otto I., Archbishop *Bruno* founded a famous school in Köln; and *Hroswitha*, perhaps a relative of the royal house, wrote in the nunnery of *Gandersheim* well-known comedies in the style of Terence. Otto II. and Otto III., partly through the influence of Adelheid and Theophanô, did a good deal to encourage learning. They founded schools, and got famous scholars, like Gerbert, to come and stay at their court. But Latin, not German, was the language in which all works of importance were written. The Saxon Kings built many churches, chiefly in the so-called *Romanesque* style; and sculpture, painting, and music were zealously cultivated in the service of the Church.

# CHAPTER VIII.

## THE FRANCONIAN EMPERORS.

*Election of Count Conrad* (1)—*good government of Conrad II.* (2) —*Conrad II. crowned King of Burgundy* (3)—*rebellion of Duke Ernst of Swabia* (4)—*wars of Conrad II.* (5)—*all fiefs made hereditary; death of Conrad II.* (6)—*strong government of Henry III.; he proclaims a general peace, and encourages learning* (7)—*wars of Henry III.* (8)—*Henry III. and the Papacy; his death.* (9)—*weak government of Agnes* (10)—*Henry IV. falls into the hands first of Hanno, Archbishop of Köln, and afterwards of Adalbert, Archbishop of Bremen* (11)—*Henry IV. irritates the Saxons* (12)—*Bertha, Henry IV.'s Queen* (13)— *the Saxons rebel; are for a time triumphant; defeated* (14)— *Henry IV. and Gregory VII.* (15)—*Henry IV. humbled by Gregory VII.* (16)—*Rudolf of Swabia elected King; Gregory VII. sides with him; Rudolf slain; his Duchy given to Frederick of Büren* (17)—*rival Kings; submission of the Saxons* (18)—*rebellion of Henry IV.'s sons; his death* (19)— *Henry V. and the Papacy; rebellion; the Concordat of Worms; death of Henry V.* (20)—*King Lothar; submission to the Pope; Henry the Proud; death of Lothar* (21)—*loss of power by the German Kings* (22)—*growing importance of the lower nobility* (23) *private war; the Truce of God* (24)—*robbery* (25).

1. **Election of Count Conrad.**—Lotharingia was now divided into two Duchies—*Upper* and *Lower;* and Carinthia had been taken by Otto III. from Bavaria and made a separate Duchy. There were thus at this time, if we take in the

Duke of Bohemia, eight Dukes in Germany. These Dukes, and the Counts and Prelates of Germany, all accompanied by their vassals, now assembled on the banks of the Rhine, between Mainz and Worms, to elect a new King. The choice of the Assembly fell on *Count Conrad*, a Franconian nobleman, and cousin to the Duke of Franconia. The two cousins sprang from the Conrad who had married a daughter of Otto I., and were thus related through the female line to the Saxon dynasty.

2. **Government of Conrad II.**—*Conrad II.*, who was forty years old at the time of his election, proved a wise and firm ruler. Soon after his coronation he rode through the kingdom administering justice and severely punishing robbers. One of the chief objects of his reign was to increase the power of the crown by lessening that of the Dukes and other princes; and in this he was very successful. He gave the Duchies of Bavaria, Swabia, and Carinthia, one after the other, in fief to his son *Henry*, who at an early period showed great strength of character, and gave promise of being able to carry out his father's plans. The burgher class was especially friendly to Conrad, for he favoured the cities, and did everything he could to make them look to the King as their natural protector against the nobles.

3. **The Kingdom of Burgundy.**—Conrad was crowned Emperor in 1027. The year before he had been crowned King of Italy. At his coronation as Emperor two Kings were present—*Rudolf III.* of Burgundy, and *Cnut* of England and Denmark. Conrad was on friendly terms with both of these Kings. His son Henry married Cnut's daughter, *Cunihild*; and he gave up to Cnut the Mark of Schleswig. Rudolf, whose niece *Gisela* was Conrad's wife, appointed Conrad, as he had before appointed Henry II., to be his successor. When Rudolf died, in 1032, Conrad met with some resistance in Burgundy; but he was

crowned King, and was soon generally acknowledged. This kingdom did not take in the *Duchy* of Burgundy, which was a fief of the French King. After Conrad's time the German King had a right to the crown of Burgundy; but owing to the weakness of later Kings the greater part of the country was in the end absorbed by France.

4. **Duke Ernst of Swabia.**—Duke *Ernst* of Swabia, who was the son of Gisela by a former marriage, believed himself to be King Rudolf's lawful heir. When, therefore, Rudolf made Conrad his heir, Ernst thought himself wronged, and tried to raise a rebellion. But his vassals refused to follow him against their King and Emperor, so that his attempt failed. Conrad took his Duchy from him, and imprisoned him in a castle in Thuringia. He was afterwards set free; and Conrad offered to give him back his Duchy if he would tell where Count *Werner*, who had helped him in trying to stir up a rebellion, was hiding. Ernst generously refused to do this. He afterwards joined Count Werner in the Black Forest, where the two nobles lived for some time by robbery. In 1030 both were killed in battle. The adventures of Duke Ernst roused a great deal of popular sympathy, and afterwards became the subject of many songs and legends.

5. **Wars of Conrad II.**—Conrad carried on many wars, and always bravely. The Duke of Bohemia several times rebelled, but he was forced to return to his allegiance. The Poles invaded Germany, but were driven back; and King *Miesko* had to do homage for his crown, and to give up *Lusatia*, which Boleslaw had received from Henry II. Conrad also caused the Slaves on the banks of the Oder and the Lower Elbe to submit. He had more trouble with King *Stephen* of Hungary; but in 1031 Conrad's son Henry made even this powerful King accept peace.

6. **Edict of Conrad II. His Death.**—Conrad visited

Italy a second time in 1037. It was during this visit that he issued the famous *Edict*, in which he decreed that fief-holders should not have their lands taken from them except by the judgment of their peers. All fiefs were thus made hereditary. The edict was meant to strengthen the lower vassals, and to make them feel that they owed a higher allegiance to the King than to their immediate lords. It applied at first only to Lombardy; but it very soon became law also in Germany. Two years after this visit to Italy Conrad died, and was buried at *Speyer*, whose fine cathedral he had founded.

7. **Henry III.**—*Henry III.*, Conrad's son, had already been crowned German King and King of Burgundy. He was now twenty-two years of age, and had many of the best qualities of a King. He continued his father's policy towards the great princes and the lower vassals, and became probably the strongest ruler since Charles the Great. The Duchies of Bavaria, Swabia, and Carinthia, which he had received from his father, he gave to princes who were content to act in all respects as the King's men. The Duchy of Upper Lotharingia having become vacant, Henry gave it also to one on whose obedience he could depend. *Gottfried*, the Duke of Lower Lotharingia, opposed this appointment; but he was overcome, and had to retire to Italy. Henry did not use his great power for selfish ends. In 1043 he proclaimed a General Peace throughout the kingdom, and succeeded, as no King did for centuries after his time, in putting down private war. He also encouraged learning, and reformed the abuses of the Church, trying to make it in every way more worthy of its great work.

8. **The Hungarians.**—Henry had to put down rebellions in Bohemia and Burgundy; but his chief wars were those carried on by him against the Hungarians. He defeated

them in 1044, and forced them to recognize King *Peter*, who had succeeded King Stephen, but had been deposed. Peter did homage to Henry for his crown. A second expedition into Hungary was less successful; but in 1057 *Andreas*, who had in the meantime become King, was obliged to follow Peter's example, and become Henry's man. Henry took the country between the *Kahlenberg* and the *Leitha*, and added it to the Mark of Austria.

9. **Henry III. and the Papacy. His death.**—In 1046 Henry was crowned Emperor by *Clement II.*, a German whom he had made Pope after deposing the three rival Popes. He also took the old title of *Patrician*. As Emperor, Henry always treated the Pope as his dependant. He raised no fewer than four Germans, one after the other, to the Papal chair. Had he lived, he might have brought the Papacy still further under the Empire, as he would certainly have added to the power of the Crown in Germany. But this great Emperor died in 1056, when still a young man, and in the the fulness of his strength.

10. **Henry IV. Agnes.**—At the time of his father's death *Henry IV.* was only six years old. His mother *Agnes* became Regent. She was an amiable and devout lady, but without the strength necessary for her high position. Her weak government enabled the princes to win back much of the power which the last two kings had taken from them. Agnes made matters worse by giving several vacant Duchies to princes who were not friendly to her. She thus prepared trouble for her son when he should be old enough to rule in his own name.

11. **The youth of Henry IV.**—*Hanno, Archbishop of Köln*, was one of those who were most unfriendly to the reigning family. In 1062 he got possession of the young King, and forced Agnes to retire from the Regency. He then proposed that Henry should live at the courts of the

Dukes, one after the other, and that the Bishop of the Diocese in which he happened to stay should be his guardian, and act as Regent. In reality he hoped to keep the chief power of the kingdom in his own hands. There was, however, another powerful Prelate, *Adalbert, Archbishop of Bremen*, who was jealous of Hanno. He had founded several bishopricks in Slavonic lands, and wished to become the strongest spiritual prince in Germany. He tried every means to take Henry from Hanno, and at last succeeded. Henry was very willing to change his guardian, for Hanno was a stern man, while Adalbert was gay and good-humoured, and lived in splendid style. Unfortunately, Henry acquired under Adalbert's influence many low tastes, and became wayward and passionate. Above all, he was taught to look on the Dukes of the kingdom as his greatest enemies, and to dislike the Saxons.

12. **Henry IV. and the Saxons.**—In 1065 Henry was declared to have reached his majority. He fixed his court at *Goslar*, where his father had usually lived, and still looked on Adalbert as his best friend and adviser. He began his reign very badly, treating the Saxons with great harshness, and acting as if he intended to add their Duchy to the royal lands. In 1066 the princes compelled Adalbert to separate from him; but Henry did not change his plans. He built forts in different parts of Saxony, making one near Goslar, called the *Harzburg*, especially strong. In 1069 Adalbert returned to court, and encouraged the King in his tyranny, so that the Saxons became more and more discontented.

13. **Bertha, Henry IV.'s Queen.**—Henry had been betrothed by his father to *Bertha*, daughter of the Margrave of *Susa*, and had afterwards been compelled to marry her. He disliked her, and wished to be divorced. The Archbishop of Mainz offered to help him to obtain a divorce if

he should compel the Thuringians to pay tithes to the See of Mainz. Henry promised to do so, and thus made the Thuringians his enemies; but the Pope would not grant a divorce. Bertha bore bravely the rudeness of her husband, and at last overcame him by her goodness, and proved his best helper during many trying years.

14. **Otto of Nordheim. War with the Saxons.**—Agnes had made *Otto* of *Nordheim*, a powerful Saxon Count, Duke of Bavaria. Henry unjustly took his Duchy from him, and gave it to *Welf*, son of the Margrave *Azzo* of *Este*, who had married a descendant of the ancient Bavarian house of Welf. Welf was a feeble prince, but became the founder of a powerful family. Otto entered into a conspiracy with Count *Magnus*, son and heir of the Saxon Duke. Both were overcome and imprisoned. Otto was soon set free, but Magnus, even after his father's death, was kept in close confinement. In 1073 a number of Saxon nobles suddenly appeared at Goslar and demanded that their young Duke should be given up to them. Henry, not knowing how strong was the feeling he had roused against himself, treated them contemptuously, and dismissed them. Almost immediately afterwards an army of 60,000 men marched on Goslar. Henry was taken by surprise, and fled to Harzburg; but he soon felt himself unsafe, and for three days wandered through the Harz mountains, accompanied by only a few faithful followers. When at last he reached Tribur, he summoned his great vassals to his aid against the rebellious Saxons. It was now that he felt how ill-advised his past conduct had been. The burghers of Worms, against the will of their Bishop, opened their gates to him, and offered to help him; but they, and the citizens of some other towns, were almost his only friends. The Saxons were thus free to do what they pleased; and they allowed their revenge to

carry them too far. They not only freed their Duke, and destroyed the fortresses built by Henry; they plundered and burned churches, and dug up and brutally insulted the remains of a brother and child of Henry. This conduct shocked even the King's enemies, so that he was soon able to gather a large army. A battle was fought near *Langensalza* in 1075. Many fell on both sides; but at last the Saxons had to fly. Promises were made to them in Henry's name which led them to submit; but Henry did not keep his word. He took the lands of many nobles, and gave them in fief to vassals of his own. He also caused the fortresses to be built again. Otto of Nordheim, his bitterest enemy, was the only noble whom he treated generously. He not only restored this prince to his Saxon lands, but made him administrator of the Duchy.

15. **Henry IV. and Gregory VII.**—Henry was now on the verge of a struggle far greater than that which, as he hoped, he had just ended. He had treated with contempt the famous decree of Pope *Gregory VII.*, condemning feudal investitures to the clergy. It was quite natural that he should do so, for if Gregory's wishes had been carried out, the spiritual princes would have owed allegiance to none save the Pope. Had Henry been a popular King, Gregory would probably not have dared to do anything against him. But Germany was deeply discontented. Saxony, although for the moment subdued, was eager to rebel; and *Rudolf* of *Swabia*, *Otto* of *Nordheim*, and a host of other enemies wished for nothing more than to see Henry humbled. Gregory resolved to take advantage of this state of things for his own ends. By overcoming Henry, he would not only settle the question of investitures; he would establish beyond dispute the principle on which he so earnestly insisted, that the Pope, as the viceroy of God, was above all earthly rulers—the Emperor, and the King who

claimed the right to be crowned Emperor, not less than other sovereigns. In 1075, therefore, Gregory summoned Henry to appear before him at Rome to answer to charges brought against him by the Saxons and others. Henry looked on this as priestly arrogance, and, at a Synod of German Bishops held at Worms early in the following year, caused Gregory to be deposed. The Pope replied not only by excommunicating Henry, but by declaring him no longer King, and by absolving his subjects from their oath of allegiance to him. Henry was not prepared for the result. Some remained true to him ; but his enemies openly accepted the Papal sentence, and such was the power of the Church that large numbers whom mere secular disputes might not have separated from him now either wavered in their loyalty or left him altogether. The whole German nation was at once divided into two hostile parties. The struggle which thus arose was to prove the bitterest and most prolonged of the Middle Ages, for it was to be a struggle of the two greatest powers on earth, the *Papacy* and the *Empire* for supremacy. The details of the struggle belong only in part to German history.

16. **Henry IV. humbled by Gregory VII.**—The first step of the princes opposed to Henry was to summon an Assembly for the purpose of electing a new King. The Assembly met at Tribur. Henry now saw the danger of his position, and tried hard to influence the Assembly in his favour. The princes at last agreed that the affairs of the kingdom should be laid before the Pope at Augsburg during the next festival of the Purification. If at the end of a year Henry remained excommunicate he was no longer to be looked on as King. The princes did not really wish Henry to be reconciled to the Pope ; but he himself felt that this was the only way in which he could now save his throne. He accordingly resolved to go and see Gregory. The

winter of 1076-7 was an unusually severe one; but Henry, accompanied by his faithful wife Bertha and their infant son, started secretly for Italy. In crossing the Alps they met with great difficulties; but at length, aided by hired guides, they safely reached Lombardy. Although Henry was warmly received by many Lombard nobles and prelates, he hastened to the castle of *Canossa*, whither Gregory had gone on hearing of his arrival. Henry had to stand three days, bare-headed and meanly clad, in the inner court of the castle, exposed to the bitter cold, waiting till Gregory should consent to see him. When at last he was admitted, the sentence of excommunication was removed; but he had to promise that Gregory should be allowed to settle the difficulties of the German kingdom, and that meanwhile he himself should not take again his position as King.

**17. Henry IV. and Rudolf of Swabia. Frederick of Büren.**—The discontented German nobles met at *Forchheim* in March, 1077, formally proclaimed their right to choose a new sovereign, and elected *Rudolf,* Duke of *Swabia*, as King. Henry hastened home, and was joined by a large party, the cities proving especially loyal friends. Rudolf was driven from Swabia, and took refuge among the Saxons, who, headed by Otto of Nordheim, bravely supported him. For a time Pope Gregory decidedly took part with neither side, but at length, in 1080, he recognized Rudolf, and once more excommunicated Henry. Henry replied as before, by summoning a council of German prelates, who deposed Gregory, and recognized the Archbishop of Ravenna, under the name of *Clement III.,* as Pope. In the same year Henry lost a battle near Zeitz; but the victory of the enemy was only in name, for Rudolf himself was killed. The Duchy of Swabia had some time before been given to *Frederick* of *Büren,* a nobleman who had built his castle on the hill of *Staufen,* in what is now the kingdom of *Würtem-*

*berg*. Frederick at the same time married Henry's daughter, *Agnes*. He was thus the founder of the great *Hohenstaufen* family, under whose rule Germany and the Empire were to rise to their highest fame and splendour.

18. **Submission of the Saxons.**—After Rudolf's death Henry's cause quickly gained ground. In 1081 he felt himself strong enough to leave the conduct of the war in Germany in the hands of Frederick of Swabia, whilst he himself went to Italy. He was crowned Emperor at Rome by Clement III., and in 1085 returned to Germany, having amply revenged the humiliation of Canossa. Meanwhile, the Saxons had recognized *Hermann* of *Luxemburg* as their King, but in 1087 he resigned the crown; and another claimant, *Eckbert*, Margrave of *Meissen*, was murdered. The Saxons were now thoroughly weary of strife, and as years and bitter experience had softened the character of Henry, they were the more willing to return to their allegiance. Peace was therefore, for a time, restored in Germany.

19. **Rebellion of Henry IV.'s Sons. His death.**—The Papacy did not forgive Henry. He was excommunicated several times, and in 1091 his son *Conrad* was excited to rebel against him. In 1104 a more serious rebellion was headed by the Emperor's second son *Henry*, who had been crowned King, on promising not to seize the government during his father's lifetime, in 1099. The Emperor was treated very cruelly, and had to sign his own abdication at Ingelheim in 1105. A last effort was made on his behalf by the Duke of Lotharingia; but, worn out by his sorrows and struggles, Henry died in August, 1106. His body lay in a stone coffin in an unconsecrated chapel at Speyer for five years. Not till 1111, when the sentence of excommunication was removed, was it properly buried.

20. **Henry V. The Concordat of Worms.**—Henry V.

was not so obedient to the Church as the Papal party had hoped. He stoutly maintained the very point which had brought so much trouble on his father. The right of investiture, he declared, had always belonged to his predecessors, and he was not to give up what they had handed on to him. In 1110 he went to Rome, accompanied by a large army. Next year Pope Paschal II. was forced to crown him Emperor; but as soon as the Germans had crossed the Alps again Paschal renewed all his old demands. The struggle soon spread to Germany. The Emperor was excommunicated; and the discontented princes, as eager as ever to break the royal power, sided with the Pope against him. Peace was not restored till 1122, when Calixtus II. was Pope. In that year, in a Diet held at Worms, both parties agreed to a compromise, called *the Concordat of Worms.* The advantage decidedly rested with the Papacy. The Prelates were still to do homage for their lands; but the Emperor renounced the investiture with ring and staff, and agreed that Bishops and Abbots should henceforth be elected by the clergy. The Church was thus made to a large extent independent of the crown. During the remaining three years of his life Henry was at peace with the Church; but he had to fight constantly with rebellious nobles. Frederick of Swabia had been succeeded by his son *Frederick;* and a second son, *Conrad,* had been made Duke of Franconia. The Emperor had given his sister Agnes, the first Frederick's wife, in marriage to *Leopold,* Margrave of Austria. He had thus secured powerful friends in the south of Germany; but in the north he never thoroughly established his authority. He died at Utrecht in 1125. He had no children, and was therefore the last of the Franconian dynasty.

21. **Lothar of Saxony.**—The nobles once more assembled

with their vassals near Mainz, to elect a new King. Ten princes from each of the four leading Duchies, Franconia, Saxony, Swabia, and Bavaria, met in Mainz, and chose *Lothar, Duke* of *Saxony.* Lothar was opposed by the Hohenstaufen princes, Frederick and Conrad. In order to put them down he submitted as no German King had before done to the Papal See. Pope *Innocent II.* even claimed that Lothar, when being crowned Emperor, in 1133, became the Pope's man. Lothar's faithful ally in this war with the Hohenstaufen was *Henry the Proud*, Duke of Bavaria, of the house of Welf. This Duke married the Emperor's daughter, held the Italian lands of the *Countess Mathilda,* and also became Duke of Saxony. He was therefore as powerful as Lothar himself. In 1134 Frederick of Swabia yielded to Lothar; and his example was soon followed by his brother Conrad. Three years afterwards Lothar died in a peasant's hut in the Tyrol on his way back from Italy.

22. **Loss of power by the German Kings.**—The German Kings were now far from being what they had been in the time of the Ottos and of Henry III. The princes were of course still the men of the King, but they had taken every opportunity to seize royal rights, and they had many opportunities during the wars of Henry IV. and his successors. A new and strong dynasty was about to arise; but in the end the far-reaching ambition of the Hohenstaufen family was itself one of the means by which the great feudal lords became practically independent of the crown and of all other earthly power.

23. **The Lower nobility.**—When all fiefs became hereditary, the vassals of the great nobles rose very much in importance. They sometimes even refused to follow their lord into the field, as the vassals of Duke Ernst did when he wished to lead them against Conrad II. This

class also came to be looked on as noble; but no one could inherit land held immediately of the crown unless both his parents belonged to the higher aristocracy.

24. **Private Warfare.**—We have seen that Henry III. proclaimed a General Peace. In the disturbed time which followed his death this was soon set aside. The nobles might lay their disputes before the Diet or a special court of their peers; but they more usually appealed to arms. All that can be said for them is that when there was no strong Government the weaker side in any quarrel could seldom obtain full justice. The Church continued to fight against a custom which did so much harm, especially to the common folk. In the eleventh century some Bishops in Burgundy proclaimed what was called *The Truce of God*, an ecclesiastical law which required all private warfare to stop every week from sunset on Wednesday till sunrise on Monday. This law was gradually brought into Germany, and, although it was not always observed, it did at least something to lessen the evils of private war. Afterwards the spiritual and secular princes of certain districts sometimes united and bound themselves by oath to keep the peace for some stated time. This also did something to prepare the way for the time when private warfare should altogether cease.

25. **Robbery.**—Private warfare was not the only public evil from which Germany suffered; for many centuries robbery was also common all over the kingdom. The petty nobles often almost lived by robbery. It was always one of the chief aims of good Kings to punish robbers; and princes who cared for the prosperity of their vassals and subject towns also tried to put down the evil within their lands.

# CHAPTER IX.

## THE HOHENSTAUFEN EMPERORS.

*Conrad of Franconia elected King; he takes Saxony and Bavaria from Henry the Proud (1)—war between Conrad and Henry; Saxony given to Henry's son; Albert the Bear (2)—Count Welf continues the war; his defeat (3)—the Welfs and Waiblings (4) —Conrad III. joins the Second Crusade; his return and death (5)—election of Frederick I.; he gives Bavaria to Henry the Lion, and makes Austria a Duchy (6)—wars of Frederick I. in Italy (7)—Frederick I. and his subject States; crowned King of Burgundy (8)—wise government of Frederick I. (9)—Frederick I. takes Bavaria and Saxony from Henry the Lion (10)—Henry the Lion submits (11)—Frederick I. joins the Third Crusade; his death (12)—the King of the Romans (13)—Henry VI. makes peace with Henry the Lion (14)—Henry VI. and the kingdom of Sicily (15)—Henry VI. and Richard I. of England (16)— Henry VI. tries to make the crown hereditary; his death (17)— Kings Philip and Otto (18)—Otto excommunicated; Frederick II. made King (19)—character of Frederick II. (20)—absence of Frederick II. from Germany (21)—rebellion of Frederick II.'s son Henry (22)—Frederick II. marries Isabella, sister of Henry III.; holds a Diet at Mainz (23)—the Moguls driven back from Silesia (24)—Frederick II. and Pope Innocent IV. (25)— election of rival Kings; death of Frederick II. and Conrad IV. (26)—conquest of Slavonic lands (27)—further loss of power by the German Kings (28)—the Seven Electors (29)—the German Kings and the Pope (30)—increase of immediate nobles (32)— leading noble houses (32)—laws of inheritance (33)—institution of knighthood* (34)—*the towns* (35)—*leagues of towns; the Hansa* (36)—*the freeing of serfs* (37)—*the "Sachsenspiegel" and "Schwabenspiegel"* (38)—*the Femgerichte* (39)—*Architecture and Literature* (40).

1. **Conrad III. takes Saxony and Bavaria from Henry the Proud.**—Henry the Proud hoped to be made Lothar's successor; but he was disappointed. In 1138, the princes friendly to the Hohenstaufen met at *Coblentz* and elected *Conrad* of *Franconia* as King. Conrad, wishing to lessen the power of Henry the Proud, ordered him to give up Saxony, on the ground that it was unlawful for one prince to hold two Duchies. When Henry refused, both his Duchies were taken from him. Conrad gave Bavaria to *Leopold*, Margrave of Austria, and Saxony to *Albert the Bear*, who had received from King Lothar the Northern Mark of Saxony.

2. **Saxony given back to Henry's Son. Albert the Bear.**—War now broke out between Conrad and Henry the Proud. As usual, the cities were the best friends of the King. They were all the more friendly to him because the opposite party looked to the Pope for help, and the cities knew from experience how much harm might come of Papal interference. Henry the Proud soon died, and left a young son, afterwards known as *Henry the Lion*. Conrad, wishing to bring back peace, made Albert the Bear give up the Duchy of Saxony to Henry, and rewarded him by separating his Mark from Saxony, and making it immediate. After this Albert steadily pushed his conquests among the Wends, and seized the town of *Brandenburg*, which gave its name to his Mark. In his time we first hear of *Berlin*.

3. **Count Welf. The women of Weinsberg.**—*Count Welf*, Henry the Proud's brother, continued the war in

Bavaria; but in 1140 he was defeated. He took refuge in *Weinsberg*, which had long been besieged in vain, but now yielded. There is a story that Conrad agreed that the women of Weinsberg might leave the town before he should destroy it, and take with them whatever they chose to carry; and that next morning, when the gates were opened, a long line of women stumbled out, each carrying her husband or lover on her back. Conrad, the story says, was so touched by this that he not only let the women and the men they took with them escape, but spared the whole city.

4. **The Welfs and Waiblings.**—It was during the siege of Weinsberg that the followers of Conrad adopted as their war-cry *Waiblingen*, the name of a village where *Frederick*, Duke of Swabia, Conrad's brother, had been brought up. The rebels shouted *Welf*, the name of their leader. These war-cries, which the Italians corrupted into *Guelf* and *Ghibelin* became the names of the two great parties which divided the Empire. The *Welfs* sided with the Popes against the Emperors; the *Waiblings* supported the Emperors against the Popes.

5. **The Second Crusade. Death of Conrad III.**—Germany had been too much taken up with her own affairs in the time of Henry IV. to take any great part in the *First Crusade*. But in 1147 Conrad joined the *Second Crusade* with an army of 70,000 men. He was accompanied by his nephew *Frederick* of *Swabia*, his old enemy *Welf*, and many other princes. Conrad shewed great bravery during this Crusade; but he gained nothing, and came home in two years, his health broken by anxiety and suffering. Before his death he had again to put down a rebellion headed by Count Welf. As he was preparing to go to Italy to be crowned Emperor, he died at *Bamberg* in 1152.

6. **Frederick I. Henry the Lion receives Bavaria. Austria made a Duchy.**—Conrad had recommended that

his nephew, *Frederick*, should be made his successor; and his advice was followed. The new King, afterwards called, from his red beard, *Frederick Barbarossa*, was thirty-one years old at the time of his coronation. He was a man of free and noble nature, but had a strong will, and could be stern and harsh in asserting what he looked on as his rights. He was the son of Henry the Proud's sister, and his cousin Henry the Lion was his personal friend, so that he was anxious to heal the differences between the *Welfs* and the *Waiblings*. With a view to this he gave Henry the Lion, who already held the Duchy of Saxony, the Duchy of Bavaria, and thus made him by far the most powerful prince in Germany. To make up to Henry, Margrave of Austria, for yielding Bavaria, Frederick took Austria from Bavaria, and made it a separate Duchy. The new Duchy was made hereditary in the female as well as in the male line.

7. **Frederick I. and Italy.**—Frederick went to Italy in 1154, and was crowned King of Italy and Roman Emperor in the following year. This was the first of a series of expeditions made by Frederick to Italy, during which he carried on his famous struggle with the Papacy and the Lombard cities. This contest took up the best part of his life, so that, although he was a great German King, the leading events of his reign belong to Italian rather than to German history.

8. **Subject States. Burgundy.**—In the first year of his reign Frederick had made the King of Denmark do homage for his crown. The King of Poland, and King *Geisa* of Hungary, also became Frederick's men. *Wladislaw*, Duke of Bohemia, was so faithful a vassal that Frederick raised his Duchy to the rank of a kingdom. Frederick married *Beatrice*, heiress of the *Free County* of Burgundy, and thus brought this part of the Burgundian kingdom to his own family. He was afterwards crowned King of Burgundy at Arles.

**9. Home government of Frederick I.**—Frederick was as strong at home as abroad. Even he could not put down private wars; but he decreed that those about to begin such a war should give the enemy three day's notice. Those who did not do this were to be treated as robbers. Frederick also encouraged the cities, making some free, and giving others important privileges. The fame of his wars, and his good government, made him one of the most popular of German Kings. The struggle between the Empire and the Papacy had always hitherto stirred up strife in Germany; and this was still more the case in the time of Frederick's successors. The Popes, however, found that, out of Italy, they had no means of harming Frederick. All parties in Germany rallied round him. When a Papal legate declared in the Diet that the Empire was dependant on the Papacy, Frederick himself had to interfere to save the legate's life. Even the Prelates remained true to Frederick. Had they always been as loyal, the history of Germany might have been very different.

**10. Bavaria and Saxony taken from Henry the Lion.**—Henry the Lion became more and more powerful. He founded new towns—among others, *Munich*—and helped those which already existed, such as *Hamburg* and *Lübeck*, to become rich and strong. He also took many lands from the Wends along the shores of the Baltic. His greatness roused the jealousy of the other princes, whom he often offended by his arrogant manner. Frederick would probably not have interfered with him if he had remained a true vassal; but in 1175, when the Emperor was in the very heat of his struggle with Lombardy, Henry, on whom he had refused to bestow the city of Goslar, suddenly left him, and went home with his followers. Frederick, who is said to have gone on his knees and besought the Duke to stay, could not forgive this, and in 1178, when he returned to Germany, two years after the battle of *Legnano*, summoned Henry to appear before the Diet at Worms. Henry refused to come. In 1180, therefore, Frederick put him to the ban of the Empire, and, with the sanction of the Diet, pronounced him to have forfeited all his lands. Some lands in the east of Saxony were given as a Duchy to *Bernard* of *Anhalt*, son of Albert the Bear. *Philip*, *Archbishop* of *Köln*, received part of the west of Saxony, and ducal rights in the lands granted to him. The Duchy of Bavaria was given to *Otto* of *Wittelsbach*, a valued friend of Frederick; but it was greatly weakened by the separation of *Styria*.

11. **Submission of Henry the Lion.**—Henry did not quietly allow his lands to be taken from him. He fought bravely in their defence; but in 1181, feeling that his cause was hopeless, he came to Frederick at the Diet in *Erfurt*, and humbly craved forgiveness. Frederick was touched by the humiliation of his old friend. He could not give Henry back his Duchies; but he allowed him to keep *Brunswick* and *Lüneburg*. Henry undertook to live for three years at the court of *Henry II.*, King of England, whose daughter he had married. During his stay in England, a son, *William*, was born to him, from whom the present royal family of England is descended.

12. **The Third Crusade. Death of Frederick I.**—In 1189, when Frederick was an old man, he set out on a *Third Crusade* at the head of a large army; but he did not again see the Holy Land. As his army was crossing the river *Calicadnus*, in *Cilicia*, in June, 1190, he became impatient at the delay caused by the blocking up of a bridge, and dashed into the river on horseback. The stream carried him away, and before help could reach him he was drowned. He was buried in *Antioch;* but a tradition afterwards arose that he slept with his knights in a cavern of the *Kyffhäuser*

*Berg*, in *Thuringia*, and that, when the ravens should cease to fly around the mountain, he would awake and restore to Germany its ancient greatness.

13. **The King of the Romans.**—Frederick had his eldest son, *Henry*, chosen as his successor. In this he followed the example of several other Emperors; but Henry was the first to take, during the life-time of the Emperor, the title of "King of the Romans." After him any one elected and crowned during an Emperor's life-time always took this title. In the end almost every Emperor tried to have his successor chosen while he himself still lived. The King of the Romans exercised no independent authority while the Emperor was alive; but when the Emperor died a fresh election and coronation were not necessary.

14. **Henry VI.**—Henry VI. had much of his fathers's strength of character, but he was harsh and cruel. At the time of Frederick's death he was fighting Henry the Lion, who had come back from England, and begun the old contest. King Henry at once made peace, and hurried to Italy to receive the Imperial crown. Henry the Lion's son afterwards married a niece of Frederick Barbarossa, so that there was peace for some time between the two houses.

15. **The Kingdom of Sicily.**—A few years before his father's death Henry VI. had married *Constance*, heiress to the Kingdom of *Sicily*. One of the chief objects of his life, after he became Emperor, was to make himself thoroughly master of this kingdom. In trying to gain this end he was a great deal out of Germany, and sacrificed much blood and treasure.

16. **Henry VI. and Richard I. of England.**—In 1193 *Richard I.* of England was given up to Henry by *Leopold*, Duke of Austria, who had seized the English King as he was passing through Austria on his way homewards. Henry

made Richard appear before the Diet, and refused to set him free until the English people had paid a great ransom.

**17. Henry VI. tries to make the crown hereditary. His death.**—Henry was very anxious that the German crown should cease to be elective, and offered the princes many privileges if they would make it hereditary in his family. Some princes would have agreed to this proposal; but the Saxons, many of the clergy, and afterwards the Pope objected, so that the scheme had to be given up. In 1197, Henry suddenly died in Sicily, in his thirty-second year.

**18. Kings Philip and Otto.**—Henry VI.'s young son, *Frederick*, had already been elected King of the Romans, but his claims were now set aside. The *Waiblings*, or Hohenstaufen party, chose *Philip*, Henry VI.'s brother, as King; the *Welfs* elected *Otto*, the second son of Henry the Lion. These rival Kings carried on war with each other for ten years, during which the country was in great confusion. Had they been left to themselves, Philip would probably have gained an easy victory; but Otto was favoured by Pope *Innocent III.*, and this greatly strengthened him. At last, in 1208, Philip was murdered by a private enemy; and Otto was generally recognized as King.

**19. Frederick II.**—Otto was crowned Emperor in 1209. But Pope Innocent was offended by his showing some signs of independence, and soon turned against him. Frederick, Henry VI.'s son, to whom, since the death of his mother, Innocent had acted as guardian, had now grown up in Sicily to be a youth of high promise. Innocent excommunicated Otto, and called upon the German princes to elect Frederick as his successor. Otto set out for Southern Italy to attack his new rival; but as he learned on the way that the German princes had obeyed the Pope's command, he turned and hastened to Germany. Frederick also went to Germany, and was received with enthusiasm by the friends of his house. After this Otto gradually lost ground, and in the end he retired into private life. In 1215 Frederick, supported by the Pope, and by the great body of the German princes, was crowned King at Aachen.

20. **Character of Frederick II.**—Frederick II. was personally one of the greatest of the Emperors. He was so highly gifted that men called him *The Wonder of the World*. He knew many languages, was a man of science and a poet, and had ideas of government far beyond those of his own day. If he had lived in happier times he would have profoundly influenced the course of history. As it was, he did very little of lasting importance. His great powers were wasted in a long struggle with the Lombard cities and with the Papacy, which, although at first friendly to him, soon saw in him its most deadly enemy.

21. **Absence of Frederick II. from Germany.**—In 1220 Frederick went to Rome to be crowned Emperor, and he did not return for fifteen years. During that time he had very little directly to do with Germany; his struggle with the Lombard cities, and with Pope *Gregory IX.*, his crusade for the deliverance of Jerusalem, and the many pleasures of his brilliant court, took up almost all his thoughts. Before he left Germany he persuaded the princes to elect his young son *Henry* King of the Romans. This child, under *Engelbert*, Archbishop of Köln, was left as Regent in Germany. The nobles, who, during the struggle between Otto and Philip, had greatly added to their power, took advantage of Frederick's long absence to establish their independence more fully. Private wars went on all over the country; and robberies became once more common.

22. **Frederick II's son Henry rebels.**—Frederick's son Henry did not inherit his father's fine qualities. He was mean, rash, and violent. He resolved to seize the German

throne, and openly declared his intention, in 1234, to the assembled princes at *Boppart.* Next year the Emperor came to Germany. Henry tried to poison him, but was found out, and sent as a prisoner to *Apulia.*

**23. Marriage of Frederick II. Diet at Mainz.**—During this visit to Germany, Frederick married *Isabella*, sister of *Henry III* of England. There had never been such festivities in Germany as those which took place in Köln, where Frederick met the bride, and at Worms, where they were married. Some time after the wedding Frederick held a great Diet at Mainz, to which many princes and nobles came. At this Diet he decreed that private warfare should be unlawful except in cases where justice could not be obtained. He also established an *Imperial tribunal*, made up of a judge with certain assessors, which was to decide all causes not affecting princes of the Empire. Frederick did not stay long enough in Germany to complete the work he had begun. In 1236 he returned to Italy, and he never again visited Germany. His son *Conrad* was left to fill the place which Henry had forfeited.

**24. The Moguls.**—Shortly after this time Germany was threatened by the *Moguls*, vast hordes of whom had broken into Europe from Asia. In 1241 they were met in *Silesia*, with a very inferior force, by *Henry* of *Liegnitz.* The Silesians were almost all cut down, and Henry himself fell; but the Moguls had met with such stubborn resistance at the very borders of Germany that they gave up all thought of entering the country, and marched southwards to Hungary.

**25. Struggle of Frederick II. with the Pope.**—Frederick found in *Innocent IV.* a foe more bitter and dangerous than even Gregory IX. had been. These Popes declared that Frederick was a heretic, and had sympathies with Mahometanism; but the real causes of their hatred were,

F

that he would not recognize the authority of the Pope as higher than that of the Emperor, and that his possession of the kingdom of Sicily, which had long been looked on as a fief of the Holy See, enabled him to attack the Papacy from the south as well as from the north. In 1245 Innocent IV. not only renewed the sentence of excommunication against Frederick, but solemnly declared him dethroned. This created great confusion in Germany. A party, now as always, sided with the Emperor; but the spiritual princes joined the Pope, and they had the sympathy of all those nobles who wished to make use of the Emperor's difficulties for the purpose of adding to their own importance.

26. **Election of rival Kings. Death of Frederick II. and of Conrad IV.**—The party in favour of the Pope met at *Würzburg*, and elected as King *Henry Raspe*, Landgrave of *Thuringia*. He was never fully acknowledged, and died in 1247. On his death the same clerical party again met, and declared *William* of *Holland*, a youth of twenty, his successor. William allied himself to the Welfic house, but in South Germany he was utterly powerless against the Emperor's son Conrad. Meanwhile, the Imperial authority almost altogether broke down. The utmost disorder prevailed throughout the kingdom. The great nobles avenged their own wrongs, and robbery became so common that a man's person and property were safe only in so far as he was able to fight in his own defence. In 1250 the Emperor, whose attention had been given to the struggle for authority in Lombardy, died at *Firenzuola*. After his death the party which had clung to him recognized his son *Conrad IV.;* but Conrad died in 1254. Conrad was the last Hohenstaufen King in Germany.

27. **Conquest of Slavonic lands.**—The Germans had long been pushing their way eastwards. Besides taking possession of *Brandenburg*, they had been slowly colonising

*Lower Silesia, Holstein, Mecklenburg*, and *Pomerania*. About the beginning of the thirteenth century a monk named *Christian* began to preach in *Prussia*. The Prussians resisted him, whereupon a crusade was preached against them, and many warriors came to Christian's help. About 1230 the Knights of the *Teutonic Order*, under their Grand Master, *Hermann* of *Salza*, came to Prussia, and began to conquer it. Another Order, *the Knights of the Sword*, had before conquered *Livonia*. In 1237 this Order joined the Teutonic Knights. *Königsberg* was founded in 1245, and received its name in honour of *Ottocar*, King of Bohemia, who took part in the crusade against Prussia. The larger part of Prussia was conquered by 1260, when a great revolt took place. Many Germans settled in the land, and in 1309 the Order was established in its seat at *Marienberg*. Warriors came from all parts of Europe and joined the Order in fighting the Prussians. Its members were bound by vows like monastic orders; but their manners were not improved by prosperity.

28. **Further loss of power by the German Kings.**—For a time it had seemed as if the German Kings were once more to become strong rulers; and if the Hohenstaufen dynasty had chosen to confine itself to Germany, it might have won back, and added to, the power of Charles the Great, of Otto the Great, and of Henry III. But, as we have seen, the Hohenstaufen Kings were almost constantly engaged in distant wars, brought about by their position as Emperors and Kings of Italy and (after Frederick I.'s time) of Sicily. While they were carrying on these wars, the German princes seized one royal right after another, and made themselves practically independent. Instead of winning back their rights, the Hohenstaufen Kings sometimes gave them up in order to add to their strength at the moment. By two *Pragmatic Sanctions* Frederick II. con-

firmed the princes in the rights they had seized; the ecclesiastical princes in 1220, the secular princes in 1232. Where he was present his authority was still to be over all; but in his absence the princes were to be almost independent sovereigns within their towns and territories. The result of the weakness thus brought about was that the German Kings lost almost all their power abroad. *Denmark, Poland,* and *Hungary* ceased to owe them allegiance, and *Burgundy* began to fall, bit by bit, into the hands of France.

29. **The seven Electors.**—As we have seen, the Kings were in early times elected by the whole body of freemen. When feudalism arose, this right passed into the hands of the nobles. If the power of the Kings had gone on increasing instead of becoming less and less, they would probably have made their crown hereditary; but their growing weakness enabled the nobles to hold fast the right of election. The Popes encouraged them to do so, for much of the Papal power would have been lost if any one family could have claimed the Imperial crown as a right. Besides, there was a general feeling that the position of Emperor was far too great and sacred to be entrusted to a single house. The fact that three successive dynasties failed of heirs male also helped to keep the crown from becoming hereditary. Although the German crown remained elective, the great body of the nobles soon lost their electoral rights. For a time the leading princes asked the aristocracy to approve their choice of a King, but in the end their choice was accepted as final. Those who thus usurped the right of electing the King were called *Electors*. There were now *seven* Electors—three *spiritual* and four *secular*. The spiritual Electors were the Archbishops of *Mainz, Köln,* and *Trier*. The Duke of *Saxony* (the small Duchy given by Frederick I. to Bernard, son of Albert the Bear), the Margrave of *Brandenburg*, the *Rhenish Palsgrave*, and the

King of *Bohemia*, were the secular Electors. The three Archbishops were Arch-chancellors of Germany, of Gaul and Burgundy, and of Italy; and each of the secular Electors held one of the great offices of the Imperial household. These offices were formerly held by the Dukes of Franconia, Bavaria, Saxony, and Lotharingia; but when the Dukes were at the height of their power, the right of electing the King had not been seized by a few. The Duke of Bavaria would probably have been an Elector, but the house of Wittelsbach held also the Rhenish Palatinate, and it would have been dangerous if the electoral dignity had belonged to two members of one family. The right of choosing the King was the most important of all the rights gained by the leading feudal lords, for the Electors could keep strong men from the throne, and make those whom they appointed confirm them and their fellow-princes in their independence. The Electors were above all other princes, and formed a separate college in the Diet.

30. **The German Kings and the Pope.**—In the time of the *Ottos* and the *Henrys*, the German Kings, as Emperors, confirmed, and even appointed, Popes. From the time of *Innocent III.* the Popes claimed the right to review the election of the German King, and to reject any one whom they did not think suitable. This was another humiliation brought upon the German kingdom by its connexion with the Empire.

31. **Increase of immediate nobles.**—The Duchies now no longer played the great part in German history that they had once played. The Duchy of Franconia had ceased to exist; and when *Conradin*, the son of Conrad IV., perished in 1268, Swabia also fell to pieces. The Duchy of Saxony, in the old sense, had never been restored after the fall of Henry the Lion. Upper Lotharingia still existed; but the Duchy of Lower Lotharingia was more nominal than real.

Bavaria had been made much less important by the separation of Carinthia, Austria, and Styria. The result of these changes was that a great many of the lower order of nobles became *immediate*. That is, many who had held their lands of the Dukes now held them of the crown. This made robbery much more common than it had been, and added greatly to the number of private wars.

32. **Leading noble houses.**—It may be well to mention some of the leading noble families who now, in immediate dependance on the crown, shared with the Church the greater part of the land of Germany. The small Saxon Duchy was divided into *Lauenburg* and *Wittenberg*. These were held by two branches of Bernard's family, each of which thought it had the best right to the electoral dignity. To the north of Wittenberg was the powerful Margraviate of *Brandenburg*. The Dukes of *Brunswick* and *Lüneburg*, and the Counts of *Oldenburg*, of *Holstein*, and of *Schwerin*, all held what had once been Saxon land, and claimed to be immediate. *Thuringia*, which had for some time been joined to Saxony, but had been made a Margraviate, became a *Landgraviate* in the time of the Hohenstaufen. The Landgraves pushed their way westwards till their territory took in *Hessen* as well as Thuringia. This was the extent of country ruled by *Lewis IV.* of Thuringia, husband of the famous *St. Elizabeth* of *Hungary*, In 1269 Thuringia was given in fief to *Henry*, Margrave of *Meissen*, the ancestor of the present royal family of Saxony; while Hessen fell to *Henry* of *Brabant*, a grandson of Lewis IV. by the female line, from whom the later Landgraves of Hessen sprang. The Duchy of Bavaria was still held by the house of *Wittelsbach*, which had also received by marriage, in 1227, the *Rhenish Palatinate*. To the east of Bavaria were the three Duchies which had at different times been separated from it—*Austria*, *Styria*, and *Carinthia*.

Styria had been united to Austria in 1192. *Frederick*, the last Austrian Duke of the house of Babenberg, died in 1246. His death was followed by a time of great confusion in the Austrian lands. After much fighting with the Hungarians, *Ottocar*, King of Bohemia, at last got possession of them for some time. The Counts of *Würtemberg* were among the greatest of the Swabian nobles. The house of *Zähringen*, the founder of which Conrad II. had placed over Burgundy, had been confined by Frederick I. to the Duchy of *Lesser Burgundy*, to the east of the *Jura*. This house died out in the thirteenth century, and many of its lands fell to the Counts of *Baden* and the Counts of *Habsburg*. The Counts of *Hohenzollern*, who held the position of Burgraves of *Nürnberg*, were also powerful Swabian nobles, and received about this time certain Bavarian lands which afterwards became the Duchies of *Ansbach* and *Baireuth*. The Counts of *Nassau* may be named among those who held ancient Franconian lands. The Duchy of Upper Lotharingia was held by the Counts of *Elsass*. The Dukes of Lower Lotharingia preferred to call themselves, after their hereditary possessions, Dukes of *Brabant*. Among the nobles in this part of Germany who claimed to be immediate were the Counts of *Luxemburg*, *Jülich*, *Geldern*, *Cleve*, and *Holland*.

33. **Laws of Inheritance.**—So long as a Duke or other prince was looked on as an officer of the crown, his lands were inherited by his eldest son; but now the lands of most princes were divided equally among all the sons. The brothers sometimes lived together and shared the power, but they more commonly divided the lands. It thus often happened that there were a number of independent principalities, ruled over by members of one family. At first each brother obtained absolute possession of his share; but as this greatly weakened the power of princely houses, it

became common for the heirs of a prince to make arrangements which kept any part of the fief from falling to the crown until the male line had wholly died out. In the end the custom of *primogeniture* was adopted by several great families—notably by the house which has become in our day the Imperial family of Germany.

34. **The institution of knighthood.**—The institution of knighthood, which the Crusades had made so important, flourished in Germany in the time of the Hohenstaufen. It was open to the lower as well as to the higher nobles to become knights, so that the institution formed a bond of union between the two orders. The son of a nobleman usually served a knight for some years as *page* and *esquire*, and was afterwards himself knighted, if possible by a noble of high rank. Those who were to be made knights prepared themselves for the ceremony by religious exercises, and vowed to obey the King or Emperor, to uphold the right, to defend widows and orphans, and to oppose the infidels. Every knight had the right to confer the honour of knighthood. He could also take part in *tournaments*, which were often held at the courts of the Emperor and princes. Knights were supposed to hold women in high reverence. They were by no means always so pure as they are sometimes said to have been; but in Germany, as elsewhere, they did much to foster a spirit of generosity, courtesy, and honour, at a time when these qualities were peculiarly valuable.

35. **The towns.**—The towns were now an element of great importance in Germany. Almost every great German town at present existing had been founded by the time of the Hohenstaufen. The Crusades had given a powerful impulse to trade, so that the burgher class generally had become very rich. When the Duchies ceased to exist or lost their old importance, many towns that had before been

mediate became immediate. The immediate towns usually tried to get rid of the bailiffs who represented the crown; and in the thirteenth century many of them succeeded in doing so, and thus became *Free Imperial Towns*, still recognizing the supremacy of the King or Emperor, but ruling themselves according to their own ideas. When a town became free, a struggle very often arose between the old families or Patricians and the Gilds, and it usually ended by the Patricians having to yield to the Gilds some share in the government. The free imperial towns became far too powerful to be left out of the national council. In the end their deputies formed a third college in the Diet, and had an equal vote with the Electors and princes.

36. **Leagues of towns. The Hansa.**—The free towns rarely quarrelled with the King; but they were almost always at war with the nobles, both secular and spiritual. This led to their forming *Leagues* or *Confederations* for mutual defence. Several of these Leagues became very powerful. The *Rhenish League*, which was formed in the middle of the thirteenth century, took in no fewer than seventy towns. But of all the Leagues of cities, the *Hansa* was by far the strongest. It is thought by some to have arisen from a treaty made between *Lübeck* and *Hamburg*, in 1241, for the protection of their commerce. Other northern towns soon joined them, and a League was formed called the *Hanseatic League*, which in the end took in upwards of eighty cities. It was divided into four groups, of which the chief towns were *Lübeck*, *Köln*, *Brunswick*, and *Danzig*. The Diet of the League met in Lübeck, which was looked on as the head town. When at its height the Hansa carried on the whole trade of the Baltic and had a principal share in that of the North Sea. It had fleets and armies, and often got the better of the Northern Kings. It even made itself

respected by the more powerful Kings of France and England; and for a time much of the export English trade was carried on by Hanseatic merchants. Here they were called *Easterlings*—whence the word *Sterling*.

37. **The freeing of serfs.**—About the time of the Hohenstaufen many serfs were made free. They were made so in various ways. Some received their freedom by joining the Crusades; others obtained it from nobles who were about to set out for the Holy Land; while others fled from tyrannical lords, and found refuge in the cities. The cities willingly took them in, and made them citizens—either *Pfahlbürger*, citizens who took up their abode in the suburbs, within the palisades that enclosed the lands of the city, or *Ausbürger*, citizens who lived outside the city, but could claim its protection. These Pfahlbürger and Ausbürger were a source of constant misunderstanding between the nobles and the towns. By and by the better class of nobles began to feel that it was more profitable, as well as more Christian, to be served by freemen than by serfs; but serfdom continued in some parts of Germany, especially the north, till quite recent times.

38. **The "Sachsenspiegel" and "Schwabenspiegel."**—There was no one system of law in use all over Germany. The princes administered justice in accordance with local customs and traditions. Early in the thirteenth century a Saxon noble, *Eike* of *Repgow*, brought together in one work the laws in use in Saxony. This work was called the *Sachsenspiegel*, and was soon looked on as a code of high authority all over Germany. Later in the century a Swabian priest wrote the *Schwabenspiegel*, which did for the usages of Swabia what the *Sachsenspiegel* had done for those of Saxony. Afterwards other collections were made in different parts of the kingdom. During the twelfth and thirteenth centuries the old Roman law was eagerly

studied in the Italian Universities; and at a later time it came into very general use in Germany.

39. **The Femgerichte.**—There was a peculiar class of courts of justice in Westphalia, called *Femgerichte*. They sprang from the old courts of Counts which Charles the Great had first appointed in Saxony, and which went on longer in Westphalia than elsewhere, because of the greater number who there continued to hold their lands by a free tenure. Towards the end of the twelfth century the Counts began to call themselves *Freigrafen* or *Free Counts;* and the judges who with a *Freigraf* formed a court were called *Freischöffen* or *Free Judges*. As feudalism advanced, many Free Counties were brought under secular or spiritual princes. The princes, however, did not gain full power over them. They appointed the Free Counts; but the latter received their authority from the King or Emperor, and dispensed justice in his name. The Femgerichte did not meet, as has often been said, at night and in caves or other hidden places. They met in open day, generally under some tree; but the proceedings of the court were kept secret. No case was taken up which was not punishable by death. If an accused person was condemned, he was hanged at once. Any one who did not appear after having been summoned three times was assumed to be guilty; and sooner or later he was certainly put to death. In those lawless times the oppressed were glad to find a court anywhere which gave them some chance of obtaining justice. Appeals began, therefore, to be made to the Femgerichte from all parts of Germany. In the end men of free birth, to whatever part of the country they belonged, were allowed to become Freischöffen, and many thousands of all classes availed themselves of the privilege. For a considerable time the Femgerichte did real good, for nobles who cared nothing for King or Emperor trembled when they

received the summons of some Freigraf to appear at a certain date before a secret tribunal. But as the power of the Femgerichte increased, they were often reckless and unjust; and many, especially the clergy, cried out loudly against them. They lost nearly all their power in the sixteenth century; but traces of them long afterwards existed among the Westphalian peasantry.

40. **Architecture and Literature.**—In spite of the wild lives of many nobles, the age of the Hohenstaufen was in some respects the most brilliant of the Middle Ages. Many churches were built in a new style of architecture called *the pointed* or *Gothic*. Of these, the Cathedral of Köln, which is not even yet finished, was the most splendid. Poetry flourished as it had never before done in Germany. This was due partly to the influence of the *Troubadours* and *Trouvères*. The *Crusades* also stirred men's imaginations by opening to them a new world of wonder and beauty. The poets were called *Minnesänger* or *Love Singers*. They wrote many romances, the favourite heroes of which, in Germany as well as in France and England, were Charles the Great and King Arthur with the Knights of the Round Table. Many lyrics were also written which are not only finely finished but show a true feeling for everything great and beautiful in nature and human life. Several of the Hohenstaufen Emperors and various princes were themselves poets. Among the most famous of the Minnesänger were *Heinrich von Veldeck*, who lived towards the end of the twelfth century and was one of the earliest of his class, *Wolfram von Eschenbach*, *Gottfried von Strassburg*, and *Walther von der Vogelweide*. There were many legends of German heroes in different parts of Germany. These legends were kept alive in the minds of the people by *wandering singers*, who long addressed themselves chiefly to the common folk, but were afterwards welcomed

# ARCHITECTURE AND LITERATURE.

to the castles of princes and nobles. Of the legends thus handed down from generation to generation some were put together about this time, and made into the great national epics of the *Nibelungenlied* and *Gudrun*. The age of the Hohenstaufen was thus one of the most remarkable epochs in the history of German literature. A more sordid time followed in which poetry almost altogether vanished.

## CHAPTER X.

### SOVEREIGNS OF DIFFERENT HOUSES.

*Death of William of Holland; election of Alfonso and Richard; the Interregnum* (1)—*election of Rudolf of Habsburg* (2)—*war between Rudolf and Ottocar, King of Bohemia* (3)—*the House of Habsburg receives Austria* (4)—*good government of Rudolf; his death* (5)—*King Adolf* (6)—*King Albert I.* (7)—*King Henry VII.; his son John becomes King of Bohemia* (8)—*Henry VII. crowned Emperor; his death* (9)—*election of Frederick of Austria and Lewis of Bavaria; war; defeat of Frederick* (10)—*struggle of Lewis IV. and Pope John XXII.* (11)—*Lewis IV. becomes sole King; is crowned Emperor* (12)—*Lewis IV. supported by his subjects against the Popes* (13)—*election of Charles IV.; death of Lewis IV.* (14)—*the Kings and their hereditary lands* (15)—*the Eidgenossen or Confederates; battle of Morgarten Pass* (16).

1. **The Interregnum.**—After the death of *Conrad IV., William* of *Holland* was the only King in Germany; but he was quite powerless. He was killed in 1256, while fighting against the Frisians. There was now no one who had any particular claim to the crown. The Electors, therefore, resolved to appoint a King under whom they and their fellow princes should be able to confirm their independence. Two foreigners—*Alfonso*, King of *Castile*, and *Richard*, Earl of *Cornwall*, brother of our *Henry III.*—were very anxious to receive the crown. As both bribed the Electors, one party chose Richard and another Alfonso. The period

which followed this double election is called the *Interregnum*. Richard was crowned King at Aachen; but after his coronation he visited Germany only three times, and he never interested himself much in its affairs. Alfonso never even came to Germany. The *Interregnum* is one of the darkest periods in German history. The princes and immediate nobles ruled their lands exactly as they chose, and carried on many wars both among themselves and against the cities. The petty independent barons, whose numbers now so much increased, were almost all robbers, so that no one worth robbing dared to travel unless he was strongly guarded. During this fierce time men thought of Frederick Barbarossa, and dreamed of the day when he should awake from his sleep and bring back peace and order to Germany.

2. **Election of Rudolf of Habsburg.**—Richard of Cornwall died in 1271. The Electors would have been in no hurry to appoint a successor; but the Pope found that the confusion caused by the absence of the royal authority in Germany was interfering with the Papal revenue. He therefore let the Electors know that if they did not choose a King he himself would appoint one. At last, in 1273, *Rudolf*, Count of *Habsburg*, was elected. Habsburg was in *Aargau* in the south of Swabia. Rudolf was a brave man, and sincerely anxious to put down the disorders which were ruining Germany. He was greatly strengthened by the support of the Church, to which he was always submissive.

3. **Ottocar, King of Bohemia.**—By far the most powerful prince of the Empire at this time was *Ottocar*, King of Bohemia. Besides his native kingdom, he now held *Austria*, *Styria*, *Carinthia*, and *Carniola*. He ruled these lands very harshly, and was generally disliked. As he had hoped to have been made King of the Romans himself, he refused to acknowledge Rudolf. During the years 1274 and 1275

he was three times summoned to do homage for his lands, but he would not yield. In 1276, therefore, Rudolf marched against him. Rudolf had a large army, for the princes were jealous of Ottocar, and anxious to see him humbled. Seeing this, Ottocar became afraid, and not only did homage for the kingdom of Bohemia, but resigned Austria and the neighbouring lands. Most of the princes, thinking the war was at an end, returned to their territories. When they had done so, Ottocar began the war again, hoping to find Rudolf unprepared. In 1278 a fierce battle was fought at the *Marchfield*, on the right bank of the Danube. Both sides fought bravely, but at last the Bohemians were defeated, and Ottocar himself was killed.

4. **The House of Habsburg receives Austria.**—Some time after his victory over Ottocar, Rudolf, with the consent of the princes, gave Austria, Styria, Carinthia, and Carniola in fief to his sons, *Albert* and *Rudolf*. Afterwards Carinthia was given to Count *Meinhard* of *Tyrol*, whose daughter was Albert's wife; and the other lands were left in the hands of Albert alone. By these arrangements King Rudolf laid the foundations of the future greatness of the house of Habsburg.

5. **Rudolf's government. His death.**—The crown lands of Germany had at one time been very extensive; but by the time Rudolf became King, they had nearly all passed into the hands of great nobles. Some of them had been sold by different Emperors to provide money for the wars carried on in Italy; others had been seized by the Palsgraves who administered them, and by neighbouring princes. Nearly all the royal dues had also been seized or granted away. Rudolf strove hard to win back the royal lands and dues which had been unjustly taken during the Interregnum; and in spite of the difficulties in his way he was to some extent successful. But he probably did most for Germany

as an administrator of justice. He revived the system of judicial procedure and police set up by Frederick II., and rode through nearly every part of the kingdom, trying to put a stop to private war, and ridding the country of robbers. In Thuringia alone he caused twenty-nine robber nobles to be executed, and destroyed sixty-nine strongholds. In 1291 he tried to get his son Albert elected King; but the Electors refused to appoint a successor during his lifetime, nominally on the ground that the revenues of the crown, which could ill support one King, could much less support two. In September of the same year Rudolf died, in the seventy-fourth year of his age. His good government had made him a great favourite with the common folk. If the royal power had not been thoroughly undermined before he became King, he would have done much more to make Germany great and prosperous.

6. **King Adolf.**—Rudolf's successor was *Adolf*, Count of *Nassau*. Adolf was very poor, and had no great personal qualities. He was elected chiefly through the influence of *Gerhard*, Archbishop of Mainz, his cousin, who hoped to use the new King as a tool for the attainment of his own ends. Like Rudolf, Adolf tried to win back some of the royal lands and dues; but he could do very little against powerful nobles. He formed an alliance with *Edward I.* of England, who sent him a large sum of money on condition that he should declare war with France. At this time Thuringia was ruled by a very worthless Landgrave, *Albert the Degenerate*. With the money received from Edward I. (for which no return was ever made) Adolf bought Thuringia from Albert. This gave rise to war, for Albert's two sons refused to give up their inheritance, and they were supported by some princes and by their own vassals. Meanwhile Adolf had been by no means so submissive to Gerhard as the latter had hoped. Taking

advantage, therefore, of the discontent aroused by Adolf's doings in Thuringia, Gerhard persuaded the Electors to dethrone him, and to elect *Albert*, Duke of *Austria*, King Rudolf's son. Adolf resisted, but in 1298 he was killed in a battle near Worms. Albert was then re-elected and crowned at Aachen.

7. **King Albert I.**—Albert had none of his father Rudolf's winning qualities. He had been a severe ruler in his own lands, and was anxious to make his house rich and great. He tried to get possession of Bohemia—his son *Rudolf* was King of Bohemia for a few months—and the county of Holland; and he entered Thuringia for the purpose of driving out *Frederick*, one of the two brothers who had resisted Adolf, and now Landgrave. Frederick bravely defended himself, and was at last allowed to keep his lands in peace. Albert's schemes for enriching his family were cut short by a violent death. His nephew, *John*, whom he kept from his inheritance, formed a conspiracy with four other nobles; and on May 1, 1308, when the King had just crossed the *Reuss*, and was within sight of the castle of Habsburg, they fell upon him and killed him. A convent was afterwards built on the spot where the murder had been committed. Albert had declared *Vienna* the capital of the realm in Austria.

8. **Henry VII.**—The Electors, being jealous of the house of Austria, chose as King, not one of Albert's sons, but *Henry*, Count of *Lützelburg* or *Luxemburg*. Henry did not live to do much for Germany; but he appears to have been one of the wisest of her Kings. His son *John*, with the consent of the Bohemian States, married *Elizabeth*, granddaughter of King *Ottocar*, and thus became King of Bohemia. Bohemia long remained in the possesssion of the house of Luxemburg, so that Henry, like King Rudolf, was the means of making his own family very powerful.

**9. Henry VII. becomes Emperor. His death.**—No German King, since Frederick II., had been crowned Emperor. King Rudolf had said, "Rome is like the lion's den in the fable—one may see the footsteps of many who have gone there, but of none who have come back." The connexion between Germany and Italy was now practically at an end; and for an Emperor to have claimed authority over any other of the leading European countries would have been ridiculous. But the Germans had long been accustomed to think of themselves as the Imperial race. For centuries their Kings had, at least in name, been rulers of the world. Although all life had gone out of the Empire, they were unwilling to lose the distinction which its connexion with their crown gave them. King Henry himself was anxious to become Emperor. In 1310, therefore, he went to Italy, and received both the Italian and the Imperial crowns. He would probably have restored the Empire to some of its old greatness, but he died suddenly at *Buonconvento* in 1313.

**10. Election of Frederick of Austria and Lewis of Bavaria.**—In choosing a successor to Henry VII., the Electors were divided into two parties. One chose *Lewis*, Duke of *Bavaria;* another, *Frederick*, Duke of *Austria*, eldest son of King Albert. Frederick was so handsome that he was known as *Frederick the Fair*. Both candidates were crowned, Lewis at Aachen, and Frederick at Bonn. The result of this double election and coronation was a terrible war, which lasted for ten years, and did great harm to Germany. The towns for the most part sided with Lewis; the nobles with Frederick. At last, in 1322, a great battle was fought near *Mühldorf*. The Austrians were defeated, and Frederick was taken prisoner, and confined in the Castle of *Trausnitz* in the Upper Palatinate.

**11. Lewis IV, and Pope John XXII,**—Frederick's

brother, Duke Leopold, and other princes, would not accept the battle of Mühldorf as decisive. Their cause was greatly strengthened by a quarrel in which Lewis became involved with Pope John XXII. The latter was angry with Lewis for acting as King of the Romans without having received the Papal sanction. Lewis maintained that he received his dignity, not from the Pope, but from the Electors. As he held by this opinion, the Pope not only excommunicated him, but placed under the interdict those parts of Germany which supported him. Thus the old quarrel between the spiritual and the secular powers once more broke out.

12. **Lewis IV. becomes sole King; is crowned Emperor.**—Anxious to obtain peace, Lewis set Frederick free in 1325, on securing a promise from him that he would give up all claims to the crown. The Pope and Duke Leopold, Frederick's brother, refused to be bound by this agreement; but Frederick remained true to his word. At last, in September, 1325, Lewis and Frederick agreed to share the power between them. This agreement was carried out; but Frederick took little interest in public affairs, and died in 1330. Lewis then became sole King. The years between 1327 and 1330 he had spent in Italy, where he had been crowned Emperor, first by two heretical Bishops, and afterwards by a Pope of his own creation, called *Nicholas V.*

13. **Lewis IV. supported by his subjects against the Popes.**—Although Lewis had appointed an anti-Pope, he tried hard to be reconciled, first to Pope John, and afterwards to *Benedict XII.*, John's successor. His efforts failed, partly because they were opposed by France, on which the Popes were at this time practically dependant, and which wished to keep the Empire weak. But the Papacy no longer held the position with respect to Germany which it had held in the days of Henry IV. and Frederick II. The cities and

many of the princes, seeing that Papal interference had always brought strife into the kingdom, had become more and more jealous of the Popes. The Popes therefore found, in their quarrel with Lewis, that they had no longer the support of public opinion, which had made former Popes all-powerful. When Lewis had failed to conciliate Benedict, the States met at Frankfurt in 1338, and openly sided with the Emperor. The Electors, with the exception of King John of Bohemia, who was jealous of the house of Bavaria, and one of Lewis's most persistent enemies, met at *Rense*, on the Rhine, and made a solemn declaration that the Emperor or King of the Romans derived his rank and power, not from the Pope, but from the choice of the Electoral princes. This meeting of the Electors was the first *Electoral League*. Their decision was accepted by the States, proclaimed by the Emperor, and became part of the law of the land. It was a decision of great importance, as it legally established the independence of the Empire.

14. **Election of Charles IV. Death of Lewis IV.**—A wise sovereign would have known how to use the popular feeling in his favour so as to strengthen his own power; but Lewis was very imprudent. In 1323 he had given the Mark of Brandenburg in fief to his son Lewis. He was anxious that this same son should receive Tyrol; but *Margaret Maultasch*, the heiress of Tyrol, was already married to a son of King John of Bohemia. Lewis dissolved Margaret's marriage, and gave her a dispensation to marry his own son. In taking this step he attacked a Papal right which all acknowledged. He therefore not only made reconciliation with the Pope impossible, but turned against him many who had hitherto supported him. He also roused the jealousy of the princes by greatly enriching his family. He had made his son Lewis a wealthy prince; and on the death of William IV. of

Holland, the brother of his second wife, he gave the counties of *Holland, Seeland*, and *Hennegau* in fief to his son *William*. The ill-will roused by Lewis found expression in 1344 at a second assembly of the Electors, where the princes brought many accusations against him. Two years afterwards Pope *Clement VI.* declared him deposed. This time the Electors were at one with the Pope, and chose to the vacant throne *Charles*, Margrave of *Moravia*, and son of King John of Bohemia. Lewis still claimed to be King and Emperor; but he died suddenly during a boar hunt in 1347.

15. **The Kings and their hereditary lands.**—Lewis had not, like most of the Kings before him, given up his hereditary lands; and after his time no German King did so. The reason was that the public revenues had become too small to support the royal and Imperial dignity. The change was not altogether good for the country. The King was now tempted to neglect the general interests of Germany for those of his own immediate subjects, and to look on the crown as little more than a means of enriching himself and his family.

16. **The Eidgenossen or Confederates.**—It was during the reign of Lewis IV. that the famous battle of *Morgarten Pass* was fought. The people of *Schwyz, Uri*, and *Unterwalden*, three districts lying round what is now called the Lake of *Luzern*, had always been free, doing allegiance to none save the King or Emperor. When the Counts of Habsburg became Dukes of Austria, they began to covet these districts, within which they already had estates, and to wish to add them to their hereditary possessions. The three districts had already, like other districts and cities of Germany, formed a *League* for mutual defence; but they now drew closer together, and prepared to fight, if necessary, for their freedom. In 1315, soon after the out-

break of war between Frederick and Lewis IV., *Leopold*, Duke of Austria, marched against the League, for the purpose of breaking it up and subduing the people. But his fine army was utterly routed in *Morgarten Pass*, and he himself escaped with difficulty. After this the League was favoured by Lewis IV. During his time it was joined by the city of *Luzern;* and soon after his death the cities of *Zürich, Zug, Glarus,* and *Bern* also joined it, one after the other. The League thus became very strong, and its various members added to their power by seizing or buying, whenever they had a chance, the lands of neighbouring nobles. The members of the League were called *Eidgenossen* or *Confederates;* the League itself was the *Old League of High Germany.* It was not till long afterwards that the whole Confederation received the name which properly belonged to the one canton of *Schwyz.*

# CHAPTER XI.

## THE LUXEMBURG EMPERORS.

*Charles IV.; crowned Emperor, and King of Burgundy* (1)—*the plague in Germany; persecution of the Jews* (2)—*Charles IV. grants the Golden Bull* (3)—*Charles IV. adds to his hereditary lands; his good government of them; his death* (4)—*the House of Austria receives Carinthia and Tyrol* (5)—*bad government of King Wenceslaus; the Swabian League* (6)—*the battles of Sempach and Näfels* (7)—*Wenceslaus deposed; King Rupert* (8) *election of Jobst and Sigmund; death of Jobst; Sigmund reelected* (9)—*the Council of Constanz* (10)—*increased power of the Eidgenossen* (11)—*the doctrines of Wycliffe in Bohemia; John Huss summoned before the Council of Constanz; he is burned as a heretic; Jerome of Prague also burned* (12)—*the Hussite War; John Zisca* (13)—*the Calixtines and the Taborites; the Calixtines accept the terms of the Council of Basel; the Taborites defeated; Sigmund becomes King of Bohemia; his death* (14) —*Frederick of Hohenzollern receives Brandenburg; Frederick of Meissen receives Sachsen-Wittenberg* (15).

1. **Charles IV.**—The house of Bavaria refused at first to acknowledge *Charles IV.;* and, with the help of the Archbishop of Mainz, got *Edward III.* of England, and afterwards *Frederick*, Margrave of *Meissen*, elected. Neither of these would accept the crown. *Günther*, Count of *Schwarzburg*, was elected in 1349, and might have proved a formidable rival to Charles; but he suddenly died, perhaps by poison, soon after his election. Charles was then crowned

again at Aachen, and reigned without opposition. In 1355 he was crowned Emperor at *Rome*, and in 1365 King of Burgundy at *Arles*.

2. **The plague in Germany; persecution of the Jews.**—In 1349 Germany suffered, like the rest of Europe, from a fearful plague, known in England as the Black Death, which had been brought to Italy by ships from the East, and quickly spread to other countries. Hundreds of thousands died within a short time. Everywhere men were anxious and disturbed, and submitted to all kinds of penances to appease what was believed to be the Divine wrath. A belief arose that the Jews had brought on the plague by poisoning springs and rivers. This led to a persecution so dreadful that many Jews set fire to their houses and perished in the flames rather than fall into the hands of their enemies. It was only when the princes, and especially the spiritual princes, interfered that the persecution gradually died out.

3. **The Golden Bull.**—Charles IV. almost wholly neglected Germany. Instead of trying to win back the crown lands, he sold what still remained of them. He also enriched himself by selling honours and privileges, raising many, in return for money, to noble and even princely rank. In 1356 he granted a charter called the *Golden Bull*, which finally settled everything connected with the election of the King. The number of the Electors was fixed at *seven*. The King of Bohemia was not only confirmed in his right of voting, but was declared the first secular Elector. The Archbishop of Mainz was made *convener* of the Electoral College. All cases were to be decided by a majority of votes. The elections were always to take place at *Frankfurt*, and the coronations at *Aachen*. The Electors had already acquired a great position; but the Golden Bull added to their importance. They received full sovereign rights

within their territories; there was to be no appeal from their courts unless they refused to dispense justice; and their persons were declared sacred. These privileges raised them still further above other princes, and made them, taken together, of more importance than the King or Emperor.

4. **Charles IV. and his hereditary lands.**—Charles greatly increased his hereditary lands. By his second wife he obtained the *Upper Palatinate;* and he united the whole of *Silesia* and *Lower Lusatia* to Bohemia. He also gained the Mark of *Brandenburg* from the house of Bavaria. While he was a bad German King and Emperor, he ruled all the lands directly subject to him in a very enlightened spirit. Bohemia flourished under him as it had done under no former King. He greatly improved *Prague*, the Bohemian capital, and founded there a University which soon became a famous centre of thought and learning. Charles died at Prague in 1378. Two years before the Electors had chosen his son *Wenceslaus* to be King of the Romans.

5. **Growing power of the House of Austria.**—The house of Austria, like that of Luxemburg, added greatly to its power about this time. In 1335 it received *Carinthia*, after the death of *Henry*, the last descendant, in the male line, of *Meinhard*, to whom King Rudolf had given the Duchy. When *Margaret Maultasch*, Henry's daughter, died in 1366, *Tyrol* was claimed by the house of Bavaria; but in 1369 it was finally given up to the house of Austria, to which Margaret had bequeathed it. From this time *Carinthia* and *Tyrol* always belonged to the Dukes of Austria.

6. **King Wenceslaus. The Swabian League.**—Wenceslaus was neither a good Bohemian nor a good German King. He was a man of coarse nature, fond of low pleasures, and sometimes savagely cruel. The result of his and his

father's neglect of Germany was that something like the confusion of the *Interregnum* returned. There were never more robber barons, and there were petty wars everywhere throughout the kingdom. The towns had to maintain their freedom by constant fighting. Those of *Swabia*, following the example of the *Eidgenossen* and of the *Rhenish* and *Hansa* towns, formed at this time a great League, which took in at first thirty-four, and afterwards forty-one towns, together with some nobles. If there had been a King in Germany wise enough to ally himself with this and the other Confederations, much of the royal power might have been won back; but Wenceslaus was too indolent to do more than give a feeble encouragement to the various Leagues. In opposition to the Leagues of towns, the princes and nobles also formed Confederations, to which they gave such names as the Society of *St. George, St. William*, the *Lion*, or the *Panther*.

7. **The Battles of Sempach and Näfels.**—During the reign of Wenceslaus, Duke *Leopold* of Austria, nephew of the Leopold who had fought at *Morgarten Pass*, made a great effort to conquer the *Eidgenossen*, who had received into their League some towns owing allegiance to Austria. Leopold was joined by many princes and nobles, who were jealous of the growing power of the League. A great battle was fought at *Sempach* in 1386. The Austrians and their allies were utterly defeated; and Leopold himself was killed. Two years afterwards an important victory was gained by *Glarus* at *Näfels*. In consequence of these victories, the *Eidgenossen* were allowed to keep the lands they had conquered and the towns which had voluntarily joined them.

8. **Wenceslaus deposed. King Rupert.**—Wenceslaus was so bad a King that in 1400 the Electors met and dethroned him, on the ground that he wholly failed in his duties. They

were stirred up to do this by *Boniface IX.*, one of the two Popes who at this time divided the Western Church, and both of whom Wenceslaus had wished to depose. By a majority of votes the Electors chose *Rupert* of the *Palatinate* as Wenceslaus' successor. Rupert was in every way worthy of his position; but a party still supported Wenceslaus, and even those who were in favour of the new King were not inclined to give him more than a nominal obedience. Consequently nothing of any importance was done during his reign. He tried to go to Rome, but was defeated at *Brescia*. In 1410 he died.

9. **King Sigmund.**—Two Kings were now elected, *Jobst*, Margrave of *Moravia*, and *Sigmund*, brother of Wenceslaus. Sigmund was Margrave of *Brandenburg*, and had been made King of *Hungary*. Jobst very soon died, so that a new election took place. This time the votes of all the Electors were for Sigmund. Great hopes were raised by his election, for he had some good qualities; but in the end he often showed himself rash and narrow-minded. He lacked firmness, and was thus led sometimes to do things probably condemned by his own better judgment.

10. **The Council of Constanz.**—There were at this time three Popes, and in Germany, as elsewhere, many abuses had crept into the Church. Benefices were often sold to the highest bidder, and the moral condition of the clergy was in many cases very bad. A *General Council* had met at *Pisa* in 1409, but Sigmund induced Pope *John XXIII.* to join him in summoning another, which assembled at *Constanz* in 1414, and sat till 1418. Sigmund took a leading part in the proceedings of the Council of Constanz, and even went to Spain to try to induce *Benedict XIII.* to carry out its wishes by resigning. While he was away from Germany at this time, Sigmund visited *Paris* and *London*.

11. **Increased power of the Eidgenossen.**—The assembling of the Council was indirectly the means of adding greatly to the importance of the *Eidgenossen*. After having promised to resign, Pope *John XXIII.* fled from *Constanz* to *Schaffhausen*, where he found refuge in the castle of Duke *Frederick* of Austria. Sigmund put Frederick to the ban of the Empire, and stirred up the Eidgenossen to make war on him. Bern at once did so; and it was soon joined by the other cantons. When Frederick made peace with Sigmund he received back many of his possessions; but the Eidgenossen refused to give up what they had conquered. They thus kept *Aargau*, in which was the castle of *Habsburg*, and other lands and towns.

12. **The doctrines of Wycliffe in Bohemia. John Huss.**—At this time a movement was going on in *Bohemia* which led to very important results. The University of Prague, which Charles IV. had founded, was divided into four *nations*—the *Bohemian*, the *Saxon*, the *Bavarian*, and the *Polish*—each possessing one vote. A strong party had grown up among the Bohemians, which held in the main the doctrines of our own *Wycliffe*. The leader of this party was *John Huss*, a professor of philosophy. As the other *nations* were opposed to the Wycliffite doctrine, there were constant disputes between them and the Bohemians. In 1409, Wenceslaus, who was still King of Bohemia, changed the constitution of the University, giving three votes to the Bohemian *nation* and only one to the others. The German students and professors felt insulted by this, and at once left Prague, going for the most part to the University recently founded at Leipzig. The reforming party was now all-powerful, and Huss, who was made Rector of the University, began to speak very strongly against the abuses of the Church. He thus roused the hatred of the clergy, and at last the Pope excommunicated

him, and placed Prague under the interdict so long as it should shelter him. When the Council of Constanz met, Huss was summoned to appear before it. The Council thought his doctrines dangerous both to Church and State, and soon after he reached Constanz caused him to be seized and thrown into prison. On July 6, 1415, he was burned. He had received a safe-conduct from the King; but Sigmund was weak or base enough to let the Council persuade him that he ought not to keep his word with a heretic. The movement in Bohemia displeased Sigmund, not only because he thought it heretical, but because it was arousing among the Bohemians a national life which must, sooner or later, tend to separate them from the Empire. In 1416, *Jerome* of *Prague*, who had first brought Wycliffe's writings to Prague, was also burned in Constanz.

13. **The Hussite War.**—The burning of Huss and Jerome of Prague caused a very bitter feeling in Bohemia, and this was increased by further attempts made by the Council of Constanz and by Pope *Martin V.* to put down the heretics. When Wenceslaus died in 1419, Sigmund claimed to be King of Bohemia. If he had tried to conciliate the more moderate Hussites he might have gained the crown at once; but, instead of doing so, he caused a crusade to be preached against all Huss's followers, and thus united them against him. The war which followed was a very fierce one, and lasted fifteen years. The Hussites were at first led by *John Zisca*, one of the greatest generals that ever lived. He became blind; but his followers had unbounded trust in him, and he led them from one victory to another. He died in 1424. After his death, his spirit seemed still to live among the Hussites, for they not only defeated army after army sent against them, but invaded and laid waste the lands lying around Bohemia.

14. **Sigmund receives the crown of Bohemia.** His

death.—The Council of *Basel* met in 1431, and soon began to negotiate with the Hussites. The latter were divided into two parties—the *Calixtines* and the *Taborites*. The chief doctrine of the Calixtines *(Kalyx, a cup)* was that laymen as well as the clergy ought to receive the cup in the communion. The Taborites went much further than this, and wished to remain for ever separate from the Church. They received their name from a hill which Zisca had made his headquarters and had strongly fortified, and which had been called *Mount Tabor*. In 1433 the Calixtines, also called *Utraquists*, came to an agreement with the Basel Council, which permitted the use of the cup; and returned to the Church. The Taborites looked on this as treachery, and turned against their old friends; but in 1434 they were utterly defeated near Prague. Sigmund then confirmed the agreement made between the Council and the Utraquists, and was acknowledged King of Bohemia. He did not, however, act fairly, for when he came to Prague he tried to put down the Utraquists, and to bring back the Catholic worship. He died in 1437. In 1433 he had been crowned Emperor.

15. **Brandenburg and Sachsen-Wittenberg.**—In 1415, in return for 400,000 Hungarian gulden, Sigmund gave the Mark of *Brandenburg* in fief to *Frederick*, Count of *Hohenzollern*. From this time the house of Hohenzollern always held Brandenburg. *Sachsen-Wittenberg* was given in 1423, also in return for money, to *Frederick*, Margrave of *Meissen* and Landgrave of *Thuringia*. Both princes received the Electoral dignity along with their new lands.

# CHAPTER XII.

## EMPERORS OF THE HOUSE OF AUSTRIA.

*Albert of Austria elected; his firm government; his death (1)—Frederick of Styria becomes King; supports the Pope against the princes (2)—Frederick III. crowned Emperor; confirms to the House of Austria the title of Archduke (3)—the Turks threaten Christendom (4)—Ladislaus, Albert II.'s son, dies; Frederick III. receives Lower Austria; George Podiebrad becomes King of Bohemia, and Matthias Corvinus King of Hungary (5)—wars in Germany (6)—disturbances in Austria (7)—Charles the Bold defeated by the Eidgenossen (8)—Maximilian, Frederick III.'s son, marries Mary of Burgundy (9)—wars of Frederick III. and Matthias Corvinus (10)—the Swabian Confederation; death of Frederick III. (11)—the Teutonic Order has to give up the western part of Prussia to the King of Poland, and to do homage for the rest (12)—character and power of Maximilian I. (13) —Marriage of Philip, son of Maximilian I., with the Infanta Joanna (14)—a perpetual peace proclaimed; the Imperial Chamber; the common penny (15)—foreign wars of Maximilian I. (16)—the Turks (17)—war of Maximilian I. with the Swiss League (18)—war of the Bavarian succession (19)—Maximilian I. takes the titles of "Emperor Elect" and "King of Germany" (20)—Germany divided into Circles (21)—the Aulic Council (22)—death of Maximilian I. (23)—the end of the Middle Ages (24)—position of the German Kings (25)—the princes; the Provincial States (26)—the free Imperial cities (27) the Diet (28)—the Roman Law in Germany (29)—Universities* of Germany; the Revival of learning (30)—the Literature of the people (31).

1. **Albert II.**—After Sigmund died, his son-in-law, *Albert*, Duke of Austria, was made King of Bohemia and of Hungary; and in 1438 he was chosen King of the Romans. From this time the Imperial crown was held without interruption by the house of Austria till the male line died out. At this time the affairs of the Church were the chief subject of interest to Germany as well as to the rest of Europe. The Council of *Basel* had quarrelled with Pope *Eugenius IV.*, who was supported by all who opposed the reformation of the Church. At first Germany took neither side in this quarrel; but in 1439 Albert, with the approval of the Diet, accepted the reforming decrees of the Council, and thus recognized its authority. If these decrees had been carried out, the Church might have been spared much future humiliation. Albert acted as wisely in civil as in ecclesiastical matters, so that his reign promised to be a very prosperous one; but he suddenly died, after a campaign against the Turks, in 1439.

2. **Frederick III.**—Albert II. was succeeded on the German throne by *Frederick*, Duke of *Styria*. Frederick reigned longer than any German King either before or after his time, but did nothing great. He was a grave and thoughtful man, but he lacked energy, and was too poor to do much without the help of the States, which were now almost always unwilling to interfere in matters not directly affecting themselves. Germany still supported the Council of Basel; but Frederick sided with the Pope. In 1445 Eugenius IV. deposed the Archbishops of *Köln* and *Trier*. The Electors felt themselves wronged by this insult to two of their number, and, meeting at *Frankfurt*, made various demands on the Pope, requiring, among other things, that he

should recognize the decrees of Constanz and Basel. Frederick III., with the help of his secretary, *Æneas Sylvius*, who afterwards became Pope, not only got the Electors to moderate their demands, but in the end reconciled them to Eugenius. He afterwards concluded with *Nicolas V.* the *Concordat of Vienna*, by which the Pope received back almost all the rights which the Basel Council had taken from him. To this Concordat the assent of the princes, one after the other, was afterwards obtained. By his friendship with the Pope Frederick hoped to gain back some of the lost rights of the German Kings. He thus turned against the princes the very weapon with which they had in former times attacked the royal and Imperial authority. But it was now too late to take this course. An alliance between the Pope and the German King would once have done great things for both; but they had quarrelled so long, and weakened each other so thoroughly, that their friendship was now of very little use to either.

3. **Frederick III. and the House of Austria.**—Frederick was crowned Emperor at Rome in 1452. He was the last Emperor crowned at Rome, and the last but one who received the Imperial crown from a Pope. When he became Emperor he confirmed to the House of Austria the title of *Archduke*, which had been first taken by Duke *Rudolf* in the time of the Emperor *Charles IV.* He also granted privileges to his family which raised it above all other princely houses except those of the Electors.

4. **The Turks.**—A great danger at this time threatened Germany. This was the advance of the *Turks*, who took *Constantinople* in 1453, and destroyed the Eastern Empire. Frederick wished to join the Pope in keeping back this powerful enemy; but the States would not support him, partly from indifference to what affected the general weal, and partly because they feared that if they should contribute

men and money the Pope and the Emperor would use these for their private ends. The defence of Christendom by land was thus left chiefly to the Poles and the Hungarians. In 1456 the Turks besieged *Belgrade;* but they were driven back with great loss by the Hungarians, who were led by their regent, *John Huniades*.

5. **Death of Ladislaus, son of Albert II.**—Ladislaus, the posthumous son of Albert II., had succeeded his father as Duke of Austria and as King of Hungary and Bohemia. He died in 1457. The Emperor then claimed, as head of his house, the whole of Austria; but he had to give up *Upper Austria* to his brother *Albert*, and to content himself with *Lower Austria*. He next tried to obtain the Bohemian and Hungarian crowns. The Bohemians, however, elected *George Podiebrad*, a Utraquist nobleman, who had already acted as regent; and *Matthias Corvinus*, son of *John Huniades*, was made King of Hungary. In the end Frederick had to recognise both of these Kings.

6. **Wars in Germany.**—The reign of Frederick was a time of great confusion in Germany, for when he interfered in its affairs he had no power to enforce his decrees. A war, called the Margraves' War, went on for seven years, from 1449, between *Albert*, Margrave of *Brandenburg*, and the city of *Nürnberg*. Many princes joined Albert; and Nürnberg was supported by the *Eidgenossen* and more than seventy cities. At last, in 1456, the war was ended by the defeat of Albert; but in the end the city had to pay to him a large sum. Another war was carried on against *Frederick* of the *Rhenish Palatinate*. He took the Archbishop of *Mainz*, when deposed by the Pope, under his protection. As usual, the Emperor sided with the Pope, and put Frederick to the ban of the Empire. *Albert* of *Brandenburg*, and *Ulrich*, Count of *Würtemberg*, undertook to execute the Imperial sentence; but, in 1462, both

were defeated, Ulrich by Frederick himself, and Albert by Frederick's ally, *Lewis*, Duke of *Bavaria*. Other wars were carried on which did much harm to all classes, but especially to the peasantry.

7. **Disturbances in Austria.**—Even in Lower Austria the Emperor was treated with very little respect. In 1462 the people of Vienna rebelled against him, and besieged him in the citadel, in which he had taken refuge with the Empress and their young son *Maximilian*. Frederick's brother *Albert* took part with Vienna. The Emperor in vain appealed to the States to help him; but at last George Podiebrad, King of Bohemia, sent an army to his relief. In 1462 he was compelled to give up Lower Austria, with Vienna, for eight years to his brother. Albert, however, made himself as unpopular as the Emperor had done; and he died in 1463. His death made Frederick master of all the Austrian lands except Tyrol.

8. **Charles the Bold and the Eidgenossen.**—The wealthiest prince of this time was *Charles the Bold*, Duke of *Burgundy*. Besides the *Duchy* of Burgundy, he held the *Free County* of Burgundy and greater part of the *Low Countries*. He wished to restore the old Lotharingia by founding a great border kingdom, reaching from the Mediterranean to the North Sea, between France and Germany. In 1476 he made war on the *Eidgenossen*, whom *Lewis XI.* of France had stirred up against him. The *Eidgenossen* never fought more bravely than in this war, for they defeated Charles in two great battles, first at *Granson* and afterwards at *Morat*. In 1477 they helped *René*, Duke of Lorraine, to win the battle of *Nancy*, in which Charles was killed. These great victories did much to draw the *Eidgenossen*, who now began to be called *Swiss*, closer together, and to give them a feeling of national life. But they still remained part of the Empire.

9. **Marriage of Maximilian with Mary of Burgundy.—** There had been negotiations between the Emperor Frederick and Charles the Bold for the marriage of *Mary*, Charles's daughter, with *Maximilian*, Frederick's son ; but some misunderstanding had arisen, and the negotiations were broken off. When Charles died, Mary gave her hand of her own will to Maximilian. Through this marriage the house of Austria received the *Low Countries* and the *Free County* of Burgundy. The *Duchy* of Burgundy had been seized by the French King when Charles the Bold died ; and it was not again given up. Mary died in 1482, leaving a son and daughter, *Philip* and *Margaret*.

10. **Frederick III. and Matthias Corvinus.—***George Podiebrad* died in 1471. The Emperor again tried to gain the crown of Bohemia ; but the Bohemian States elected *Wladislaus*, son of *Casimir IV.*, King of Poland. Frederick had been won over by Pope *Paul II.* against Podiebrad, and had stirred up *Matthias Corvinus*, King of Hungary, to make war on Bohemia. But Frederick was jealous of the great power of Matthias, and now not only left him, but supported Wladislaus against him, and excited rebellion in Hungary, hoping in the end to gain the Hungarian crown for himself and his house. Matthias twice made war on Austria, and the second time (1485) not only overran the Archduchy, but took Vienna. At this time the Emperor, nominally the greatest of earthly rulers, had to fly for his life, and was glad to find shelter in the monasteries and towns he passed. Matthias kept possession of Austria till his death in 1490. Frederick then recovered his lands, and tried to get either himself or his son Maximilian elected King of Hungary. The Hungarian States, however, were jealous of the house of Austria, and chose as their King *Wladislaus*, King of Bohemia.

11. **The Swabian Confederation. Death of Frederick III.**

—There had been so many private wars in Frederick's time that the nation was longing for peace. At a Diet held in 1486, therefore, a *public peace* was proclaimed for ten years. Two years afterwards, partly through the efforts of Frederick, a great new Confederation was formed in Swabia. It took in many princes, nobles, and cities. About this time the Duke of Bavaria had seized *Regensburg*, and was threatening other free towns. The Confederation soon compelled him to submit; and it gradually became so powerful that it did more than could have been done by either the Emperor or the Diet to keep the peace in South Germany. Frederick died in 1493, having reigned upwards of fifty-three years. For some time he had given up the government, both of Austria and Germany, to his son, *Maximilian*, who had been elected King of the Romans in 1486.

12. **Prussia and the Teutonic Order.**—For a long time Prussia flourished under the Teutonic knights. But the Order gradually got corrupted by prosperity, and began to rule badly. In the beginning of the fifteenth century it was defeated and humbled by the Polish king, *Jagellon*. In 1454, the towns and nobles rebelled against the Order, and called in *Casimir IV.*, King of Poland, to their help. A war followed which did not end till 1466. The Order had then, in the *Peace of Thorn*, to give up the western part of Prussia to Casimir, and to do homage for the eastern, which it was allowed to keep.

13. **Maximilian I.**—*Maximilian I.* was a very different man from his father. He was eager and restless, fond of war and adventure, and always forming some scheme or other for adding to his own power. Even if he had not been King of the Romans, he would have been a powerful prince. He was, in his own right, Archduke of Austria, Duke of Styria, Carinthia, and Carniola, and Count of

Tyrol; and he had lands in Swabia and Elsass. As guardian to his son *Philip*, he also ruled the Low Countries and the County of Burgundy.

**14. Marriage of Philip with the Infanta Joanna.**—The year after he succeeded to the throne, Maximilian gave up the government of the Low Countries to his son Philip. Philip afterwards married *Joanna*, daughter of Ferdinand and Isabella, who had united by their marriage the kingdoms of *Aragon* and *Castile*. This marriage led to very important results. Philip and Joanna had two sons, *Charles* and *Ferdinand*. These sons afterwards became Emperors, one after the other; and from them sprang the Austrian and Spanish branches of the House of Habsburg.

**15. The Diet of Worms, 1495.**—In 1494, *Charles VIII.* of France made his famous expedition into Italy. Maximilian was eager to oppose him, and to assert the old Imperial rights over the southern kingdom. As he could do very little without the help of the States, he summoned a Diet at *Worms* in 1495. This was one of the most famous of all the Diets. All good men in Germany now were sincerely anxious that the custom of private warfare should be put down. At this Diet, a perpetual *public peace* was proclaimed, and the right of private feuds declared at an end. The States then urged Maximilian to set up some court by which disputes might be finally settled, so that there should be no excuse for carrying on private war. Maximilian was very unwilling to give up any of his royal rights; but at last, in the hope that by yielding he might gain the support of the States against the French, he agreed to set up a court of appeal called the *Imperial Chamber*. This court was to be made up of a *judge*, or *president*, and sixteen *assessors*. The judge was to be appointed by the King; but the assessors were to be named by the States, and only to be confirmed by the King. If any one should refuse to submit to a decision of the court, it was to have the power of putting him to the ban of the Empire. A tax called the *common penny*, to be raised in all the States of Germany, was to be partly devoted to the support of the tribunal. Maximilian never liked the court, and did everything he could to make it fail; but it went on after his time until the Empire was broken up. It had usually, however, too little power, and was too slow and formal in its proceedings to be very useful.

16. **Foreign Wars of Maximilian I.**—Maximilian took part in many wars in which Germany was not directly mixed up. They had almost all to do with Italy, which several French kings, one after the other, and Ferdinand of Spain, tried hard at this time to conquer. In 1508 Maximilian joined the *League of Cambray*, formed for the purpose of breaking up the Venetian Republic. He afterwards helped the so-called *Holy League* against *Lewis XII.* of France. In almost all his foreign wars Maximilian was very unsuccessful. The chief cause of this was his want of money. He often tried to get the States to help him; but they usually insisted that what Germany really needed was peace and order, not war. He had therefore to trust chiefly to his hereditary possessions. Although these were very great, they did not enable him to fight on equal terms with Kings like Lewis XII., or Ferdinand, especially as he was lavish in his habits, and often wasted great sums of money in foolish display. His poverty led him sometimes to act in a way that was unworthy of his great position. At the siege of *Terouenne* he served under *Henry VIII.* of England for the pay of 100 crowns a-day.

17. **The Turks.**—In the latter part of Frederick III.'s reign, the Turks had, over and over again, entered Carinthia, Carniola, and Styria, and had done much harm. Maximilian always professed to be anxious to lead a crusade

against them, in order to drive them altogether from Europe; but the States, distrusting both him and the Pope, who supported him, refused to help him, so that his schemes came to nothing. During his reign, however, the Turks did not invade any of the lands held by the House of Austria.

18. **Maximilian I. and the Swiss League.**—In 1499, Maximilian made war on the *Swiss League*, as we may now call the League of the *Eidgenossen*, partly because it would not acknowledge the Imperial Chamber, but chiefly because it helped the French in their attempt to conquer Italy. In this, as in his other wars, the States supported Maximilian very unwillingly; and his own troops were defeated at *Dornach*. He was therefore obliged to conclude a peace, by which the members of the Confederation were declared free from Imperial taxation and the jurisdiction of the Imperial Chamber. The League was still nominally part of the Empire for about a century and a half; but from this time it was practically independent.

19. **War of the Bavarian succession.**—The house of *Bavaria* was still divided into two lines, the *Palatine* and the *Bavarian;* and the latter took in the two branches of *Landshut* and *Munich*. When *George*, Duke of Bavaria-Landshut, died, in 1503, the Dukes of Bavaria-Munich claimed to be his lawful heirs; but he had left his lands to his daughter, *Elizabeth*, and her husband, *Rupert*, and they were supported by the Rhenish Palsgrave, Rupert's father. The matter came before the Imperial Chamber, but Rupert and his father would not accept its decision. Maximilian made war on them; and he was joined by the Swabian League and some powerful princes. This was the most successful of all Maximilian's wars. He defeated the forces of the enemy, and in the end not only got the dispute settled according to his wish, but added

various Bavarian towns and lands to his hereditary possessions.

**20. Maximilian I. takes the titles of "Emperor Elect" and "King of Germany."**—In 1508, Maximilian was about to march to Rome to be crowned Emperor; but the Venetians refused to let him pass through their territory. With the sanction of Pope *Julius II.*, therefore, he took the title of "Emperor Elect" without being crowned Emperor at all. He also added to his other titles that of "King of or in Germany"—a title that does not occur before his time.

**21. Germany divided into Circles.**—Albert II. had tried to divide Germany into *Circles*, that he might be the better able to put down private war; but he had not lived long enough to carry out his plan. In Maximilian's time it was again taken up; and, in 1501, the Circles of *Bavaria*, *Swabia*, *Franconia*, the *Upper Rhine*, *Westphalia*, and *Lower Saxony*, were formed. In 1512, at a Diet in *Köln*, it was agreed that the hereditary dominions of Maximilian and the Electoral princes, which had hitherto been left out, should also be divided into Circles. Thus the four new Circles of *Austria, Burgundy,* the *Lower Rhine,* and *Upper Saxony*, were added to those already existing. Each of these ten Circles had its own *States*, presided over by one or more *Directors*. The duty of the Government of a Circle was to carry out the decisions of the Imperial Chamber, and generally to maintain order. It was some years before the Circles were thoroughly formed. They never did so much as many hoped they might do; but they were a great advance on the disorder of the time of Frederick III.

**22. The Aulic Council.**—Maximilian ruled his hereditary lands with great vigour. Amongst other things he set up a tribunal which was to receive appeals from lower courts. This tribunal was afterwards called the *Aulic Council*, and became a court of appeal for the whole of Germany. It lasted, like the Imperial Chamber, till the Empire broke up; but, as its judges were appointed by the Emperor, it never thoroughly gained the confidence of the country.

23. **Death of Maximilian I.**—Maximilian went on almost till his death forming great schemes, which he was never able to fulfil. He seems at one time even to have had the idea of getting himself elected Pope. At his very last Diet held in *Augsburg* in 1518, he did everything he could to rouse the States to join him in a crusade against the Turks. He also tried, but in vain, to get his grandson, *Charles*, elected King of the Romans. While on his way home from the Diet of Augsburg, Maximilian died in 1519, at *Wels*, in Upper Austria.

24. **The end of the Middle Ages.**—The Middle Ages may now be said to have nearly come to an end in Germany. The *Empire* was no longer looked on as a universal monarchy; and, as we shall see, the *Church* was soon to be broken up by the great movement of the *Reformation*. Some of the chief features of *feudalism* had also begun to disappear. The forms of feudalism were still, to some extent, kept up; but feudal lords no longer received direct service in war from their vassals in return for their lands. Princes now for the most part made war by means of hired troops. This change was brought about by the discovery of *gunpowder*, which made a body of common men on foot more than a match for an equal number of even the bravest knights on horseback armed in the old way. The demand for fighting men led many to give themselves up to a life of war. Those who did so were called "*Landsknechte*," a word first applied to mercenaries from the lowlands of Austria as opposed to those of Switzerland. The *Landsknechte* served under those princes who paid them best, no matter what might be the cause for which they had to fight. They made good soldiers, but were usually men of wild

lives, and when not in active service were a cause of great annoyance to honest people both in the towns and in the country.

25. **Position of the German Kings.**—The German King had now no certain revenue as King, and he exercised very little real power in Germany. Since the *Interregnum* the princes had greatly strengthened the independence whose foundation they had laid at that time and in the troubled reigns that had gone before it from the days of *Henry IV.* Many Imperial cities had also become *free.* Nevertheless the German Kings took a far higher place in Europe after the time of Maximilian I. then they had done for a very long time before. This was not because they were German Kings or Emperors, but because they were great princes altogether apart from their royal and Imperial position. It was not always good for Germany that the crown was held by princes so powerful in their own right, for the Austrian Emperors as a rule tried to use their position as a means of adding to the greatness of their house. Above all, they tried to drag Germany into wars waged by Austria against other countries, but with which the kingdom of Germany had really little or nothing to do.

26. **The princes. The provincial States.**—Although the princes owed only a nominal allegiance to the King, they were not usually altogether absolute rulers, for in almost every principality there were now *States* holding the same relation to the prince that the *Diet* held to the King. The States of a principality were made up of the vassals of the prince, and of representatives from its free cities. The prince had to get the approval of his States before he could lay on taxes; and in some cases he had even to give an account of the way in which he spent public money. The nobles for the most part refused to pay taxes, on the plea that it was service in war, not money, they owed their lord for

their lands. The burden thus fell chiefly on those who held *allodial* lands, on the citizens of towns, and on the peasantry. The latter class had no part in the provincial Diets, and were usually treated with great harshness. The tyranny of their lords roused deep discontent in the minds of the peasants; and more than once during Maximilian's reign they formed secret Leagues in different parts of the country, which had to be put down by force.

27. **The Free Imperial Cities.**—The free Imperial cities now held a very high place in Germany. They had become rich and powerful, and could hold their own against the greatest princes. The *Hansa* was about this time at the height of its fame. Within the cities themselves contests had long been going on between the old families, who formed a sort of civil aristocracy, and were called *Patricians*, and the *Gilds*. The *Gilds* had not only won for themselves a share in the government in almost all cities, but had in very many got the upper hand, and made the government thoroughly democratic.

28. **The Diet.**—The Diet was now made up of three *Colleges*—the Electors, the princes, and the representatives of free Imperial cities. It was still nominally a national council; but in reality it did very little. The princes and free Imperial cities were now at all times too jealous of each other and of the Emperor to do much for the common good.

29. **The Roman law in Germany.**—A great change had taken place in Germany in the administration of justice. During the greater part of the Middle Ages, as in earlier times, justice was administered in accordance with old usages. If the sovereign had remained a King and nothing more, these usages would gradually have given rise to a body of German law; but, as he was Roman Emperor as well as King, his subjects came to believe that they were

bound by Roman law. Thus the Roman law gradually came into use, first in the free Imperial cities, and afterwards in the tribunals of princes. From 1495 the Imperial Chamber was to judge according to the law of the Empire and written (*i.e.* Roman) law. The Emperors did everything they could to encourage its use, for it gave them great power. Without doing away with the feudal law of the land, it was now appealed to in the greater part of Germany.

30. **Universities of Germany. The Revival of Learning.** —The example of *Charles IV.*, in founding the University of *Prague*, had soon been followed by a number of princes in Germany. Universities were founded in the fourteenth century in *Vienna*, *Heidelberg*, *Köln*, and *Erfurt;* and, in the fifteenth, in *Rostock*, *Greifswald*, *Tübingen*, *Leipzig*, and other towns. For a long time the chief studies at the universities were Theology and the Scholastic Philosophy; but towards the end of the fifteenth century a great movement began, called the *Revival of Learning*. The leading Latin authors had always been more or less studied; but men now began to read eagerly, in addition to these, the Greek classics, and to think more freely on almost all subjects. Those who did so were called *Humanists*. The movement had begun in Italy, and had been greatly helped by the invention of *printing*, made by *John Guttenberg* of *Mainz* in the middle of the fifteenth century. Among the greatest of the *Humanists* were *John Reuchlin*, *Desiderius Erasmus*, and *Ulrich von Hutten*.

31. **Literature of the people.**—It was not only at the universities that a new spirit of inquiry was awakened about this time; the people also began to think and read for themselves. Their favourite books were *Tyll Eulenspiegel*, *Reineke Fuchs*, and the *Narrenschiff* of *Sebastian Brant*. The two first were written originally in

Low Dutch dialects. All of them were more or less satirical, and attacked with especial delight the vices of the clergy. They thus gave expression to, and deepened, a popular feeling which had long been preparing the way for the Reformation.

# CHAPTER XIII.

## CHARLES V.—THE REFORMATION.

*Election of Charles V. (1)—Martin Luther protests against indulgences; beginning of the Reformation (2)—Luther is excommunicated; burns the Pope's Bull (3)—Charles V. sides with the Catholic Church (4)—Luther before the Diet of Worms (5)—formation of an Administrative Council: a Matricula (6)—wars of Charles V. and Francis I. (7)—Luther's doctrines accepted by princes and cities; marriage of Luther; the Diet of Speyer, 1526; changes in the Church in various States (8)—Franz von Sickingen (9)—the war of the peasantry (10)—Albert of Brandenburg becomes Duke of Prussia (11)—the Archduke Ferdinand becomes King of Bohemia and Hungary (12)—the Lutherans receive the name of Protestants (13)—the Reformation in Switzerland (14)—the Diet of Augsburg, 1530; the Augsburg Confession; decree condemning Luther's doctrines (15)—the Archduke Ferdinand is elected King of the Romans (16)—the Schmalkaldic League (17)—the Turks threaten Germany; the Religious Peace of Nürnberg (18)—foreign wars of Charles V. (19)—further progress of the Reformation (20)—Charles V. and the Protestants prepare for war (21)—death of Luther (22)—the Schmalkaldic war; triumph of the Emperor (23)—the Interim (24)—rebellion of Maurice of Saxony; Henry II. of France seizes German lands; flight of Charles V. (25)—the Treaty of Passau (26)—Charles V. tries to take the territory seized by Henry II., but fails (27)—the Religious Peace of Augsburg (28)—abdication and death of Charles V. (29)—political effects of the Reformation (30)—Literature and Art (31).*

1. **Election of Charles V.**—After Maximilian's death,

was away from Germany. The Diet of Worms also drew up a *Matricula*, which settled the number of troops, at a certain rate of pay, that were to be raised by the States of the realm. This *Matricula* continued in force till the fall of the Empire. Before the Diet broke up Charles divided the hereditary Austrian lands between himself and his brother *Ferdinand*. Soon afterwards Ferdinand received all these lands, and thus became the founder of the *Austrian* branch of the house of Habsburg, while Charles became the founder of the *Spanish* branch.

7. **Charles V. and Francis I.**—Immediately after the Diet of Worms, Charles left Germany, and he did not come back for about eight years. During this time his thoughts were chiefly taken up by his great struggle with *Francis I.* of France, who had seized the Duchy of *Milan*. In 1525 Francis was made prisoner at the *battle of Pavia*. He was taken to *Madrid*, and was not set free till he had agreed to very hard terms; but he did not keep the treaty he had signed. At last, after repeated defeats, he had to give up for a time all hope of gaining a footing in Italy; and in 1529 the *Peace of Cambray* was concluded. In 1530 Charles was crowned Emperor and King of Italy at *Bologna*. After him no Emperor received the Imperial crown from a Pope.

8. **Progress of the Reformation.**—As Luther was on his way home from Worms, he was taken, by order of Frederick of Saxony, to the *Wartburg*, near *Eisenach*. Frederick wished him to stay there in quiet till the storm he had raised had to some extent passed away. In Luther's absence some of his friends began to act in a way he did not approve of. In 1522, therefore, he left the Wartburg, and went to Wittenberg, where he again took his place as leader of the Reformation. He published a translation of the New Testament, which he had written in the Wartburg, and

afterwards translated the whole Bible. He also wrote many theological books which were read in all parts of Germany. Thus his doctrines became more and more popular, and were adopted by several powerful princes, among whom were *John*, Elector of Saxony, Frederick's successor, and *Philip*, Landgrave of *Hessen*. Some great Imperial cities also became Lutheran. In 1525 Luther married *Catherine* of *Bora*, a nun. His example was followed by many of the clergy who sided with him, so that the breach between the reforming party and the Church went on widening. Charles by no means gave up his purpose of crushing the Lutheran heresy; but while he was fighting with Francis I. he had little time to think of Germany, and he could not afford just then to make the States who supported Luther his enemies. In 1526 a Diet met at *Speyer*, presided over by the Archduke Ferdinand, which ended by agreeing that, till a General Council should be summoned, the government of each State should be allowed to act in religious matters as it saw fit. After this the Elector John, Landgrave Philip, and other princes, made great changes in the Church in their dominions. They brought in new forms of Church government, did away with the saying of Mass, caused religious services to be conducted in the language of the people, and gave a much higher place to preaching than it had hitherto held. Convents were suppressed; and Church lands were seized, and only in part applied to ecclesiastical uses. Of course Luther took a prominent part in bringing about these changes. His chief helper was his friend *Melanchthon*, a man of much gentler character than himself, but one of the ablest and most learned of the Reformers.

9. **Franz von Sickingen.**—One of Luther's earliest and best friends was *Franz von Sickingen*, a famous knight. He offered to protect the Reformer in his castle of *Ebernburg*, in case his life should be endangered. In 1522,

Sickingen made war on the Elector of *Trier*. Luther entreated him to remain at peace; but he collected an army of 12,000 men, entered the Electorate, and laid great part of it waste. A large number of knights joined him. This class was profoundly discontented with the rule of the princes, and vaguely hoped, under Sickingen's guidance, to improve its position. The Elector of Trier, however, was aided by the Elector Palatine and Landgrave Philip of Hessen. Sickingen was defeated, and in 1523 besieged in his castle of *Landsstuhl*. This was soon taken; and in a few days afterwards he died, having been severely wounded. Ulrich von Hutten, who had warmly supported Sickingen, went to Switzerland after the death of his friend. In a few months he also died.

10. **The War of the Peasantry.**—We have seen that the peasantry were as a rule very ill used by the princes. By the heavy taxes laid on them they were kept in utter poverty, and their fields were often destroyed by hunting-parties. No class in Germany joined the Reformation more heartily. They hoped that it might somehow help them to obtain their rights, for by the freedom of which Luther and the other Reformers spoke so much they understood political and social as well as spiritual freedom. In 1524 a great rising took place among them in *Swabia;* and it soon passed to *Franconia*, *Elsass*, and *Thuringia*. Never had the peasantry seemed so near throwing off the yoke under which they had lain for centuries. Some knights—among others *Götz von Berlichingen*—joined them. They looked to Luther for help; but although a Reformer in the Church, he had no wish to see changes brought about in the State, and not only refused to help the peasants, but sided strongly with the princes and urged them to put down the rebellion by force. Unhappily, the peasants hurt their own cause by rashness and violence. At last, in 1525, a number of princes

united against them, and in several battles thoroughly defeated them. The rising was thus utterly crushed, and the burdens laid on the peasantry, instead of being lessened, were, if possible, made heavier than before.

**11. Albert of Brandenburg becomes Duke of Prussia.**—When the Reformation began, the Grand Master of the Teutonic Order was *Albert*, a prince of the house of *Brandenburg*. He became a Lutheran, and in 1525 made a treaty with *Sigmund I.*, King of Poland, whereby the Teutonic Order came to an end as a sovereign power, and Albert received the eastern part of Prussia in fief of Sigmund as a hereditary Duchy. The Teutonic Order looked on Albert's conduct as treachery; but he kept the new Duchy, and handed it on to his children. In the end, as we shall see, it passed into the hands of the *electoral* branch of the Brandenburg family, and became independent of Poland.

**12. The Archduke Ferdinand becomes King of Bohemia and Hungary.**—In 1522 the Archduke Ferdinand had married a daughter of *Wladislaus*, King of Bohemia and Hungary. *Lewis II.*, the son and successor of Wladislaus, was killed at the battle of *Mohacs* in 1526. Ferdinand was then elected and crowned King of *Bohemia*. He was afterwards chosen, by a party of Hungarian nobles, King of *Hungary*. Another party had already raised *John*, Waiwode of *Transsilvania*, to the Hungarian throne. This double election gave rise to war, in the course of which John craved help from the Sultan *Suleyman*, and consented to hold the crown as his vassal. Suleyman came to Hungary in 1529, at the head of a great army, and not only overran the country, but entered Austria, and besieged *Vienna*, which, however, he was unable to take. Even after Suleyman left Austria and Hungary, Ferdinand was not acknowledged by the whole Hungarian nation; but his party continued to support him. From this time the crown of Hungary was always held by an Archduke of Austria. It was still for some time nominally elective; but in the end it was made hereditary. The house of Austria also always held Bohemia after Ferdinand's time. Thus the German branch of the Austrian family became very great, and took its place, apart from the Imperial crown, as one of the leading powers of Europe.

13. **The Lutherans receive the name of "Protestants."**—The Reformation had made so much progress, and the reforming party had given up so many old beliefs and ceremonies, that the Catholics were now thoroughly alarmed, and Charles was more than ever resolved to do everything he could to uphold the Church. In 1529 the Diet again met at Speyer under the presidency of the Archduke Ferdinand. As there were more Catholics than Lutherans present, a decree was passed forbidding further changes in religion, and requiring that Mass should be said in all churches. The Lutheran princes and cities entered a formal *protest* against this decree, whence they were called *Protestants*—a name which was afterwards given to all who had left the Church of Rome.

14. **The Reformation in Switzerland.**—Meanwhile a Reformation had been going on in some Swiss Cantons which was not guided by Luther. It was begun in *Zürich* in 1519 by *Ulrich Zwingli*, who differed in some points from Luther, especially as to the nature of the Lord's Supper. A controversy arose between the two theologians and their followers, and a very bitter feeling sprang up. In 1529 Luther and Zwingli met at Marburg; but no understanding was arrived at. In the end two churches were formed, the *Lutheran* and the *Reformed*, each of which disliked the other for a long time almost as much as both disliked the Catholics.

15. **The Diet of Augsburg, 1530.**—When Charles had driven the French from Italy, and received the Imperial crown, he at last turned his thoughts seriously to Germany. In 1530 he crossed the Alps, and opened a great Diet at *Augsburg*. He hoped to gain over the chief Lutheran states without much difficulty, but he soon found that he had mistaken the strength of the new movement. The Lutherans laid before the Diet a statement of their belief, which had been drawn up by Melanchthon, and approved by Luther. This statement was afterwards called the *Augsburg Confession*, and became the chief standard of faith among the Lutheran churches. A great deal of discussion went on between the two parties; but neither side would give way. At last the Elector John and Landgrave Philip left Augsburg. Soon afterwards Charles issued a decree in which he condemned the Lutheran heresy, and commanded all who had accepted it to return to their allegiance to the Church. All Church property that had been seized was to be given back, and suppressed convents were again to be set up. Those who refused to obey this decree were to be put to the ban of the Empire.

16. **The Archduke Ferdinand is elected King of the Romans.**—As the administrative council had been friendly to the Lutherans, the Catholics wished that a King of the Romans might be appointed, and urged Charles to get one elected. He proposed his brother *Ferdinand* to the Electors. John of Saxony opposed the election; but the other Electors voted for Ferdinand, and he was crowned at Aachen in 1531.

17. **The Schmalkaldic League.**—While the negotiations for Ferdinand's election were going on, the Lutheran princes met at *Schmalkalden*, and formed a League for mutual defence. After the election they met again, and confirmed their League, which was joined also by the Lutheran cities.

This League was called the *Schmalkaldic League*. Some of its members would at once have appealed to arms; but the more moderate opposed this, so that war was for a time avoided.

18. **The Religious Peace of Nürnberg. The Turks.**—Although Suleyman went back to Constantinople in 1529, he did not intend to leave Hungary and Germany in peace. In 1532 he returned at the head of a much greater army than before. His approach caused great alarm; but the Lutheran princes refused to help Charles unless he withdrew the decree of Augsburg. Charles was very unwilling to yield; but it was necessary that he should raise a force strong enough to drive back the Turks. In 1532, therefore, he granted the *Religious Peace of Nürnberg*, by which full freedom of worship was given to the Lutherans until a General Council or the next Diet should have met. The Lutheran States then hastened to join the Emperor against the Turks. Suleyman, finding all parties united against him, hastily marched back to his own dominions. Afterwards, however, the Turks returned to Hungary, supported the party opposed to Ferdinand, and conquered a large part of the country.

19. **Foreign Wars of Charles V.**—During his second absence from Germany, Charles made two famous expeditions against *Hayraddin Barbarossa*, a pirate who had made himself master of *Algiers* and *Tunis*, and held many thousands of Christians as prisoners. During part of the interval between these expeditions, Charles had to carry on another war with Francis I., who again laid claim to the Duchy of Milan. A truce was concluded for ten years at *Nice* in 1538; but in 1542 war broke out again. In 1544 the *Peace of Crespy* was concluded, and after this there was no more open war between the two sovereigns.

20. **Further progress of the Reformation.**—The Reforma-

tion continued to make progress, especially in the north of Germany. *Joachim II.*, Elector of *Brandenburg*, who succeeded his father, a bigoted Catholic, in 1534, became a Lutheran. *Frederick II.*, Elector Palatine, and Duke *George* of *Saxony*, also brought the Lutheran doctrine into their dominions. Even Archbishop *Hermann* of *Köln* had sympathy with the Reformation, and did nothing to put it down among his subjects. Thus nearly all the northern part of Germany became Lutheran. In the south *Württemberg* was Protestant. Duke *Ulrich* of Württemberg had been driven from his dominions in 1520 by the Swabian League, but was restored in 1534 by the intervention of Landgrave Philip of Hessen.

21. **Charles V. and the Lutherans prepare for war.**—So long as Charles was at war with Francis I. or the Turks, and needed the help of all the German States, he did nothing to offend the Lutherans. He even confirmed more than once the Peace of Nürnberg. But he never really gave up his purpose of crushing out heresy in Germany. At last, when the peace of Crespy had been signed, in 1544, he felt he was strong enough to undertake the task in earnest. He had got Pope Paul II. to summon a General Council; and it met at *Trent* in 1545. The Lutherans refused to recognise it, on the ground that the Pope was a party to the dispute, and had already condemned them as heretics. Charles therefore began secretly to prepare for war, and made a treaty with the Pope, by which the latter undertook to help him with men and money. He succeeded in getting the Elector of Brandenburg, the Elector Palatine, and other Lutheran princes to remain neutral; and with *Maurice*, Duke of Saxony, Duke George's successor, he made a separate treaty. The *Schmalkaldic League*, however, remained true to its principles; and its leading members began, like the

Emperor, to collect troops. Charles tried hard to make the Lutheran cities believe that he did not intend to war against their religion, but only against certain rebellious princes. But they, distrusting him, raised an army, and placed it under *Sebastian Schärtlin*, one of the greatest generals of the day.

22. **Death of Luther.**—Before war actually broke out, Luther died in 1546 at *Eisleben*, whither he had gone to settle a dispute between the Counts of *Mansfeld*. He had striven to preserve peace; but the movement he had started had long passed to some extent beyond his control.

23. **The Schmalkaldic War.**—The war began in the summer of 1546. Charles was then at *Regensburg*, where he had for some time been holding a Diet. If the Lutheran leaders had acted vigorously, they might have gained an advantage at once, for at first the Emperor had a much smaller body of troops than they. But they were disunited, and wavered so much in their plans that the Papal troops and an army from the Low Countries both managed to join Charles. The latter acted with much energy. In a few months he had conquered all the free Imperial cities connected with the Schmalkaldic League. Meanwhile the Lutheran princes had separated, and gone with their troops to their own territories. In 1547 Charles defeated the Saxon army in the battle of *Mühlberg*, and took the Elector John Frederick prisoner. Philip of Hessen, seeing that he had then no chance of success, yielded, and was also kept as a prisoner by Charles. The Schmalkaldic War thus ended in the complete triumph of the Emperor.

24. **The Interim.**—In 1548 Charles held a Diet at *Augsburg*, before which he laid a plan for uniting the Lutherans to the Church, known as the *Interim*. Some few points were yielded to the Lutherans; but on the whole matters were to return very much to the position in

which they had been before the Reformation began. No one in the Diet formally opposed this plan. Charles therefore acted as if it had become law, and insisted on its being introduced into all the Lutheran States. Most of the Lutheran princes nominally accepted the *Interim.* The Lutheran cities resisted for a time; but in the end they also were compelled to yield.

25. **Charles V. and the Elector Maurice.**—The position of Charles now seemed very splendid. He had broken up the Schmalkaldic League, and had forced on the Lutherans a scheme which was meant to undo everything they had done towards the reformation of the Church. In reality he was by no means so safe as he seemed. He had made Duke *Maurice* the successor of John Frederick in the Electorate of Saxony. For a time this young prince, whose motives it is not always easy to understand, seemed to be the Emperor's best friend. Gradually his feelings changed, and he resolved to turn against Charles, and to become the upholder of the Lutheran faith. He got some other princes to join him, but, what was more important, he made a secret treaty with *Henry II.* of France, whereby the latter undertook to help him against the Emperor. Suddenly, in 1552, when Charles was at *Innsbruck*, Maurice began to march southwards with a large army, part of which he had been put at the head of for the purpose of compelling *Magdeburg* to accept the *Interim.* At the same time Henry II. entered *Lorraine* as "*Protector of the Liberties of Germany,*" and seized the three bishoprics of *Metz*, *Toul*, and *Verdun*. Charles was wholly unprepared to meet this sudden movement. He had raised the fears of even the Catholic States by the greatness of his power, and had offended them by trying to get his son *Philip* elected King of the Romans in place of his brother Ferdinand. Thus not a single Catholic prince or city offered to help him in

his hour of need, and he who had just seemed so great had to fly, as Maurice approached, in order to escape being made prisoner. He did not feel himself safe even in *Trent*, but pressed forward over wild mountain paths, accompanied by only a few followers, till he reached the village of *Villach*, in *Carinthia*.

26. **The Treaty of Passau.**—Although he was brought so low, Charles was very unwilling to yield to the demands of ·Maurice. At length he was persuaded to do so, and signed the *Treaty of Passau*. By this treaty he lost all he had gained in the Schmalkaldic War, for he had to promise that a Diet should be summoned within six months for the settlement of religious disputes, that meanwhile those who held the *Augsburg Confession* should be allowed full freedom of worship, that Lutherans should be admitted with Catholics as members of the Imperial Chamber, and that if the forthcoming Diet should fail to reconcile Lutherans and Catholics the stipulations in favour of the former should continue in force for ever.

27. **Charles V. and Henry II. of France.**—When peace had been restored in Germany, Charles at once gathered an army for the purpose of winning back the district in Lorraine seized by Henry II. *Metz* was besieged for some months, but could not be taken. In the end the three bishoprics were allowed to remain in the hands of the French King. Thus France, which had already got possession of the greater part of the kingdom of Burgundy, began to increase its territory at the expense of Germany.

28. **The Religious Peace of Augsburg.**—The Diet which the Emperor had promised to summon met in Augsburg in 1555. After much discussion, it concluded the *Religious Peace of Augsburg*. This Peace freed the Protestants from the jurisdiction of the prelates, allowed them to keep the ecclesiastical property that had been seized,

and gave to the government of each State the right to set up either the Catholic or Protestant religion. A State might tolerate both religions if it chose; but each prince received the right to drive out those who did not agree with him in religion. The treaty also provided that if a spiritual prince became a Protestant he should at once have to give up his office and its revenues. This was called the *Ecclesiastical Reservation*, and was not allowed by Protestants to be binding upon them.

29. **Abdication and death of Charles V.**—Charles had for some time failed in almost all his schemes, and his health was quite broken. He resolved, therefore, to give up his various crowns, and to spend his last years in private life. In 1555 he made over the Low Countries, and in 1556 Spain and the Two Sicilies, to his son Philip. He still hoped to get Philip elected King of the Romans; but in the end he saw that all parties were opposed to this, and in the autumn of 1556 gave up the government of Germany to King Ferdinand. After this Charles had no more to do with Germany. He died in 1558, in a small building near the monastery of *San Yuste*, in *Estremadura*, whither he had retired after his abdication.

30. **Political effects of the Reformation.**—There were now two parties strongly opposed to each other in Germany, the Catholics and the Protestants. A sort of peace had been patched up between them; but they were as far as possible from being reconciled. The Catholics continued to look on the Church property which Protestants had seized as rightfully theirs; and each party believed the other to hold deadly error. The Emperor did not hold the position of an impartial judge between the two parties. He was not only a Catholic, but in virtue of his office the Protector of the Catholic Church. The Protestants therefore came to look on him as an enemy to be watched and

opposed. The Protestant princes had thus a new motive for trying to weaken the Imperial authority; and in this the Catholic princes were not unwilling to join them. From the time of Charles, therefore, the Imperial government became weaker and weaker, while the States became more and more independent. Even the Diet lost most of its power. Any proposal laid before it was sure to be opposed by one party or the other, so that it could do very little. The courts of justice were also weakened by the difficulty of appointing judges and assessors trusted by both parties.

31. **Literature and Art.**—The writings of Luther are by far the most important literary works of the time of the Reformation. They—and especially the translation of the Bible—were so much read that the High-Dutch dialect in which they were written became the literary dialect of Germany for all future time. The writer whose works were most read next to those of Luther was the poet *Hans Sachs*, a shoemaker of *Nürnberg*. He wrote many pieces, and did good service to the Reformation by his wit and humour. There were several great painters in Germany about this time. Of these the chief were *Albert Dürer, Hans Holbein*, and *Lucas Kranach*. Music was also a good deal cultivated; and some fine buildings were erected in the so-called *Renaissance* style.

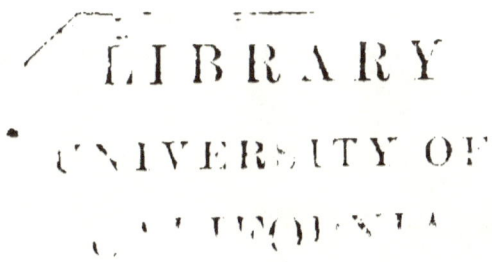

# CHAPTER XIV.

## THE THIRTY YEARS' WAR.

*Ferdinand I. tries to conciliate the Protestants; the Protestants divided among themselves; death of Ferdinand I.* (1)—*progress of Protestantism during the reign of Maximilian II.; his death* (2)—*Rudolf II. a violent Catholic; power of the Jesuits; weak government of Rudolf II.; his brothers recognize Matthias as head of the House* (3)—*the Protestant Union and the Catholic League; the Elector of Brandenburg becomes Duke of Prussia* (4)—*Rudolf II. concedes religious freedom to Bohemia: his death* (5)—*Matthias crowned; Ferdinand of Styria made his coadjutor* (6)—*disturbances in Bohemia; death of Matthias* (7)—*Frederick V., Elector Palatine, chosen King of Bohemia; Ferdinand crowned Emperor; war with Bohemia; the Bohemians defeated; punishment of Bohemia* (8)—*progress of the war; apparent triumph of the Emperor* (9)—*renewal of the war; Albert von Wallenstein raises an army; his victories; he is unable to take Stralsund* (10)—*the edict of Restitution* (11)—*dismissal of Wallenstein; Gustavus Adolphus comes to the help of the Protestants; defeat of Tilly* (12)—*Gustavus defeats Tilly a second time, and takes possession of Munich* (13)—*Wallenstein raises a second army; battle of Lützen; death of Gustavus Adolphus* (14)—*murder of Wallenstein* (15)—*treaty of Axel Oxenstiern with Cardinal Richelieu* (16)—*death of Ferdinand II.; progress of the war* (17)—*the Peace of Westphalia; terrible results of the war; no party satisfied with the peace; gains of France and Sweden; independence of Switzerland and the United Provinces recognized; changes within Germany* (18)—*indepen-*

dence of the princes; power of the Diet; it becomes a permanent body (19)—*International Law* (20)—*Literature and Science* (21)—*Superstitions* (22).

1. **Ferdinand I.**—Ferdinand was crowned in 1558. He did not receive the Imperial crown from the Pope; but he took the title of Emperor immediately after he ascended the throne of Germany. In this his example was followed by all German Kings who came after him. He was acknowledged by the Pope on condition that he should not observe the Treaty of Augsburg; but Ferdinand knew the strength of Protestantism, and he was too much taken up with the affairs of Hungary to raise up enemies needlessly. He tried to make the Protestants as friendly towards him as possible, and would have been glad if the *Council of Trent* had given way to them on some points. The Protestants were now broken up into parties. The Lutheran and Reformed Churches were very jealous of each other; and the former was divided into a moderate and an extreme party. These divisions did much harm; but in spite of them Protestantism made great progress. After doing his utmost to keep the Empire in peace, Ferdinand died in 1564.

2. **Maximilan II.**—Ferdinand had broken up the Habsburg possessions into three unequal parts, giving one to each of his sons. The eldest, *Maximilian*, who received Austria proper and became King of Bohemia and Hungary, succeeded Ferdinand as King of Germany and as Emperor. During his reign the *Jesuits*—an order recently instituted—worked hard to keep Protestantism from spreading; but Maximilian was a man of very enlightened opinions, and had no wish to favour the Catholics any more than his other subjects. He was even suspected of being a Lutheran. The result of his mild government was that even in Austria Protestantism became very powerful, and that it increased

its strength in all other parts of Germany. The larger number of Germans were now probably members of one or other of the Protestant Churches. So many adopted arms as a profession at this time that Maximilian wished to prevent foreign States from enlisting troops in Germany; but the Diet would not consent to this, and the country suffered a great deal from large numbers of "Landsknechte" who were too idle to live by honest industry. Maximilian died in 1576, having got his son *Rudolf* some time before elected King of the Romans.

3. **Rudolf II.**—Rudolf was very different from his father and grandfather. He had been brought up in the Spanish Court, and was of a gloomy disposition. He was a bigoted Catholic, and most anxious to root out the new faith from his hereditary lands. The Jesuits became very powerful, and redoubled their efforts against Protestantism. Rudolf, however, was a man of weak will, and although he issued many decrees against the Lutherans, they never came to anything. His weakness was such that Imperial government, and government in his hereditary possessions, were at last almost at an end. His kinsmen became seriously alarmed for the power of their House, and wished to appoint a colleague or successor to the Emperor. Roused by these proposals, Rudolf tried to prove that he could still rule, by taking strong measures against the Protestants in Bohemia and Hungary. The Hungarians were so oppressed that they appealed for help to the Turks, who were always only too glad to find an opportunity to injure the House of Habsburg. The Archdukes met in 1606, and formally acknowledged *Matthias*, the Emperor's brother, as head of the House. Spain assented to this arrangement. Rudolf was still Emperor; but he was forced to resign all his dominions except Bohemia to Matthias.

4. **The Protestant Union and the Catholic League.** The

**Elector of Brandenburg becomes Duke of Prussia.**—Many Protestants were alarmed by the attempts Rudolf had made to put them down, and especially by his allowing the Duke of Bavaria to seize the free city of *Donauwörth*, formerly a Bavarian town, and make it Catholic. In 1608 a number of Protestants joined together and formed, for ten years, a league called *The Union*. Its formation was due chiefly to the exertions of Prince *Christian* of *Anhalt*, who had busily intrigued with *Henry IV.* of France; but its head was the Elector Palatine. As the latter belonged to the Reformed Church, the Lutherans for the most part treated the Union coldly; and the Elector of Saxony would have nothing to do with it. It soon had an opportunity of acting. Duke *William* of *Jülich*, who held Jülich, Cleve, and other lands, died in 1609. John Sigmund, Elector of Brandenburg, and the Palsgrave of Neuburg, both members of the Union, claimed to be his heirs, and took possession of his lands. The Emperor Rudolf sent his brother, the Archduke *Leopold*, Bishop of *Passau*, to drive out these princes. The Union thereupon formed an alliance with *Henry IV.* of France, and, coming to the aid of its members, scattered the forces of the Archduke in 1610. The Catholics now took fright, and hastened to form a *League* which should hold the Union in check. It was formed for nine years, and the supreme command was given to *Maximilian*, Duke of Bavaria. The death of Henry IV. took away from the Union its chief source of strength, so that it shrank from a general war. The two princes, however, who had given rise to the quarrel, kept for a time the Jülich-Cleve territory. In 1611 the power of the Elector of Brandenburg was further increased by his succeeding to the Duchy of Prussia. From this time East Prussia was always joined to the Mark or Electorate of Brandenburg. It was now, therefore, that the house of Brandenburg laid the foundations of its future greatness.

**5. The Letter of Majesty. Death of Rudolf II.**—Matthias, in order to pacify the Austrian States, granted them full religious liberty. In 1609 the Bohemian States also obtained from Rudolf a Royal Charter, called *The Letter of Majesty*, conceding to nobility, knights and towns perfect freedom in religious matters, and the right to build Protestant churches and schools on their own and on the royal lands. Bohemia showed no gratitude for this favour. Suspecting his designs, the Bohemians even shut Rudolf up in his castle at Prague in 1611, and asked Matthias to come to their aid. He did so, and seized the supreme power. Next year Rudolf died.

**6. Matthias.**—Matthias was crowned at Frankfurt with great pomp, but he was no better fitted for the throne than his brother. He was compelled to yield much to the Protestants, yet favoured the Jesuits in their continued efforts to convert Germany. His government was so feeble that his brothers at length made him accept *Ferdinand*, Duke of Styria, as his coadjutor. In 1617 Ferdinand was elected as Rudolf's successor to the crowns of Bohemia and Hungary; and from this time all real power in the Habsburg possessions was wielded by him. Ferdinand was a young man, but had already given proof of great energy of character. He was most anxious to become Emperor after the death of Matthias, and hoped to bring back the Empire to something like its old power and greatness. The Protestants looked forward with dread to his reign if he should receive the Imperial crown. Styria had become almost wholly Lutheran. When Ferdinand succeeded his father, he had driven out the Protestant families, and made the land altogether Catholic. No Catholic prince had ever shown himself more reckless as to the means by which he served his Church. The Protestants, therefore, had good reason to fear that if he became Emperor he would renew the policy of Charles V., and try to bring back the old state of things, in which there was but one Church as there was but one Empire. Events proved that these fears were well founded.

7. **Disturbances in Bohemia. Death of Matthias.**—The last days of Matthias were very troubled. Two Protestant churches were built in Bohemia, one in the territory of the Archbishop of Prague, the other in that of the Abbot of Braunau. These princes, with permission of the Emperor, pulled down one of the churches, and shut up the other. The Protestants complained; but their appeal was met by the reply that the Letter of Majesty did not permit them to build churches on the lands of ecclesiastics. This answer excited great indignation in Bohemia; and a rumour was got up that it had not come from the Emperor, but had been written in Prague. On May 23, 1618, a number of Protestants, headed by Count *Thurn*, marched to the Council Hall of the Royal Castle, and demanded to be told the real facts. When the councillors hesitated, two of them, with the private secretary, were seized, and thrown out of the window. The Protestants then took possession of the Royal Castle, drove the Jesuits out of Bohemia, and appointed a council of thirty nobles to carry on the government. Matthias would have made peace; but Ferdinand refused to do so, and began at once to gather troops. The Union sent Count *Mansfeld*, a distinguished soldier, with 3,000 men to aid the Bohemians. They themselves, led by Count Thurn, actively prepared to defend their rights. In the midst of these disturbances, Matthias died in 1519.

8. **Ferdinand II. War with Bohemia.**—The Bohemians refused to accept Ferdinand as King, and chose *Frederick V.*

of the Palatinate. They did so, partly because the young prince was believed to be bold and generous, partly because they hoped his father-in-law, *James I.* of England, would help them in the approaching struggle. Meanwhile Ferdinand went to Frankfurt, and there had his wish gratified by being elected and crowned Emperor. He resolved utterly to crush Protestantism in Bohemia, and afterwards to attack it in all parts of the Empire. On his way to Frankfurt he had visited *Maximilian*, Duke of Bavaria, and come to an understanding with him that, if the Union should support Bohemia, the Catholic League would take arms on the side of the Emperor. He also obtained promises of help from Spain. The young King of Bohemia, instead of putting forth every effort to meet his great enemy, wasted his time and energies in frivolous amusements, and wantonly offended the religious scruples of many of his subjects. The Protestant States of Germany acted with shameful indifference. The Elector of Saxony was easily bought over by the Emperor; and the Union, seeing that the war was likely to be a fierce one, agreed to disarm before the struggle began. Thus the Bohemians had to trust to themselves. In 1620 they were defeated in a great battle on the *Weissenberg*, near Prague, by Count *Tilly*, Duke Maximilian's general, an able soldier troubled with few scruples as to the means by which he gained his ends. Frederick, who was called the *Winter King*, fled with his family. He was put to the ban of the Empire, and his lands were held by Spanish troops. Ferdinand dealt with Bohemia as hardly any land has been treated in modern times. Many of the Protestant leaders were put to death ; lands were confiscated ; the Protestant clergy were banished ; and in the end every form of worship except the Catholic was forbidden. Bohemia quite changed its character. It ceased to be a seat of learning, and its commerce was ruined. An attempt was made to treat Upper Austria with the same severity. In 1626 a Peasants' Insurrection took place there, and was put down with difficulty by the Austrian and Bavarian troops.

**9. Progress of the war.**—The war was continued, on the part of the Protestants, by Count *Mansfeld*, *Christian* of *Anhalt*, and other nobles, with bands of troops made up of men who often cared less for the objects of the war than for the opportunities of plunder which it afforded. Tilly was defeated in 1622, but he afterwards overthrew both Mansfeld and Christian, and obliged them for a time to disband their forces. In 1622 the Union was broken up; and in the following year the Emperor attached Duke Maximilian more closely to himself by raising him to the electoral dignity which the Elector Palatine was supposed to have forfeited. Surrounded by powerful friends, and with his enemies crushed, the Emperor appeared to have overcome all obstacles; but in reality the *Thirty Years' War* had begun, and it was to prove one of the most fearful struggles in history.

**10. Albert von Wallenstein.**—Other Protestants besides those of Germany now began to watch Ferdinand with alarm. *Christian IV.* of Denmark tried to unite the northern powers against him; but the scheme failed, mainly through the indecision of James I. of England. Count Mansfeld, Christian of Anhalt, and others, were, however, sufficiently supported to enable them once more to take the field; and they were powerfully aided by Christian IV., who was placed at the head of the army of the Circle of Lower Saxony. Up to this time the Emperor's troops had done little in the war. It had been carried on almost solely by the army of the Catholic League, led by Tilly. Ferdinand was anxious to raise an Imperial force, but was too poor to do so. At last a wealthy nobleman, *Albert von Wallenstein*, came forward, and offered to gather an army on condition that he should have the supreme command. The Emperor accepted his services, stipulating that the men should be paid, not from the Imperial revenues, but by the plunder of conquered lands. Wallenstein soon had at his command an army of 30,000 men. With these he attacked Count Mansfeld in 1627 at *Dessau*, and defeated him. Mansfeld died soon afterwards. Christian of Anhalt died in the same year; and the Danish King was routed at *Lutter* by Tilly with the army of the League. Wallenstein pursued Christian IV., who was compelled to ask for peace. The two victorious generals then overran Holstein and Mecklenburg. Wallenstein was made Duke of the latter State, and probably intended to win over the Hansa towns, partly by bribery, partly by force, to the Imperial side, so that Austria should be as great by sea as by land. For this purpose he tried to make himself master of *Stralsund;* but the brave town held out, and Wallenstein had to retire after having suffered great loss. Peace was finally concluded with Christian at Lübeck in 1629.

11. **The Edict of Restitution.**—In spite of the check received at Stralsund, the Emperor now seemed to have reached almost the summit of his wishes. Nearly all Germany appeared to be in his power. He took advantage of his position to issue an edict called the *Edict of Restitution*. Two archbishopricks, twelve bishopricks, and other ecclesiastical lands had fallen into the hands of the Protestants since the Treaty of Passau. By the Edict of Restitution, Ferdinand decreed that all these should be given back to the Catholic Church. This did not contradict the letter of the Passau Treaty; but it was felt by all Protestants to be an act of gross tyranny.

12. **Dismissal of Wallenstein. Gustavus Adolphus.**—

General *Horn*, and *Bernard*, Duke of *Weimar*. Wallenstein now lost a great deal of time, and laid himself open to many suspicions on the part of the Emperor's supporters. At last, in 1634, he was removed a second time from his command, and murdered. The Emperor rewarded the murderers, and issued a document setting forth all the deeds and purposes of which Wallenstein was accused.

16. **Treaty of Axel Oxenstiern with Cardinal Richelieu.**— The Imperial forces were now commanded by *Ferdinand*, the Emperor's son, and King of the Romans. A battle was fought at *Nördlingen* in 1634, in which the Swedes were defeated, and General Horn was made prisoner. After this the Elector of Saxony made peace at Prague with the Emperor, and other princes did the like. The war would probably have ended altogether, for all parties were longing for peace; but Cardinal *Richelieu*, who had long watched the struggle, and who thought this a good opportunity of humbling the house of Austria, had already concluded a treaty with Oxenstiern, by which France was to receive German territory in return for aid in carrying on the war. Duke Bernard, who thus entered the French service, collected a fine army in the Rhine country, while the Swedish General Baner fought in Saxony and Thuringia.

17. **Death of Ferdinand II. Progress of the War.**—Ferdinand II. died in 1637, and was succeeded by his son *Ferdinand III.*, who was compelled to continue the war, not to secure the ends for which it was begun, but to save as much as possible from the Swedes and the French. In 1639 Duke Bernard suddenly died, having several times defeated the Catholic army. General Baner was also successful against the Imperialists; and after him *Torstenson*, and later on *Wrangel*, led the Swedes to many brilliant victories. Generals *Turenne* and *Condé* carried on the war on behalf of France.

18. **The Peace of Westphalia.**—Negotiations for peace seriously began in 1643. If the matter had depended on Germany alone, all difficulties would soon have been overcome; but France and Sweden both claimed to be rewarded for their share in the struggle, and their demands were so great that conferences went on from year to year without anything being done. The negotiations with the Swedes were carried on at *Osnabrück;* those with the French at *Münster.* At last, on October 24, 1648, peace was concluded. This peace is known as *The Peace of Westphalia.* The war which it ended was one of the most terrible that Europe has ever seen. Half, if not two-thirds, of the population of Germany had perished while it was going on. Every part of the country had been laid waste; many cities were in ruins; trade had almost died out. In 1630 the Hansa League was virtually broken up on the ground that the towns composing it could no longer pay the expenses which connexion with the League involved. In spite of all this, the Peace of Westphalia was liked by no party in Germany. The Lutherans and Calvinists received the same freedom of conscience as the Catholics; all Church property which the Protestants had possessed in 1624 was to remain in their hands; and Protestants and Catholics were to be equally represented in the Imperial Chamber. These concessions so irritated the Catholics that Pope *Innocent X.* protested against the Peace of Westphalia through his legate, and afterwards issued a bull declaring it void. On the other hand, the Protestants lost Bohemia. Both there and in his hereditary Austrian dominions the Emperor refused to tolerate Protestantism. While the religious parties of Germany had their own causes of complaint against the Peace of Westphalia, it brought heavy losses on the country as a whole. France was confirmed in her possession of the Lorraine bishopricks, *Metz, Toul,* and *Verdun,* and received as much of *Elsass* as belonged

to Austria. By these acquisitions, and by the destruction of various fortifications on the Upper Rhine, France secured to herself an open passage into Germany. In addition to the towns of *Wismar* and *Stettin*, Sweden received *Western Pomerania*, and the Sees of *Bremen* and *Verden*—territory which placed in her hands the most important points on the coasts of the Baltic and the North Sea. She was also promised the sum of five million thalers. In virtue of the territory ceded to Sweden, she became a member of the German Diet; but the lands which France received were wholly severed from Germany. Both France and Sweden obtained the right of interfering in the affairs of Germany whenever they thought, or affected to think, that the provisions of the treaties of Osnabrück and Münster were endangered. *Switzerland* and the *United Provinces* were already practically independent of the Empire; but their independence was now expressly acknowledged. Within Germany itself some changes were effected. The Elector of Bavaria kept the Upper Palatinate; but *Charles Lewis*, the son of Frederick V., was restored to the rest of his hereditary territories, and an eighth electoral title was created for his family. The Elector of Brandenburg received *East Pomerania*, the archbishoprick of *Magdeburg*, and the bishopricks of *Halberstadt*, *Minden*, and *Kamin*. Concessions were also made to Mecklenburg, Hessen-Cassel, and Brunswick-Lüneburg.

19. **Condition of the Empire.**—The Empire now ceased to exist, except in name, even in Germany. As we have seen, the tendency of the Reformation was to strengthen the independence of the princes, both Catholic and Protestant. By the peace of Westphalia the Emperor fully recognised that independence. They were even to have the right of concluding treaties of alliance with foreign States, if not directed against Emperor or Empire. The

authority of the Aulic Council, which was entirely subject to the Emperor, was made merely nominal. The power of passing and interpreting laws, of making war or peace, of raising troops—these, and other rights relating to the Empire or Confederation as a whole, were now to belong, not to the Emperor, but to the Diet. Even the Diet, however, was to have no great power. In 1654 it was made a permanent body; and it became more and more famous for its formality and trifling, and for the solemnity and pomp with which it managed to do nothing. Difficulties connected with religion were not henceforth to be decided by a vote of the Diet, but by negotiations between the States in which the difficulties arose.

20. **International Law.**—There was one good result which sprang from the division of Germany into a vast number of petty independent States. It became necessary that there should be some code which should protect the weaker States from the stronger. Such a code was gradually formed, and it worked so well that, although there was practically no central authority to keep down the unruly, the weakest prince felt himself safe even when his nearest neighbour was a powerful Elector or King. The system which thus regulated the intercourse of the States of Germany gradually became the foundation for a system of International Law.

21. **Literature and Science.**—German literature and science were not altogether crushed by the horrors of the Thirty Years' War. *John Kepler*, one of the most illustrious of modern astronomers, and *Otto von Guerike*, the inventor of the air-pump, both belong to this period. *Jacob Boehm*, a half-mystical thinker, wrote works which have exercised considerable influence on later German philosophy. *Martin Opitz*, a writer who strove to maintain the purity of the German language, was the founder of

what is called the *First Silesian School* of Poets. To this School belonged the versatile *Paul Flemming*. *Paul Gerhardt* takes his place among the best religious poets of Germany.

22. **Superstitions.**—In spite of the Reformation, and of the schools that the Reformers had founded, the majority of the German people were still ignorant and superstitious. Even yet many eagerly sought for the philosopher's stone, and a belief in astrology was very general. Witchcraft was almost universally believed in, and nothing was more common than for women to be tortured and burned as witches. Good men occasionally protested against this barbarous custom; but it continued even into the eighteenth century. It finally gave way only before the light of advancing science.

## CHAPTER XV.

### WARS WITH FRANCE.

*Abolition of most provincial Diets; bad government of the princes; decay of the free towns (1)—weak character of Leopold I.; the Great Elector; war with Lewis XIV.; the battle of Fehrbellin; the peace of Nimwegen (2)—robbery of German territory by Lewis XIV.; Strassburg seized (3)—rebellion of Hungary; the Turks make war on the Emperor; Vienna besieged; the crown of Hungary made hereditary (4)—new war with France: brutality of the French soldiers; coalition of European Powers against France; the Peace of Ryswick (5)—ninth Electorate; George Lewis, Duke of Brunswick and Lüneburg, becomes King of England; Augustus II. of Saxony elected King of Poland (6)—Frederick, Elector of Brandenburg, crowned King of Prussia (7)—the war of the Spanish Succession; the Electors of Bavaria and Köln join France; the battles of Donauwerth and Blenheim (8)—Joseph I.; victory of Prince Eugene at Turin; battles of Oudenarde and Malplaquet; demands of the allies (9)—Charles VI.; the treaties of Utrecht, Rastatt, and Baden (10)—the Pragmatic Sanction; war with the Turks; war with France; Lorraine given up to Stanislaus Leszczynski; it afterwards falls into the hands of the French (11).*

1. **The States of Germany.**—Germany was now broken up into a large number of States, almost independent of the nominal head of the Empire. The history of these States is for a long time very uninteresting. Most of the Diets were put an end to, and those which continued

to exist were without real power. The princes were thus absolute rulers within their territories. Each had his own courts of justice, his own hired troops, his own coinage, customs, tolls, and taxes. Most of them were very bad rulers. They imitated the pomp and grandeur of the court of *Lewis XIV.* of France, and in order to keep up their extravagance laid heavy taxes on their subjects. Thus trade, instead of reviving after the harm done to it by the Thirty Years' War, withered more and more. The free cities, no longer strengthened by their combination in Leagues, prospered no better than the principalities. Many of them became petty oligarchies; others lost their freedom altogether, and were made subject to neighbouring princes.

2. **Leopold I. The Great Elector.**—Nothing of great importance happened in the last years of Ferdinand III.'s reign. He died in 1657, and was succeeded by his son *Leopold*. Lewis XIV. tried hard to get himself elected; but the temporal Electors refused to be bribed. Leopold was well-meaning, but very weak both in intellect and character. This was the more unfortunate for Germany, because during his whole reign he had in Lewis XIV. a crafty and ambitious enemy, who lost no opportunity of enriching himself at the expense of the Empire. When Lewis invaded the Netherlands in 1667, he met with no resistance from any German State, and by the Peace of *Aachen*, in 1669, compelled Spain to give up part of the country. In 1672 he made war on the *United Provinces*. At this time the ablest prince in Germany was *Frederick William* of *Brandenburg*, usually called the *Great Elector*. In 1657 he had concluded the *Treaty of Welau*, by which Prussia was declared independent of Poland; and in 1666 he received, by the settlement of the dispute respecting the Jülich-Cleve territory, the Duchy of *Cleve*, and the counties of *Mark* and *Ravensberg*. Fearing for the safety of these lands, he

joined the United Provinces against Lewis. The Emperor and King *Charles* of *Spain* did the like. The Austrian army was placed under *Montecuculi*, a famous general. Leopold's chief councillor, Prince *Lobkowitz*, was bribed by the French, and he, acting with the spiritual Electors and the Bishop of *Münster* (who openly sided with Lewis), hampered the army so much that in 1673 Frederick William made peace. After the dismissal of Prince Lobkowitz, Montecuculi acted with more freedom, and gained some advantages on the Lower Rhine; but on the Upper Rhine the Austrians were defeated by the French general *Turenne*. In 1674 Frederick William again joined the allies against France. Denmark took the same side; but Sweden made a treaty with Lewis, and invaded Brandenburg. Various German princes also disgraced themselves by siding with the French. Frederick William had to return from the Rhine and defend his own country against the Swedes, and in 1675 defeated them in a great battle at *Fehrbellin*. After this he conquered the greater part of Pomerania. Meanwhile the war on the Rhine went on. By the death of Turenne the French lost ground for a time; but, on the whole, the allies were not successful. In 1678 the United Provinces and Spain made peace with France at *Nimwegen*, and next year the Emperor also did so. He had to give up *Freiburg* in Breisgau to the French; and Frederick William was obliged to restore to the Swedes nearly all his conquests in Pomerania. The Great Elector, however, was a firm and wise ruler, and under him his subjects prospered so much that he may be looked on as the chief founder of the greatness of the House of Hohenzollern. He died in 1688.

3. **Strassburg seized by Lewis XIV.**—During the years that followed the Peace of Nimwegen, Lewis would not leave Germany alone. Pretending that the treaties by

which France had received the Austrian lands in Elsass and other territories had given up not only these possessions but all places that had ever been united to them, he seized many towns, villages, and lands on both sides of the Rhine. To give an appearance of fairness to his proceedings, he established "Chambers of Reunion" to decide what places lawfully belonged to him. A great outcry was raised in Germany against these robberies. Lewis consented to have the whole matter laid before a congress in Frankfurt; but nothing came of its discussions. Of all German towns, he was most anxious to possess *Strassburg*, the key to the whole of South Germany. In 1681, when many of the people were at the Frankfurt fair, he suddenly took possession of it, having before gained the support of a party within the city by means of bribes. All Germany deplored the loss of this strong and beautiful town. It remained in the hands of France till our own day.

4. **Austria, Hungary, and the Turks.**—The Emperor might at last have been roused to put a stop to the robberies of Lewis; but at this time the affairs of Hungary demanded all his energies. He had treated the Hungarian Protestants with so much harshness that at length, in 1678, they had rebelled. Lewis, although he persecuted Protestants in his own country, helped those of Hungary against their King. Their chief allies, however, were the Turks, who were also incited by Lewis to make war on the Emperor. In 1683 a great Turkish army marched through Hungary, and made for Vienna. The Emperor and many of the people fled; but the city prepared to defend itself, and for several months, under Count *Rüdiger* of *Stahrenberg*, it baffled every effort of the besiegers. It was nearly overcome when at last Duke *Charles* of *Lorraine*, and *John Sobieski*, King of *Poland*, came to its aid. The Turks suddenly took fright, and fled without offering battle. The war did not

come to an end; but the Turks were several times defeated, and in 1699 they made peace at *Carlowitz*. In 1687 the crown of Hungary, which had before been nominally elective, was made hereditary.

5. **New war with France.**—In 1688 Lewis made war again on the Emperor, nominally because one whom he wished to be made Elector of Köln was not accepted. This time the Diet declared war against Lewis. The French army entered the Palatinate, and by the King's orders was guilty of great outrages. The country was overrun by wild troops, and the people begged in vain for mercy. Their homes were set on fire, and they themselves were either murdered or driven almost naked into France. *Heidelberg*, with its beautiful castle, and many flourishing towns on the Rhine, were destroyed. At *Speyer* the soldiers opened the graves of the Emperors, stole the silver coffins, and scattered the bones on the ground. These acts roused throughout Germany so much hatred and anger that their effects can hardly be said to have died away even in our own day. The Emperor bestirred himself, and he was powerfully supported by *Frederick* of *Brandenburg*, the Great Elector's son, and other princes. A coalition of European Powers, in which *England*, under *William* of *Orange*, took the leading place, was formed. The great struggle which followed belongs more to general European history than to that of Germany. For seven years it was carried on by sea and land with varying fortune. At length, in 1697, peace was concluded at *Ryswick* between France, England, Spain, and Holland. The Emperor soon followed the example of his allies. France kept *Strassburg*, but she had to give up *Freiburg*, *Breisach*, *Philipsburg*, and also places that had been annexed on the ground of having formerly belonged to Elsass. A promise was obtained that the Catholic religion, which had been established in these

places by France, should be maintained in them under the Empire.

**6. Two German princes ascend foreign thrones.**—During the progress of this war, the Emperor had created a ninth electorate in favour of *Ernst August*, Duke of *Brunswick-Lüneburg* or *Hanover*. The College of Princes, jealous of this elevation of one of their number, refused to recognize the new title; but *George Lewis*, who succeeded his father in 1678, was universally acknowledged as Elector in 1705. In 1714 he ascended the English throne, as George I. Another German prince who ascended a foreign throne about this time was *Augustus II.*, called "The Strong," Elector of *Saxony*. In 1697, more than a year after the death of Sobieski, he was chosen King of Poland. He became a Catholic. All his successors in Saxony have been Catholics; but the body of the Saxon people were and still are Protestants.

**7. The Elector of Brandenburg becomes King of Prussia.**—The Electors of Hanover and Saxony were not the only German princes who became Kings. The Great Elector was succeeded by his son *Frederick*. Frederick was a very vain man, fond of pomp and show. He could not become King of Brandenburg, because as Elector of that country he nominally owed allegiance to the Emperor; but as Duke of Prussia he was independent, and there was nothing to hinder his becoming Prussian King if he could obtain from the Emperor a promise to recognize the new title. In ordinary circumstances the Emperor would probably have hesitated to sanction so great an advance on the part of one who was, at least in name, a subject; but he knew that he would soon be involved in another war, and he was anxious to secure as much support as possible. On condition, therefore, that Frederick should aid him in the approaching contest, he at last consented that the Prussian Duchy should be changed into a kingdom. On January 18, 1701, and in circumstances of great splendour, Frederick was crowned King at *Königsberg*. Few thought this an event of much importance, but it was followed by very grave consequences both for Germany and Europe.

**8. The War of the Spanish Succession.**—The struggle which had for some time been foreseen was the famous *War of the Spanish Succession*. Charles II. of Spain had named the son of the Bavarian Elector as his successor; but the young prince died before Charles himself. Charles died on November 11, 1700. Shortly before his death he was induced, almost against his own will, to declare as his heir *Philip* of *Anjou*, the grandson of Lewis XIV., whose first wife, *Maria Theresa*, was a sister of Charles. The Emperor would not submit to this arrangement. His wife, *Margaret Theresa*, was also a sister of Charles; and she had not, like Maria Theresa, renounced her rights. He therefore claimed the Spanish crown for his son, the Archduke *Charles*. The Protestant Powers sided with the Emperor, for they thought that if the thrones of France and Spain were held by members of one family the freedom of the whole of Europe might be endangered. The Emperor had at this time a general of high military genius. This was *Francis Eugene*, Prince of *Savoy*, who had already been made field-marshal for distinguished services. In the spring of 1701, Eugene crossed the Alps with an Austrian army, aided by Prussian and Hanoverian troops, in order to drive the French out of Italy. A few months afterwards Austria was joined by England and Holland; and on October 2, 1702, the States of the Empire formally declared war against France. *Maximilian Emmanuel*, the Elector of Bavaria, and his brother, the Elector of Köln, joined France. In 1703 the French crossed the Rhine and joined the

Bavarian troops. Instead of marching with the French into Austria, the Elector undertook an expedition into Tyrol. He at first had some success; but the Tyrolese soon recovered themselves, and drove out the Bavarians, after having slain large numbers. In 1704 *Lord Marlborough*, who had already become famous from his doings in the Netherlands, and Prince Eugene united their forces at Heilbronn. A battle was fought near *Donauwerth* on July 2, in which the Elector and Marshal *Marsin* were defeated. They were soon joined by Marshal *Tallard;* and on August 13, a still greater battle took place. The French and Bavarians took up their position near *Höchstädt*, Tallard, with the right wing of the French, occupying *Blenheim*, from which the battle has received its name. Both sides fought bravely; but at length the English and Imperial troops succeeded in driving back the enemy at all points. No fewer than 20,000 French and Bavarians were killed or drowned, whilst more than half as many more surrendered as prisoners. Amongst the prisoners was Marshal Tallard himself. The result of this battle was that the seat of war was removed in great part from Germany. The defeated allies rapidly crossed the Rhine, the Bavarian Elector taking refuge in the Netherlands, whilst the Imperialists seized Bavaria and the neighbouring countries. Marlborough was made a prince of the Empire; and he became as well known and popular in Germany as in England.

9. **Joseph I.**—In 1705 the Emperor Leopold died. He was succeeded by his son, *Joseph I*. The new Emperor was in every way a much stronger man than his father, and, unlike him, put full confidence in Prince Eugene. He continued the war with France, and had also to put down civil wars in Hungary. The Austrians had treated the Bavarians with so much harshness that the peasantry had

at length revolted. After an obstinate contest this insurrection was quelled, and the Elector and his brother were put to the ban of the Empire. Prince Eugene met with serious reverses in Italy; but, on September 7, 1706, he more than made up for them by a great victory over the French at *Turin*. This success was largely due to the Prussians, who, under Prince *Leopold* of *Dessau*, formed the left wing of Eugene's army. Prince Eugene and Marlborough once more united their armies in the Netherlands, and gained in 1708 and 1709 the brilliant victories of *Oudenarde* and *Malplaquet*. In the interval between these battles, peace would probably have been made but for the demand of the allies that, in addition to other concessions, Lewis XIV. should aid them by force of arms in driving his grandson, Philip V., from the throne of Spain.

10. **Charles VI. Treaties of Utrecht, Rastatt, and Baden.** —Joseph I. died on April 17, 1711. As he had no children, his brother, the Archduke *Charles*, was elected his successor. The allies were as unwilling that the Spanish crown should belong to the chief of the house of Austria as that it should belong to the Bourbons. For this, and other reasons arising out of the home politics of England, Marlborough was recalled, and on April 11, 1713, the Peace of *Utrecht* was signed. Charles VI. complained that he was betrayed by his allies, and continued the war; but the Imperial troops were so unsuccessful in the following campaign that Austria at length consented to come to terms, and, on March 7, 1714, the Peace of *Rastatt* was concluded. Austria gave up her claims to Spain in favour of Philip V., but received the Spanish *Netherlands*, *Naples*, *Milan*, and *Sardinia*. In a separate treaty which was concluded between France and the Empire at *Baden* in *Aarau* on September 7, 1714, the Empire had to cede to France the Imperial fortress of *Landau*. The Electors of Bavaria and

Köln were pardoned, and restored to all their titles and possessions.

11. **The last years of Charles VI.**—Charles had no son. In 1713, therefore, he drew up, in favour of his daughter, *Maria Theresa*, a Pragmatic Sanction, a law providing that the Austrian dominions, in case the male line should die out, should be heritable by the female line. After many efforts he at last induced the leading European Powers and the Empire to guarantee this arrangement. In a war with the Turks, carried on between 1715 and 1718, Prince Eugene again distinguished himself. By the Peace of *Passarowitz*, Austria received *Belgrade* and other towns and lands. A new war with France broke out in 1733, on account of the claim of *Augustus III.*, Elector of Saxony, to the throne of Poland. France supported *Stanislaus Leszczynski*, Lewis XV.'s father-in-law, whom a considerable party in Poland had chosen as their King. The Emperor, anxious to gain the support of the Saxon Elector to the Pragmatic Sanction, took his side. The result of this war was that, besides exchanging *Naples* and *Sicily* for *Tuscany* and *Parma*, the Emperor had to give up the beautiful province of *Lorraine* to Leszczynski, through whom it came in the end into the hands of the French. Charles died on October 21, 1740. He was the last Emperor, in the male line, of the house of Habsburg.

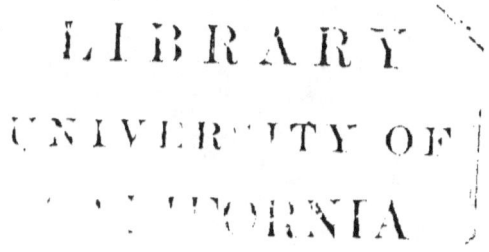

# CHAPTER XVI.

### FREDERICK THE GREAT.

*The Austrian territories claimed by Charles Albert, Elector of Bavaria; claims of Augustus III. of Saxony; action of Frederick II. of Prussia (1)—Frederick I., King of Prussia (2)—Frederick William I. of Prussia; his character; his attention to the army; territory won by him (3)—youth of Frederick II. of Prussia (4)—the first Silesian war; battle of Molwitz (5)—alliance formed against Maria Theresa; the Elector of Bavaria crowned Emperor; Maria Theresa supported by the Hungarians; battle of Czaslau: peace with Frederick II. (6)—successes of Maria Theresa; death of Charles VII.; the second Silesian war; victories of Frederick II.; Peace of Dresden (7)—Francis, Grand Duke of Tuscany, elected Emperor; Peace of Aachen (8)—home government of Frederick II. (9)—hostility of the European powers to Frederick II.; alliance between Prussia and England, and between Austria and France (10)—beginning of the Seven Years' War; Frederick II. invades Saxony; battle of Lowositz (11)—victory of the Prussians near Prague (12)—the battle of Kolin; greater part of Silesia seized by the Austrians; the Convention of Closterseven (13)—battles of Rossbach and Leuthen (14)—battles of Crefeld, Zorndorf, and Hochkirchen (15)—battles of Minden and Kunersdorf (16)—battles of Liegnitz and Torgau (17)—movements of Prince Henry and Frederick in 1761 (18)—alliance of Frederick II. with Peter III. of Russia; victory over the Austrians; withdrawal of the Russians; siege of Schweidnitz; advantages gained by Frederick II. (19)—Peace of Hubertusburg; results of the Seven Years' War (20)*

—*Joseph II.; government of Frederick II.* (21)—*First Partition of Poland* (22)—*the "Potato War"* (23)—*death of Maria Theresa; vigorous government of Joseph II. ; League formed by Frederick II.* (24)—*death of Frederick II.; Frederick William II.* (25)—*Joseph II.'s schemes; his death* (26)—*Leopold II.* (27).

1. **The claims of Maria Theresa to the Austrian inheritance disputed.**—On the death of her father, *Maria Theresa*, Queen of Hungary, took possession of the Austrian territories. But, in spite of the solemn promises which Charles VI. had received in favour of his daughter, she found that she would have to defend her rights. *Charles Albert*, the Elector of Bavaria, a descendant of the eldest daughter of the Emperor Ferdinand I., claimed that he had a better title to the Austrian dominions than Maria Theresa. Augustus III., Elector of Saxony, and King of Poland, also put forth claims to the Austrian inheritance. Before these princes had taken any practical steps in support of their demands, a more dangerous rival had taken up arms and actually conquered one of the fairest provinces of the young princess. This was *Frederick II.*, who had recently succeeded to the throne of Prussia.

2. **Frederick I., King of Prussia.**—Frederick I. of Prussia died in 1713. In imitation of Lewis XIV., he had lived in a style of great splendour, and, by his reckless extravagance, did much to keep his people poor. Nevertheless, he did a great deal for Prussia. By raising it into a kingdom, he secured that his successors should always have an inducement to strengthen and extend their inheritance. It is thus to him that much of the greatness to which Prussia afterwards rose may be indirectly traced. Among the benefits directly conferred by him on Prussia were the University of *Halle*, the *Academy of Sciences* in Berlin, and various other institutions intended to promote the higher culture.

3. **Frederick William I. of Prussia**—*Frederick William I.* was in almost all respects the opposite of his father. He was a man of coarse and violent nature, given to fierce outbursts of anger. Even those who had the strongest claims on his tenderness he treated with great harshness, if they in any way thwarted his plans. He had a contempt for learning and learned men, and was fond of brutal practical jokes. One of the good points of his character was his rigid economy, and even this he carried too far. No King ever lived in plainer style. After his father's death he dismissed a host of Court servants, whom he looked on as mere encumbrances. His evenings were spent in what he called his tobacco-college. His ministers and generals met him in a plainly-furnished room, where, amidst clouds of tobacco smoke, important affairs of state were discussed. Although arbitrary and tyrannical, he did much to add to the power of Prussia. The result of his efforts was that, at the time of his death, the Prussian army consisted of 80,000 men, fully equipped and thoroughly organized. He took especial delight in the "Potsdam Guard," which was made up of very tall men, brought together, at great expense, from all parts of Europe. His agents even kidnapped giants for his service from foreign countries. He died on May 31, 1740. In 1720 he had acquired from Sweden the city of *Stettin*, the southern part of *Hither-Pomerania*, and the islands of *Usedom* and *Wollin*.

4. **Frederick II. of Prussia.**—Frederick William was succeeded by his son *Frederick II.*, usually called *Frederick the Great*. Frederick was twenty-eight years old when he became King. He had great natural abilities, and had acquired considerable culture. His youth had not been a happy one. His tastes were so different from those of his narrow-minded father that the latter had treated

The Austrians, taking advantage of their unexpected victory, advanced into Silesia, and seized greater part of the province. The Russians defeated the army which had been left in defence of Prussia, and the Swedes threatened the country from the north. As if these misfortunes were not enough, Frederick's cause was further injured by the base Convention of *Closterseven*, by which the Duke of *Cumberland* agreed to disband his army and to yield to the French *Hanover*, *Hessen*, and the Duchy of *Brunswick*.

14. **Battles of Rossbach and Leuthen.**—A weaker man would have been utterly overwhelmed by such trials; but they only called into full play Frederick's great powers. The French had united with the Austrian troops; and as, since the convention of Closterseven, there was no enemy to check their progress, they were advancing to take possession of Saxony. Frederick determined, if possible, to drive them back. Marching rapidly towards the *Saal*, he came up with the allied armies on November 5, near the village of *Rossbach*. His troops were greatly outnumbered by those of the enemy, who looked forward to an easy victory. The French even hoped they might have the pleasure of sending Frederick as a prisoner to Paris. As they joyfully advanced, the Prussians, who occupied a height, appeared to pay no attention to their movements. The King himself quietly sat at table with his generals. When, however, the French were near enough, a terrible fire was opened by the Prussians; and the cavalry, under the brave General *Seidlitz*, swept down upon the enemy. The French had not looked for such rapid movement. They scarcely even offered battle, but turned and fled. This victory secured Saxony, and raised the spirits of the Prussian army; but Frederick did not feel that he had yet done enough. It was necessary that Silesia should now be delivered. Exactly a month after the battle of Rossbach, the battle of

*Leuthen* was fought. The Prussians numbered 30,000, the Austrians 80,000. Nevertheless, the latter were utterly defeated, and driven out of Silesia. Frederick had thus in a short time swept back the tide of invasion which had threatened to overwhelm his country. Having no wish to continue the war a day longer than was necessary, he made proposals of peace to Austria; but the Empress rejected his offers, and began to prepare for a new campaign. The supreme command was taken from Prince Charles of Lorraine, and given to Daun, who, although the victor of Kolin, was not a general of high ability.

15. **The Battles of Crefeld, Zorndorf, and Hochkirchen.**—The campaign of 1758 was opened by *Ferdinand*, Duke of Brunswick, who, with an army maintained by England, attacked the French, and gradually drove them out of the country to the east of the Rhine. In a battle fought at *Crefeld*, the Duke, with greatly inferior numbers, gained a decided victory. Frederick himself attempted, by a bold stroke, to seize Olmütz; but he was unsuccessful. The Russians had entered Prussia, and were treating the people very cruelly. Frederick, leaving Marshal *Keith* to defend Silesia, came up with the Russians near *Zorndorf* on August 28. A fearful battle was fought, in which neither side gave quarter. From morning till night the slaughter lasted; but in the end the Prussians were victorious, and the Russians retreated into Poland. The King hastened to the help of his brother *Henry* against the Austrians in Saxony. Daun took up a strong position, whilst Frederick incautiously encamped on an open plain near the village of *Hochkirchen*. His generals expostulated with him; but he would hardly listen to their complaints. The Austrians did not fail to take advantage of the mistake. Early in the morning of October 14, whilst it was still dark, they attacked the advanced posts, and, seizing a battery which

commanded the chief street of Hochkirchen, turned the cannon against the Prussians. The latter made brave efforts to defend themselves; but, knowing nothing of the position of the enemy, they were thrown into helpless confusion, and thousands, with some of Frederick's best generals, were cut down. After sunrise there was a dense mist. When at length this cleared away, Frederick saw that nothing remained but to retreat. His army did so in such excellent order that the Austrians obtained no further advantage. Although defeated, Frederick continued his march towards Silesia, and his operations there were so successful that at the end of the year the Austrians had to leave the province in his hands, and to take up their winter quarters in Bohemia.

16. **The Battle of Minden. The defeat of Kunersdorf.**—The year 1759 was an eventful one for the Prussians. Frederick's enemies were more than ever resolved to crush him. The Russians advanced in great numbers, under General *Soltikow*, towards the Oder, whilst the Austrian army, commanded by *Daun* and *Loudon*, was strongly reinforced. The French tried to win back the territory from which Prince Ferdinand had driven them; and for a time they seemed to be almost certain of success. The two bodies into which their army was divided crossed the Rhine at different points, and, uniting near *Giessen*, seized *Cassel* and other towns. Ferdinand retreated as far as *Bremen*, but he at length resolved to offer battle, and, on August 1, came up with the French near *Minden*. The French cavalry, which was placed in the centre, was attacked by the English and Hanoverian infantry, and routed. A crushing defeat would have been the result, but *Lord George Sackville*, whom Prince Ferdinand ordered to pursue the French, either from cowardice or jealousy refused to obey, and the enemy thus managed to retreat

in good order. But Ferdinand's victory was complete enough to enable him to regain the whole of the ground he had lost. King Frederick was by no means so successful. This was for him the most unfortunate campaign of the Seven Years' War. For some time his great object was to prevent the union of the Russians with the division of the Austrian army under Loudon. When the former succeeded in crossing the Oder, he sent General *Wedel* to oppose their further progress. On June 23, Wedel attacked the enemy at *Kay*, and was defeated. As the Russians and Austrians now united their forces, Frederick resolved to proceed against them himself, and to attack them with his whole strength. He seems to have regarded this as a supreme effort, on which everything depended; for he made provision for the government of his kingdom in case he should either be killed or taken prisoner, and charged his brother Henry on no account to conclude a peace disgraceful to Prussia. The great battle was fought on August 12, near *Kunersdorf*. After a long and fierce contest, the left wing of the Russians was put to flight. Frederick's troops were already worn out by long marches, and his generals entreated him not to ask them to do more that day. But he hoped to succeed, and ordered the battle to go on. The Russian right wing and the Austrians were still fresh, and the Prussians in vain tried to break their ranks. The attempt was again and again made, but always with the same result. At length the Prussians themselves gave way. Their numbers had been fearfully reduced, and, instead of retreating in their usual good order, they fled in wild confusion. Not fewer than 17,000 Prussians fell in this battle. Frederick appeared almost broken-hearted as he saw his brave army break up and disperse in all directions, pursued by the Austrian cavalry. When he was brought, almost against his will, to a place of safety, he wrote in pencil to his minister *Friesenstein*, "All is lost: save the royal family." Shortly afterwards he despatched a second note: "The consequences of this battle will be worse than the battle itself. I shall not survive the ruin of the Fatherland. Adieu, for ever!" Fortunately the King's forebodings were not realized. Although allies, the Russians and Austrians were very jealous of each other; and this feeling prevented them from taking full advantage of their victory. The defeat of Kunersdorf, however, was not Frederick's only misfortune in this campaign. A body of troops was sent by him to defend *Dresden;* but before they arrived Count *Schmettau*, in order to save the military chest, had delivered up the city to the Austrians. Somewhat later, General *Fink* was compelled to surrender himself and his army, consisting of 5,000 men, to the Austrians at *Maxen;* whereupon General Daun took possession of Dresden, and determined to winter in Saxony. Frederick harassed him for some time; but in January, 1760, the excessive cold compelled even the King to go into winter quarters.

17. **The Battles of Liegnitz and Torgau.**—The position of Frederick became daily more trying. Prussia was at this time a small kingdom, and its resources appeared now almost exhausted. On the other hand, there appeared nothing to prevent his enemies from continuing the war for an indefinite time. But a peace concluded after so many misfortunes could not but be unfavourable. Frederick therefore resolved to go on with the war, making the most of the small means at his disposal. In the summer of 1760 he had to meet a fresh disaster. The force of General *Fouqué*, who had been entrusted with the defence of Silesia, was surrounded by the Austrians at *Landshut*. The Prussians never fought more bravely, but they could not hold out against greatly superior numbers. General Fouqué

himself was taken prisoner. Frederick tried to make up for this defeat by bombarding Dresden; but, as Daun came to its relief, he had to raise the siege. He hastened to Silesia, where the successes of General Loudon made his presence necessary. The Austrians under *Daun* and *Lasci* accompanied him, a division marching on either side of his army. At *Liegnitz* these generals were joined by Loudon, and they resolved to surround and cut down the Prussian army. Early in the morning of August 15, Loudon marched silently towards the heights of *Pfaffendorf*, whence he expected to be able to attack the enemy in the rear. But during the night Frederick had taken possession of these very heights. Loudon gave battle, hoping to be assisted by Daun; but the latter was ignorant of what was going on, so that the Prussians were soon victorious. When Daun advanced from another side, he was attacked by the Prussian right wing under the brave General *Ziethen*, and driven back. Frederick's victory was thus complete. But he had no sooner gained this advantage, which made Silesia safe, than he had to meet new difficulties. The Russians, joined by the Austrians under Lasci, advanced to Berlin, and on October 4 they entered it in triumph. In a few days they retreated, a rumour having arisen that Frederick was marching to the relief of his capital. On Nov. 3 another battle was fought between the army of Frederick and that of Marshal Daun, who occupied a strong position near *Torgau*. The Prussians attacked the Austrians in two divisions, the one led by Frederick himself, the other by Ziethen. Frederick's division suffered fearfully; and he was under the impression at night that the battle would have to be renewed in the morning. But in the morning it was found that the Austrians had silently retreated. Daun marched to Dresden; but the greater part of Saxony now fell anew into Frederick's hands, and he took up his winter quarters at Leipzig.

18. **Movements of Prince Henry and Frederick in 1761.**—During the summer of 1761 Prince Henry, whom Frederick afterwards declared to have been the only general who made no mistakes during this war, succeeded in thwarting all the plans of Marshal Daun for the recovery of the part of Saxony which the Prussians had conquered. Much of the year was spent by Frederick himself in preventing the Russians under *Butterlin*, and the Austrians under *Loudon*, from joining their forces. On August 12 the two armies succeeded in uniting, and Frederick was for some time shut up in his quarters near *Bunzelwitz*. But the allies did nothing. They were still jealous of each other, and soon separated. They did far more damage when acting apart than when together. Loudon, by an unexpected movement, hastened to *Schweidnitz*, which, on October 1, fell into his hands. By the possession of this town he commanded a large part of Silesia. On the other hand, the Russians wintered in Pomerania. The important town of Colberg resisted them for four months; but, on December 1, it had to surrender.

19. **Alliance of Frederick with the Russians.**—The year 1762 brought with it new hope for Frederick. On January 5, the Empress *Elizabeth* of Russia died. Her successor, *Peter III.*, not only made peace, but entered into an alliance with Frederick. As Sweden also signed a treaty of peace with Prussia, Frederick could now devote himself wholly to the task of overcoming the Austrians. When joined by his Russian allies, he advanced to attack Daun at *Buckersdorf.* During the march the unwelcome news came that Peter III. had been murdered; and *Czernitschef*, the Russian commander, received orders from the Empress *Catherine II.* to return with his army at once to Poland. Frederick persuaded Czernitschef to conceal his instructions for three days. Before that time had passed the Austrians

were attacked and defeated. The Russians then withdrew; and Frederick besieged Schweidnitz. It held out for nine weeks; but on October 9, its provisions being exhausted, it surrendered. The position of Prussia was still further improved by a victory gained by Prince Henry over the Austrians at *Freiberg* on October 29, and by the continued successes of Prince Ferdinand in his opposition to the French, who had made great but vain efforts to subdue him. Whilst Frederick went into winter quarters, having previously agreed to an armistice with Austria, General *Kleist*, with an army of 10,000 men, carried the war into Franconia, and compelled the hostile German princes to conclude peace.

20. **The Peace of Hubertusburg.**—The Empress Maria Theresa, notwithstanding all that had passed, would gladly have continued the war; but she knew she soon would have to do so alone. The Empress Catherine had confirmed the peace concluded with Frederick by her husband; and France, exhausted by its struggle with England, was about to give up the contest. Negotiations between Austria and Saxony on the one hand, and Prussia on the other, were therefore entered into, and, on February 15, 1763, a few days after the conclusion of the *Peace of Paris*, the *Treaty of Hubertusburg* was signed. The chief article of this treaty was the confirmation of Frederick in his possession of Silesia. One of the most destructive wars in history thus left the two chief combatants in apparently the same position as that in which it had found them. But it was not really so. For seven years Prussia, trusting mainly to her own resources, had maintained her independence against the combined forces of several of the leading European Powers. A struggle so bravely carried on could not, when triumphantly closed, leave things exactly as they had been. As the result of the Seven Years' War, Prussia rose from the

position of a petty kingdom, which no one much respected or feared, to that of a Great Power. She also learned her own strength, and prepared the way for those great achievements by which she has since made her name famous. From this time Prussia became the rival of Austria in Germany; and the minor States grouped themselves around these two Powers according to their tastes and sympathies. The question which of the two Powers was in the end to be supreme gradually became the leading question in German politics. It did not receive a final answer till our own day.

21. **Joseph II. Home government of Frederick the Great.**—Francis I. died in 1765. He was succeeded in the same year by his son, *Joseph II.* Maria Theresa had associated the latter with her in the government of the hereditary Austrian lands; but during her lifetime he had very little authority. Under the vigorous government of Frederick II., Prussia gradually recovered from the effects of the Seven Year's War. Order was everywhere established, and those who had been ruined were helped by gifts of money and corn. The King's measures were by no means always popular. A Government monopoly of tobacco and coffee was especially disliked. On the whole, however, his rule was wise and disinterested, and encouraged the energies of the people to flow in a variety of new directions. To Silesia, which had cost him so many sacrifices, Frederick always devoted special attention; and he was rewarded by seeing the population steadily increase in numbers and wealth.

22. **First partition of Poland.**—During the interval of peace that followed the Treaty of Hubertusburg, Austria and Prussia joined Russia in doing a great public wrong. Without the smallest provocation, these Powers seized, in 1772, a large part of *Poland*, and divided it between them.

Poland was very badly governed; but that was no reason why it should be robbed of a third of its territory by neighbouring nations. By this *first partition* Austria received *East Galicia* and *Lodomiria;* Frederick, what was called *West Prussia*, but without the important towns of *Danzig* and *Thorn*.

23. **The "Potato War."**—A few years afterwards the peace of Germany was for a short time broken. On the death of *Maximilian Joseph*, Elector of Bavaria, in 1777, the Emperor Joseph asserted a claim to Lower Bavaria, and, marching into the country, took possession of it. The true heir, *Charles Theodore*, the Elector Palatine, was taken by surprise, and gave up to Austria two thirds of his inheritance on condition that he should retain the remaining third. The Elector Palatine's heir, the *Duke of Zweibrücken*, protested against this arrangement, and appealed to Frederick II. for help. Frederick, who was unwilling that Austria should become too powerful, sided against the Emperor, and once more marched into Bohemia. But no battle was fought. On receiving the Circle of *Burgau*, Austria consented to yield the rest of Bavaria. Peace was therefore, at *Teschen*, concluded on May 13, 1779. The war thus ended was nicknamed "the potato war," because the soldiers were said to have nothing to do except to cook their potatoes.

24. **Death of Maria Theresa. Attempted reforms of Joseph II.**—Joseph's mother, Maria Theresa, died on November 29, 1780. He then became sole ruler of the Austrian dominions. He was full of good wishes for his subjects, and had long meditated daring schemes of reform. He instantly began to put his ideas into practice. No fewer than 624 monasteries were closed, and an edict of toleration was proclaimed, by which freedom of worship was granted to all Christain sects. The Emperor's attacks

on the supposed rights of the Church excited such violent opposition that Pope *Pius VI.* himself visited Vienna. He was received with enthusiasm by the people; but the Emperor treated him with marked coldness, and conceded nothing. It was not only the Church that Joseph tried to reform. He attempted to simplify the administration of justice, to do away with the privileges of the nobility, and to introduce a uniform system of government throughout his hereditary states. In all this he was too rash. He forgot that great reforms cannot be effected all at once, and that it is impossible, even if it were desirable, to force nationalities, whose circumstances are widely different, into one mould. In 1785 he made another attempt to obtain possession of Bavaria; but his plans were again thwarted by Frederick, who formed a League for the preservation of the Imperial constitution. This League was joined by the majority of the temporal princes and by the Elector of Mainz, and may be regarded as the first attempt of Prussia seriously to contest with Austria the leading place in Germany. It came to an end immediately after the death of Frederick.

25. **Death of Frederick the Great. Frederick William II.**—Frederick was now an old man, and had survived most of those who had shared his former triumphs and defeats. Years had not softened his character. His mind, however, remained active to the last, and he never lost his interest in affairs of state. He died on August 17, 1786, and was succeeded by his nephew *Frederick William II.* The latter proved a weak King, under the dominion of unworthy favourites.

26. **Failure of Joseph II.'s schemes. His death.**—The Emperor Joseph soon found himself in circumstances of extreme difficulty. In 1788 he engaged in an unwise war with the Turks. He himself accompanied the Austrian

troops; but nothing creditable either to him or his army was done. Meanwhile, discontent had been rapidly growing up, especially in Hungary and the Austrian Netherlands. The people of the latter country—with the exception of *Luxemburg*—at length rebelled, and, on October 22, 1789, formed an independent Government at *Breda*. The Hungarian nobles, indignant at the attack of the Emperor on their privileges, roused the peasantry to revolt; and they so far succeeded that Joseph had to undo in Hungary all the reforms he had tried with so much zeal to carry out. His health had been seriously injured during the campaign against the Turks. The anxiety caused by the opposition of his subjects to his well-meant schemes on their behalf greatly increased his weakness, and he died, almost broken-hearted, on February 20, 1790.

27. **Leopold II.**—*Peter Leopold*, Grand Duke of Tuscany, Joseph II.'s brother, succeeded to the Austrian inheritance. He was more cautious than Joseph, and, by returning to the principles which had always hitherto regulated Austrian policy, he soon restored his States to peace. On September 20, 1790, he was elected Emperor.

# CHAPTER XVII.

## THE FALL OF THE EMPIRE AND OF THE KINGDOM OF GERMANY.

*The French Revolution; how regarded in Germany; resolution of Leopold II. and Frederick William II. to support the French King; death of Leopold II. (1)—war declared by France against Austria; Prussia joins Austria; successes of the allies; their reverses; Mainz taken by the French (2)—the campaigns of 1793 and 1794 (3)—Second Partition of Poland; Austria is jealous of Prussia, and intrigues with Russia against her; coldness of Frederick William II. in prosecuting the war; secret treaty between Austria and Russia; Peace of Basel; gains of Prussia and Austria by the Third Partition of Poland (4)—campaigns of 1796 and 1797 in Italy and Germany; preliminaries of peace signed at Leoben; Treaty of Campo Formio; Congress of Rastatt (5)—Austria joins England and Russia against France; successes of the allies in 1799; Russia withdraws from the war; battles of Marengo and Hohenlinden; Peace of Lunéville (6)—alliance against France in 1805; surrender of General Mack; battle of Austerlitz; Peace of Pressburg (7)—the Confederation of the Rhine (8)—Francis II. resigns the Imperial Crown; end of the Roman Empire and the Kingdom of Germany (9).*

1. **The French Revolution. Death of Leopold II.**—The French Revolution caused great excitement in Germany. Many thought it the beginning of better times for the whole of Europe; but the princes naturally looked on it with fear and hatred. The French refugees, of whom there were a

great number, tried to strengthen the latter feelings, and urged the princes to make war on France. Some time passed before the great German Powers, who were very jealous of one another, would consent to act together. At last the Emperor *Leopold* and *Frederick William II.* of Prussia met at *Pillnitz*, near Dresden, and resolved to support the French King. Before anything was done, however, Leopold died, early in 1792.

2. **War with France.**—Leopold was succeeded by his son *Francis II.* The French, irritated by foreign interference in their affairs, had already declared war against Austria, in April, 1792. Austria was joined by Prussia; and a Prussian army, under *Ferdinand*, Duke of *Brunswick*, and accompanied by Frederick William II. himself, soon marched into France. The Prussians were aided by many French refugees and 6,000 Hessians. The war, which was to grow into a contest unparalleled for the greatness of its operations and of the issues depending on it, was at first favourable to the German Powers. *Valenciennes*, *Longwy*, and *Verdun* all fell into the hands of the Prussian general; and a rapid advance might easily have been made on Paris. But fortune soon changed. The Duke of Brunswick issued a proclamation calling upon the French people to submit to their lawful King, and threatening Paris with the fate of ancient Jerusalem if the slightest affront were offered to the royal family. This manifesto roused deep indignation throughout France, and thousands flocked from all parts of the country to drive back the invader. A slight action took place at *Valmy*, after which the Duke of Brunswick, the Prussians having been much weakened by disease, gave orders for a retreat. The dispirited troops hastened towards the Rhine, which they crossed at *Coblentz*. The Austrians were even less fortunate than their allies. They were overtaken by the French at *Jemmappes*, where, on November 5,

1792, a battle was fought. After an obstinate fight the Austrians had to fly ; and in a few days the French entered Brussels. Since the time of Joseph II. the Netherlands had never been really loyal to Austria, so that they gladly threw off the yoke of that country, and proclaimed a Republic. In the meantime, *Mainz* had fallen into the hands of the French, who were warmly welcomed by a considerable number of the people.

3. **Progress of the War.**—Almost immediately after the execution of *Lewis XVI.*, France made war on Great Britain, Holland, and Spain. After much discussion the States of the Empire declared war against France, but they had little real share in the struggle that followed. The Austrian army in the Netherlands was commanded by the Duke of *Coburg*. On March 18, 1793, it defeated the French at *Neerwinden*. A second victory was gained by the Austrians, aided by a British division, at *Famars;* and the towns of *Condé* and *Valenciennes* were taken by the allies. These advantages were not followed up with much energy, so that the French soon won back lost ground. After being defeated at *Wattignies*, on October 16, the Austrians retreated. The Austrian army on the Middle Rhine, commanded by *Wurmser*, was routed on the 26th December by *Hoche*, in the neighbourhood of the *Lauter*. The Prussians had, after a long siege, recovered Mainz, and gained a victory at *Kaiserslautern;* but, after the defeat of Wurmser, they had to fall back, and were able to hold only a small district round Mainz. In 1794 the Emperor Francis joined the Austrian troops in the Netherlands ; and, together with the allies, they gained several advantages. The town of *Landrecies* fell into their hands. But fortune again turned in favour of the French. On May 22 *Pichegru* defeated the allies at *Tournay;* and on June 26 a still greater victory was gained by *Jourdan* at *Fleurus*. Whilst

the former general prepared to invade Holland, the latter forced the Austrians back upon the Rhine, and compelled them to cross it on October 5. The left bank of the Middle Rhine had already been given up to the French by the Austrians and Prussians, who, after having been victorious at *Kaiserslautern* on May 22, had been defeated at the same place on July 15.

4. **The Second and Third Partitions of Poland. Prussia makes peace with France.**—Whilst the war with France was going on, the attention of the German Powers was much occupied by the affairs of Poland. In 1793 Prussia joined Russia in effecting the *Second Partition* of that kingdom, receiving the larger part of *Great Poland*, with the cities of *Thorn* and *Danzig*. Austria was filled with jealousy at the increased power of her ally, and *Thugut*, the minister who directed the Austrian policy, intrigued so much with Russia against Prussia that King Frederick William II. began to prosecute the war with France coldly, and to think of withdrawing altogether from the struggle. In 1794 a great revolt, headed by *Kosciuszko*, took place in Poland. Prussia tried to put it down; but it was finally quelled by Russian troops. Early in 1795 Russia and Austria concluded a secret treaty, dividing Poland for the third and last time. The Prussian King, suspicious of the policy of the courts of Vienna and St. Petersburg, resolved to make peace with France; and on April 5, 1795, the *Treaty of Basel* was signed. Prussia ceded to France all her possessions on the left bank of the Rhine. A little later Hanover and Hessen-Cassel also made peace with France. The secret understanding of Austria and Russia with respect to the *Third Partition of Poland* was made known to Prussia on August 8, 1795. By this arrangement *New East Prussia*, with *Warsaw*, was added to the Prussian monarchy; and Austria received *West Galicia*.

## 5. The Peace of Campo Formio.

—During the summer of 1795 there was a lull in the war between Austria and France; but in September the Austrians were driven across the *Main*. They soon rallied, and by a victory at *Höchst*, near Frankfurt, compelled the French to retire to the opposite side of the Rhine. In the campaign of 1796 Austria had to put forth her whole strength. Her army in Italy was commanded by General *Beaulieu*. Opposed to him was *Napoleon Buonaparte*, a young general who soon became the foremost man in Europe. Having forced Sardinia to accept peace, Buonaparte advanced against the Austrians, and, after a fearful struggle, defeated them at the bridge of *Lodi*. Marshal *Wurmser* was sent with a considerable army to their relief; but he was several times defeated, and on September 9 was obliged to take refuge in *Mantua*. Meanwhile important operations had been going on in Germany. Two French armies, under the command of *Moreau* and *Jourdan*, had gone far into the country; but on August 22 Jourdan was defeated at *Neumark* by the Archduke *Charles*. Two days afterwards a second victory was gained by the Archduke over the same general. Moreau, being thus left alone, retreated towards the Rhine. In Italy the Austrian arms continued unsuccessful. An army, which was placed under Marshal *Alvinzi*, gained some advantages; but on November 17 it was driven with great loss from *Ascole*. When fighting was begun again in January, 1797, Alvinzi was once more defeated at *Rivoli;* and on February 2 Mantua capitulated. Buonaparte now conceived the bold project of carrying the war into the hereditary territories of Austria. In this he succeeded. Crossing the Alps between Italy and Carinthia, he entered the latter country, and took up his head quarters at *Leoben*. As he was thus cut off from all help, a vigorous effort on the part of Austria might perhaps have freed her from her great enemy; but she had been thoroughly humbled, and the Government now trembled for Vienna itself. Negotiations were therefore entered upon; and the preliminaries of peace were signed at *Leoben* on April 18. Various difficulties afterwards arose; but on October 17, 1797, the Treaty of *Campo Formio* was agreed upon. The Austrian Netherlands were ceded to France. In return for her Italian possessions, which were formed into the *Cisalpine Republic,* Austria received *Venice, Friuli, Istria, Dalmatia,* and the islands off the Dalmatian coast. By a secret article the Emperor consented to cede the left bank of the Rhine to France, and to settle compensations for the deprived princes. Immediately after the conclusion of this treaty, a Congress was opened by Buonaparte at *Rastatt,* for the purpose of settling the terms of peace between France and the Empire. At this Congress the German princes were treated with much insolence by the French envoys, and had to yield every demand of the conqueror, however unreasonable. The conditions of peace, however, were still under consideration, when a change in the aspect of affairs suddenly brought the proceedings of the Congress to a close.

6. **Austria joins England and Russia against France. Peace of Lunéville.**—After the conclusion of the Peace of Campo Formio, Austria watched with great jealousy the violent doings of France in Italy and Switzerland. She therefore willingly formed an alliance with Russia and England against the common enemy; and war broke out again in 1799. It began brilliantly for the allies. The Archduke Charles delivered Germany from the French by a great victory gained over General Jourdan at *Stockach* on March 25; and soon afterwards the army of *Masséna* was driven out of the western part of Switzerland. In Italy Marshal *Kray* was victorious over the French, under

## PEACE OF LUNEVILLE.

*Scherer*, at *Verona* and *Magnano*. When the great Russian commander, Marshal *Suwaroff*, had joined the Austrians, the allies defeated the French in battle after battle, and freed almost all Italy from their yoke. Next year these advantages were quickly lost. The Russian Emperor, whose forces were not so successful in Switzerland, withdrew from the war; and Buonaparte, whose very name now struck fear into the hearts of his enemies, had returned from *Egypt* to take the command of the French. On June 2, 1800, *Genoa* opened its gates to the Austrians; but on that very day, after his daring march across the Alps, Buonaparte entered *Milan* in triumph. On June 14 the great battle of *Marengo* was fought. The defeat of the Austrians was so complete that by this one battle the French regained almost all they had lost in Italy. At the same time General Moreau was advancing victoriously through Germany. On December 3 he gained the splendid victory of *Hohenlinden*. The Austrian Government no longer felt itself able to continue the war, and on February 9, 1801, the Peace of *Lunéville* was signed. This peace confirmed that of Campo Formio. The Emperor again yielded the Austrian Netherlands. He also consented to recognise the *Batavian, Helvetic, Cisalpine*, and *Ligurian* Republics; and gave the Margraviate of *Breisgau* to the Duke of *Modena*, and the archbishoprick of *Salzburg* as a secular principality, together with the title of Elector, to the Grand Duke of *Tuscany*. Besides these concessions, Austria consented to the German lands on the left bank of the Rhine being yielded to France. They were formally given up by the States of the Empire, whose plenipotentiaries began their inglorious labours at *Regensburg* on August 24, 1802. France thus gained for a time the long-coveted Rhine boundary. The princes who lost territory by the arrangement received gifts of secularised Church property and mediatised free cities on the right bank. The Landgrave of *Hessen-Cassel*, the Duke of *Würtemberg*, and the Margrave of *Baden*, were made Electors. Of the spiritual Electors, only the Archbishop of Mainz kept his offices; and his See was transferred to *Regensburg*. Lübeck, Hamburg, Bremen, Frankfurt, Augsburg, and Nürnberg, were the only cities allowed to remain free. The freedom of not less than 48 had been suppressed.

7. **New Alliance against France. Battle of Austerlitz. Peace of Pressburg.** — Germany had never been so thoroughly humbled as now. Her territory was divided, and the people handed from one ruler to another at the bidding of a foreign conqueror. The disunion of the various members of the Empire had thus at last borne bitter fruit. Little more was needed to put an end to the Empire altogether; and the unavoidable change soon came. Buonaparte, while ruling France with wisdom and energy, showed more and more contempt for the rights of all other nations. In 1803 he seized *Hanover*, as if it had been a part of Great Britain. Prussia protested against this outrage, but in general held selfishly aloof, hoping to gain through the losses of her neighbours. The territory of the Empire was violated in 1804 by the seizure of the Duke of *Enghien*, but the Diet adjourned to avoid interference in the matter. Austria, however, was preparing for war. In 1805 she once more formed an alliance with *England* and *Russia;* and the three Powers, which were joined by *Sweden*, resolved to make a grand effort that should utterly crush their opponent. But, by his rapid movements and well-arranged plans, Buonaparte got the better of the allies. He hastened towards the Rhine, and at once crossed into German territory. Fidelity to the Empire was so entirely a thing of the past on the part of many of the princes, that he had no difficulty in bringing *Bavaria*, *Würtemberg*, and

## THE PEACE OF PRESSBURG.

*Baden* over to the side of France. General *Mack* commanded an Austrian army near *Ulm*. He allowed himself to be cut off from all communication with Vienna, after which he was several times defeated. Taking refuge in Ulm, he was compelled, on October 17, to capitulate with his whole army, which was then made up of 30,000 men. On November 13 Buonaparte was in the palace of *Schönbrunn* in Vienna; and a few days afterwards he had crossed the Danube in order to attack the Austrians and Prussians, who had united their forces in *Moravia*. The battle of *Austerlitz* was fought on December 2. The allies outnumbered the French, but mere numbers were not a match for skilful generalship and the trust of French soldiers in their leader; and the battle ended in a great victory for Buonaparte. The war, however, need not have ended, if the Emperor Francis had been courageous enough to persevere. The Russians were willing to go on fighting; the Archduke *Ferdinand* was at the head of an army of 20,000 men, with which he completely overcame the Bavarians; and a short time before the French navy had been made powerless by the great victory of the English at *Trafalgar*. Besides, it seemed not improbable that Prussia might at last be aroused to a sense of her duty to the Empire and to Europe. But the Emperor wished for peace, and, in a personal interview with Buonaparte, arranged preliminaries. A treaty was signed at *Pressburg* on December 25. Austria had never before accepted terms so humiliating. Besides ceding Venice to Italy, she gave up *Tyrol*, *Vorarlberg*, and other lands to Bavaria, and her territory in *Swabia* to Würtemberg and Baden. In return for these sacrifices she received *Salzburg*, the Elector of Salzburg being transferred to *Würzburg*, which was given up to him by Bavaria. Not content with these changes, Buonaparte raised the Electors of Bavaria and Würtemberg to the rank of Kings. The Emperor had to recognize them and the Elector of Baden as sovereigns wholly independent within their territories. In return for *Hanover*, Prussia yielded *Ansbach* to *Bavaria*, *Cleve* and *Neufchatel* to *France*. Soon afterwards Buonaparte gave *Cleve* and *Berg*—received from Bavaria in return for Ansbach—to his brother-in-law, *Joachim Murat*, and Neufchatel to his friend and councillor, *Alexander Berthier*.

8. **The Confederation of the Rhine.**—The Holy Roman Empire still existed in name; but a step was now taken which brought about its fall. Buonaparte knew how much it would help him to have a Power within Germany itself whose friendship he could always trust. It would once have been impossible to form such a Power; but now all was changed. To their utter shame, German princes were found who could consent, for their own selfish ends, to support a foreigner against the Fatherland. On June 12, 1806, the Kings of *Bavaria* and *Würtemberg*, the Elector of *Baden*, the Landgrave of *Hessen*, the Duke of *Berg*, the Archbishop of *Regensburg*, and other princes, formally declared themselves separated from the Empire, and acknowledged the French Emperor as their protector. The league received the name of the *Confederation of the Rhine*, and undertook to aid Buonaparte in war with an army of 63,000 men. The Archbishop of Regensburg, who had hitherto been Electoral Archchancellor, was appointed by Buonaparte, with the title of *Prince-Primate*, his representative in the Confederation.

9. **The fall of the Empire and of the Kingdom of Germany.**—The final stroke had now been delivered, and the ancient Empire, the true representative of the Empire of the Cæsars, fell to pieces. On August 6, 1806, Francis II. formally resigned the Imperial crown. The kingdom of Germany, as well as the Roman Empire, thus came to an

end. In 1804 Francis, wholly mistaking the meaning of the word *Emperor*, had added to his existing title that of *Hereditary Emperor of Austria*. In the Treaty of Pressburg he is called *Emperor of Germany and Austria*. From 1806 he was simply *Emperor of Austria;* and his successors have borne the same title. After his resignation of the true Imperial crown Germany was no longer, even in name, a united State acknowledging a common head.

# CHAPTER XVIII.

## THE STRUGGLE WITH BUONAPARTE.

*Desire of Buonaparte to humble Prussia; war between France and Prussia; battle of Jena (1)—terror of the Prussians; Buonaparte enters Berlin (2)—battle of Friedland; Peace of Tilsit (3)—war between Austria and France in 1809; battle of Wagram; Peace of Schönbrunn (4)—loyalty of the Tyrolese; bravery of Hofer; shot by the French (5)—preparation for war in Prussia (6)—Frederick William III. appeals to the Prussian people to arm against the French; alliance between Prussia and Russia (7)—battles of Lützen and Bautzen; armistice; the allies joined by Austria and Sweden (8)—victory of Blücher at the Katzbach; defeat of the allies before Dresden; defeat of Vandamme and Ney (9)—the battle of Leipzig (10)—the war carried into France; the First Peace of Paris (11)—the Congress of Vienna; escape of Buonaparte from Elba (12)—the battle of Waterloo; the Second Peace of Paris (13)—changes of territory in Germany (14)—the German Confederation (15)—German writers (16)—Music in Germany (17).*

1. **War between Prussia and France. The Battle of Jena.**—The selfish withdrawal of Prussia from the struggle with Buonaparte had hitherto saved it from disaster; but its turn now came. Frederick William II. had died on November, 1797. He was very extravagant, and died deeply in debt. His son *Frederick William III.*, who was twenty-seven years old at the time of his accession, was a man of much worthier character. This sovereign was deeply

mortified by the formation of the Rhenish Confederation, partly because it threatened to destroy the supremacy of Prussia in North Germany. Buonaparte was at no pains to make him friendly. In fact, the French Emperor was jealous of the independence of Prussia, and anxious for an opportunity to humble it. He made proposals for the restoration of Hanover to the King of Great Britain, and was even unmanly enough to assail the character of *Louise*, the beautiful and popular Prussian queen. Stung by these and many other insults, Frederick William at length, in 1806, placed his army on a war footing, and demanded that the French troops should quit Germany. Unfortunately the Prussians were altogether unfit for the struggle into which they were thus hurried. The main body of the army had never had experience of actual warfare, while the leaders were for the most part slaves to mere form, puffed up with the glories of their fathers, and without any true notion of the strength of the enemy they had to deal with. The aged *Ferdinand*, Duke of *Brunswick*, who again commanded, took up his station to the north of the Thuringian Forest, and awaited the approach of the French. On October 10, a preliminary engagement between the French and a Prussian corps under Prince *Lewis*, the King's cousin, took place near *Saalfeld*. Prince Lewis was defeated and slain. This victory made the French masters of the Saal, and enabled them to cut off the Prussians from communication with Saxony, which was an unwilling ally of Frederick William in the war. On October 14 a great battle was fought at *Auerstädt* and *Jena*. The Duke of *Brunswick* commanded at the former place, and *Prince Hohenlohe* at the latter. Neither was aware of the movements of the other; and both were defeated. At the beginning of the battle the Duke of Brunswick was mortally wounded. A few regiments fought bravely; but in the Prussian army as a whole there was the utmost confusion. Great numbers were slain, and afterwards 20,000 men were made prisoners.

**2. Buonaparte enters Berlin.**—The results of the battle at Jena were even more disastrous than the battle itself. A few generals distinguished themselves by their brave resistance. Although *Blücher*, who afterwards became so famous, was obliged in the end to give in, he did not do so till, with a small body of troops, he had done much harm to the French in and near *Lübeck*. Generals *Gneisenau* and *Schill* continued to defend *Colberg* against a greatly superior force, and, when *Courbière*, who held *Graudenz*, was told that there was no longer a King of Prussia, and that he had better yield, he replied, "If there is no longer a King of Prussia, then *I* will be King in Graudenz." These, however, were exceptions. The campaign had been begun without any definite plan; and now the whole country seemed overwhelmed with fear. Even *Magdeburg*, with its garrison of 22,000 men, capitulated without striking a blow. The King and Queen fled to Königsberg, and Buonaparte took possession of Berlin. The people of the capital submitted so readily that Buonaparte affected to doubt whether he ought to be proud or ashamed of having conquered such a nation. He surpassed himself by his robberies at this time. Amongst other things, he took away the sword of Frederick the Great, which he pompously declared was worth more than twenty millions of dollars, and the car of victory above the Brandenburg gate.

**3. The Peace of Tilsit.**—What remained of the Prussian army, under *Lestocq* and *Kalkreuth*, joined the Russians on the Prussian frontier. On February 7 and 8, 1807, a battle was fought at *Eylau*, near Königsberg. On the whole, the advantage seemed to rest with the allies; but nothing came of the battle. The decisive contest took place on June 12 near *Friedland*. The French gained a complete victory, and in a few days held *Königsberg* and *Tilsit, Danzig* having been compelled to yield in the last days of May. Buonaparte had an interview with the Russian Emperor on a raft in the middle of the Niemen, and induced him to make peace. As Prussia could not hold out without help, the Peace of *Tilsit* was signed on July 9. Hard terms were exacted of Prussia by this treaty. The whole of the territory between the Elbe and the Rhine was taken from her, and, together with *Brunswick*, *Hessen-Cassel*, and part of *Hanover*, formed into a new kingdom, called the Kingdom of *Westphalia*, of which Buonaparte's youngest brother *Jerome* was made King. The Polish territory of Prussia was called the *Grand Duchy of Warsaw*, and given to the Elector of Saxony, who, in return for having deserted Prussia after the battle of Jena, was raised to kingly rank by Buonaparte. Danzig was declared a free town. The Prussian King thus lost the better part of his territory, and no fewer than 5,000,000 subjects. He was obliged also to reduce his army to 42,000 men, and to pay an indemnity of 140,000,000 francs. That a country so humbled should ever recover itself, and strike another blow for freedom, seemed impossible.

4. **New war between Austria and France. Battle of Wagram. Peace of Schönbrunn.**—Austria had never looked on the results of the battle of Austerlitz as final. She was all along resolved to recover, if possible, her lost territory. Whilst Buonaparte was occupied in *Spain*, Francis made great preparations for the forthcoming struggle. The army was strengthened, and the people roused by every means that could excite their enthusiasm to come forward and join the newly established *Landwehr*. No effort was spared to make the war in every sense a people's war. The hopes of Germany were raised to a high pitch; but, as the event proved, the time of her deliverance had not yet come. On

April 9, 1809, the campaign was opened by the Archduke *Charles*, who commanded the whole army, crossing the *Inn* in order to take possession of Bavaria. Several battles were fought in quick succession, and in each the Archduke was defeated. After a battle at *Eckmühl*, he fell back on *Regensburg;* but he was driven from this position also, and obliged to retreat towards Bohemia. The right bank of the Danube was thus left open to the French, and Buonaparte at once hastened to Vienna, which, after a slight resistance, he entered in triumph for the second time, on May 12. The Archduke Charles was soon in motion at the head of his troops; and the French crossed the Danube on a bridge of boats, in order to give him battle. A fierce battle was fought on May 21 and 22, on the plain between *Aspern* and *Esslingen*, in which Rudolf of Habsburg had formerly defeated King Ottocar of Bohemia. This time the Austrians were victorious; and there is reason to suppose that, if their movements had been somewhat more rapid, the whole French army might have been cut off. On July 4 Buonaparte again crossed the Danube, his army having meanwhile received vast reinforcements; and, on July 5 and 6, the battle of *Wagram* was fought. Crowds anxiously watched the progress of the battle from the towers of Vienna. The Austrian right wing was victorious; but, the left wing having been surrounded, the Archduke Charles had to retreat. The Austrian Emperor now felt that he would be no longer justified in continuing the war, and a few days afterwards an armistice was concluded. The Peace of *Schönbrunn* was signed on October 14. Besides ceding *Carniola, Friuli, Croatia*, part of *Dalmatia*, and *Trieste*, Austria yielded *Salzburg* to *Bavaria*, and the greater part of *Galicia* to Russia and the King of Saxony.

5. **Loyalty of the Tyrolese. Hofer.**—During this war several brave struggles had been carried on in different

parts of Germany. *Schill* harassed the enemy for some time in *Brunswick* and *Mecklenburg;* but in the end he was obliged to take refuge in *Stralsund*, where he was killed. *Baron von Dörnberg* tried, but in vain, to rouse the Hessians against King Jerome. *Frederick William* of *Brunswick*, the son of the Duke who fell at Auerstädt, brought together a body of men which received the name of the *Black Troop*, and fought hard for the recovery of his lands. But he and his comrades had at last to embark for England. More memorable than these isolated efforts was the great struggle of the *Tyrolese*. Although their country had been annexed to Bavaria, they had remained loyal to the House of Habsburg, and at the outbreak of war rose as one man, under the leadership of *Hofer*, *Speckbacher*, and *Straub*. The Bavarians and French were defeated, and driven from the country. After the battle of Wagram, Marshal *Lefebvre* regained possession of *Innsbruck*; but the Tyrolese again succeeded in freeing their country, and Hofer became for some time head of the Government. By the peace of Schönbrunn, Bavaria was confirmed in her possession of Tyrol; and Austria herself induced the people to lay down their arms. Hofer again rebelled; but his contrymen were no longer able to support him, and he was obliged to conceal himself in the snows of the Alps. Here he was betrayed to the French, who, in 1810, basely shot him, at Mantua, as a traitor.

6. **Preparation for war in Prussia.**—Germany now seemed to have reached the lowest depth of humiliation. Some Germans pretended to believe that the state to which Buonaparte had brought them was the best for their country. The general feeling of the nation was more healthy. In Prussia especially many hopeful signs were showing themselves. The bitter experience through which that country had passed brought forth good fruit. After the Peace of

Tilsit, the King dismissed *Haugwitz*, the minister who was chiefly responsible for the policy which Prussia had before followed. Haugwitz's successor, *Stein*, was one of the ablest statesmen of his age. He abolished serfdom, threw open civil offices to all classes, and induced the King to concede various municipal rights to the towns. The King was finally obliged to dismiss him as an enemy of France, and he took refuge in Russia. By the efforts mainly of *Wilhelm von Humboldt*, the school system of Prussia was placed on a basis which even yet makes it the envy of other nations. All the leading public men strove to awaken in the hearts of the people a patriotic feeling which should lead them at the proper moment to aid in throwing off the French yoke from Germany. The "Tugendbund" or "League of Virtue" did good service to the national cause. It was joined by men of all ranks, but especially by professors and students, who thirsted for an opportunity to undo the disasters caused by the faults and mistakes of the past. The military system of Prussia was as efficiently re-organized as the civil. Under *Gneisenau* and *Scharnhorst* the provision that the Prussian army should not exceed 42,000 men was skilfully evaded. The army was nominally kept at this figure; but so soon as one set of men was sufficiently trained, it was replaced by another. Thus all the men of the country were silently made ready for the great struggle to which every one looked forward.

7. **Frederick William appeals to the Prussian people. Alliance of Russia and Prussia.**—Some years passed before the fitting time for attacking Buonaparte came. In 1810 he annexed to France the free towns of *Bremen, Hamburg,* and *Lübeck*, and the whole northern coast of Germany as far as the Elbe. After the disastrous retreat from Russia, Germans felt that they would probably never have a more favourable opportunity for freeing themselves. Prussia was the first

to act. Berlin being in the power of the French, Frederick-William went to *Breslau;* and from thence, on February 3, 1813, he issued an appeal to the youth of Prussia to arm in defence of the Fatherland. On February 18 he met the Russian Emperor at *Kalisch;* and there an alliance was formed against the common enemy. Years before the same monarchs had met at midnight at the grave of Frederick the Great, and solemnly sworn to be true to each other in the struggle for the deliverance of Germany and Europe. The time had now come for the fulfilment of their vow. On March 15 war was formally declared by Prussia against France. Frederick William had not overrated the patriotism of his subjects. Young men from all parts of the country flocked to the national standard. They breathed a very different spirit from that of the troops whom Buonaparte had so easily crushed at Jena. The Prussian army was by this time equipped and disciplined in accordance with the wants of the age; and it was moved by a common impulse, the desire to avenge the injuries the French had inflicted on Germany, and the resolve that, cost what it might, they should be driven from German soil. The foundations of the Prussian military system had been laid by the creation of the *Landwehr* and *Landsturm*, the latter intended for the defence of the homes of the people in case of utter defeat on the field.

8. **Victories of the French. Armistice. The Allies joined by Austria and Sweden.**—The first important engagement took place on May 2, 1813, near *Lützen*, where Gustavus Adolphus was killed nearly two hundred years before. Both Russians and Prussians, fighting in view of their sovereigns, who shared the fortunes of the whole campaign, behaved well. Blücher especially distinguished himself by the bravery with which he led his troops from assault to assault. But the allies were greatly outnumbered by the

French, and retreated in good order to *Bautzen*. The King of Saxony, who had hitherto hesitated, was now compelled by Buonaparte to join him. On May 21 a second battle was fought at *Bautzen*. The allies, being still inferior in numbers to the French, were again defeated; but they did more harm to the enemy than they themselves suffered, and their retreat was so skilfully conducted that the French were unable to secure a single trophy. Buonaparte pursued the allies into Silesia; but on June 4 he consented to an armistice for three weeks. Whilst the armistice lasted both sides prepared vigorously for a renewal of the contest. Austria came forward and offered her services as mediator. In the negotiations which followed she was represented by Prince *Metternich*, a diplomatist of high distinction, whose ability Buonaparte already knew. A Congress was opened at *Prague* on July 5, and the armistice was prolonged till August 10. Terms of peace, however, could not be agreed upon; and it was resolved to go on with the war. But there was now a great change in the relative position of the various parties. Austria, which Buonaparte had hoped to keep neutral, formally joined the allies. *Bernadotte*, the Crown Prince of Sweden, had also come to their aid.

9. **Progress of the War.**—When the war began again Buonaparte sent Marshal *Oudinot* with an army of 80,000 men to seize Berlin. On August 22 this army halted at *Gross-Beeren*, hoping to enter the capital next day; but during the night it was fiercely attacked by a Prussian force under General *Bülow*, and driven towards the Elbe. Buonaparte himself had set out for Silesia in order to attack *Blücher;* but, learning that the main division of the allied army, under Prince *Schwartzenberg*, was advancing from Bohemia on Dresden, he was obliged to retreat on the very day on which Marshal Oudinot was defeated. He left in

Silesia, under Marshal *Macdonald*, an army of 80,000 men. Blücher, who had avoided an engagement with the main French army, at once advanced to meet Macdonald. On August 26 the two armies stood opposite each other, separated by a stream called the *Katzbach*. Blücher allowed a number of the enemy to cross this stream, and then exclaimed, "Now my lads, there are enough of them—forward!" The Prussians and Russians obeyed heartily, and the French were utterly routed. From this day, Blücher, who was a great favourite with the soldiers, was known as Marshal "*Vorwärts*." He was created Field Marshal, and afterwards Prince *Wahlstadt*. While the battle of the Katzbach was being won, and on the following day, another was fought before Dresden. On both days the allies were unsuccessful. Having suffered great losses, they retreated towards Bohemia. A few days afterwards they partly made up for this defeat by a victory gained over General *Vandamme* near *Töplitz*. Vandamme himself and 10,000 men were made prisoners. Buonaparte now tried a second time to gain possession of Berlin. On September 6, Marshal *Ney* came up with the Prussians at *Dennewitz*, and at once attacked them. The French army was almost double that of the Prussians, and fought with great bravery; but the Prussians stoutly resisted till the Russians and Swedes, under Bernadotte, arrived, when the French were forced to give way. They lost a large number of men, and were pursued as far as the Elbe.

10. **The Battle of Leipzig.**—During the month of September, Buonaparte strove hard to bring the main allied army to a general engagement; but this the allies cautiously avoided. At length Blücher, after some successful fighting, joined the army of Bernadotte at *Düben*. About the same time the main army, leaving Bohemia, marched through the passes of the Erz mountains, and reached the plains of

Saxony. It was obvious that the allies intended to concentrate behind Buonaparte, and cut off his communication with France. He therefore left Dresden, and retreated towards Leipzig, which he entered on October 14. He did this partly because he had been deserted by the Bavarians, who, now that he had begun to be unsuccessful, entered into an alliance with Austria. The greater part of the allied army was already in the neighbourhood of Leipzig, so that the decisive contest was evidently at hand. Prince Schwartzenberg and Buonaparte, aware of the great issues depending on the approaching battle, did everything they could to arouse the enthusiasm of their troops; and their efforts were not without effect. The battle began on the morning of October 16. In the evening the position of the armies was very much the same as in the morning, except that Blücher had got the better of Marshal Ney at the village of *Möckern.* But this time the French were greately outnumbered by the allies, and the latter expected fresh troops. Buonaparte saw therefore how the battle must end, and on the 17th made proposals for an armistice, offering terms highly favourable to the allies; but the latter declined to grant his request. On the 18th, Bernadotte having meanwhile joined the allies, the battle was renewed. Whilst it was going on, the troops of Saxony and Würtemberg went over to the enemy. On this terrible day the French kept up their old fame; but in spite of all their efforts they were steadily forced back, and when night put an end to fighting it was plain that a retreat could not be avoided. It began at dawn on the 19th. As the troops were crossing the *Elster*, the allies stormed the gates of Leipzig, and caused much confusion. A large part of the army had not yet crossed when the only bridge open to them was, probably by mistake, suddenly blown up. Many of those left behind were slain; others were drowned, and upwards of 15,000 were made prisoners. Great quantities of cannon and ammunition fell into the hands of the allies. In this fearful battle Buonaparte lost upwards of 70,000 men; and the allies not fewer than 40,000. As the Emperor Alexander and King Frederick William, and, a few hours afterwards, the Emperor Francis, with their generals, triumphantly entered Leipzig, all felt that the chief part of their task was fulfilled, and that the deliverance of Germany was now a question of only a very short time.

11. **The War carried into France. The First Peace of Paris.**—As the French were retreating, the Bavarian General *Wrede* tried to stop their passage at *Hanau*, but was himself defeated. Buonaparte was thus enabled to push on towards the Rhine, which he crossed at Mainz on November 2. His power in Germany was now for ever at an end. The German princes who had adhered to him deserted him. The fortresses garrisoned by his troops on the Elbe, Oder, and Vistula surrendered; the Rhenish Confederation was broken up; the Kingdom of Westphalia disappeared; the Elector of Hessen and the Dukes of Brunswick and Oldenburg took possession of their hereditary territories, and Hanover was given back to the King of Great Britain. But the allies were not satisfied. They felt that, so long as Buonaparte occupied the throne of France, they were not safe. They therefore resolved to carry the war into France itself, and not to sheathe the sword till the power of their enemy had been for ever crushed. A Prussian army, under Bülow, marched northwards to the aid of the Dutch. Schwartzenberg, with the main army, crossed the Rhine at Basel. Between these two was Blücher, who entered France between Mainz and Coblentz. On January 29, 1814, he was defeated by Buonaparte; but on February 1 his army joined that of Schwartzenberg, and the two together gained a brilliant victory at *La Rothière*. They then

separated. The result of their separation was that Buonaparte gained several victories. On March 9 and 10, however, the French were defeated at *Laon* by Blücher, who had joined the army of Bülow. Having attackèd Prince Schwartzenberg at *Arcis-sur-Aube* on March 20 without any definite result, Buonaparte formed the bold plan of getting behind the main allied army, in the hope that by cutting off their communication with the Rhine he would induce them to give up the idea of advancing on Paris. This scheme was found out by the allies. Fortune had thus thrown a great opportunity into their hands, and they did not let it escape them. A force of 10,000 men, under the Russian General *Winzingerode*, was left to deceive Buonaparte, while the armies of Schwartzenberg and Blücher marched rapidly towards the capital. They arrived there on March 29; next day Paris surrendered; and on the 31st the Emperor Alexander and King Frederick William entered the city at the head of their troops. Two months afterwards the *First Peace of Paris* was concluded between the allies and *Lewis XVIII.* of France, Buonaparte having in the meantime abdicated and been banished to *Elba*. By this treaty all the territory taken from Germany since 1792 was given back. No money indemnity was demanded; and France was allowed to keep even the art treasures which had been stolen from Germany.

12. **The Congress of Vienna. Escape of Buonaparte from Elba.**—The task now before the conquerors of Buonaparte was to bring back order to Germany. The great *Congress of Vienna* was opened on October 1, 1814. Besides the Emperors of *Austria* and of *Russia*, there were present the Kings of *Prussia*, of *Denmark*, of *Bavaria*, and of *Würtemberg*, most of the German Princes, and the representatives of the various German States and of all European Powers except *Turkey*. The Congress soon found that it would

have to overcome great difficulties. Prussia wished to be rewarded for its sacrifices by the annexation of Saxony; Russia asked the whole of Poland. The other Powers would not listen to these demands, and disputes ran so high that the peace of Europe seemed to be once more threatened. Suddenly, on March 7, 1815, when a compromise was being arrived at, all were startled by the alarming news that Buonaparte had escaped from Elba, was gathering around him the military strength of France, and preparing to begin another war. The subjects of dispute which had before seemed so important were at once forgotten in the thought of the common danger. Buonaparte was declared an outlaw. A new coalition was formed by the Great Powers represented at Vienna; and measures were taken for the raising of enormous armies. Germany prepared enthusiastically for her own defence. She was resolved that the present should be the last time Buonaparte should disturb Europe.

13. **The Battle of Waterloo. The second Peace of Paris.**—When the campaign began, in June, 1815, Prince *Schwartzenberg* held the Lower and Middle Rhine, and the *Duke of Wellington* had taken up his post in Holland; *Blücher's* headquarters were at Liege. The allies were not at first successful. On June 16 the Prussians were attacked near *Ligny*, and defeated with great loss. Blücher himself narrowly escaped being killed or made prisoner. On the same day an engagement took place at *Quatre Bras;* but in this the French were unsuccessful. At Quatre Bras the Black Troop of Frederick William of Brunswick again distinguished itself; but Frederick William himself was killed. On June 18 the great battle of *Waterloo*, called by the Germans *La Belle Alliance*, was fought. On the night before the battle Blücher promised to come to the help of Wellington, and, although he had great difficulty in

doing so, he kept his word. For eight hours the English army defended itself with splendid bravery; when Blücher came up, Buonaparte knew that all was lost. The defeat of the French was complete. They were pursued so vigorously by the Prussians under *Gneisenau*, and cut off in such vast numbers, that this single battle put an end to the war. Even Buonaparte felt that further resistance was impossible. On July 7 the allies were once more in possession of Paris; and on November 20 the *Second Peace of Paris* was signed. The German Powers wished to recover Elsass and Lorraine; but they had to content themselves with the boundaries which existed before 1790, and which differed only slightly from those fixed by the First Peace. France undertook to pay an indemnity of 700 million francs, to be divided among the allies. She had also to restore the art treasures which Buonaparte had stolen.

**14. Changes of territory in Germany.**—Whilst the armies of the allies carried on the war, the Congress of Vienna had continued its sittings. The renewal of the struggle made all parties more moderate, so that the deliberations of the Congress were brought to an end in June. Besides her former *Italian* and *Illyrian* possessions, Austria received *Tyrol*, *Salzburg*, *Vorarlberg*, and the *Innviertel*. Prussia obtained all that she gave up in the Treaty of Tilsit, and the Grand Duchy of *Posen*, *Swedish Pomerania*, the northern part of *Saxony*, the Duchies of *Westphalia* and *Berg*, and the Rhine country between *Mainz* and *Aachen*. Bavaria kept *Ansbach* and *Baireuth*, and, in return for territory ceded to Austria, received *Würzburg* and *Aschaffenburg*, together with the *Upper Rhenish Palatinate*, thenceforth known as *Rhenish Bavaria*. Hanover also received some new lands, and, as Bavaria, Würtemberg, and Saxony had already been, was made a Kingdom. The remaining German States kept very much the same boundaries as those they had possessed during the time of the Rhenish Confederation.

15. **The German Confederation.**—The jealousies of Austria and Prussia, and the unwillingness of Bavaria and Würtemberg, did not permit that the Empire should be restored. The States of Germany, therefore, joined in a great *Confederation*. It was made up of thirty-nine States, taking in the free towns of *Lübeck, Hamburg, Bremen,* and *Frankfurt.* Each State was to remain independent in matters affecting itself alone, the object of the Confederation being merely the regulation of those affairs common to all German States equally. A permanent Diet, consisting of the plenipotentiaries of the States, was to hold its sittings in *Frankfurt-on-the-Main,* the representatives of Austria presiding. The members of the Confederation agreed never to declare war against each other, or to form alliances with foreign powers which should in any way be hurtful to a German State. All subjects of dispute between the various States were to be referred for settlement to the Diet. Each State was to contribute, according to its population, to the Confederate army, whose commanders the Diet were to appoint. The fortresses of *Luxemburg, Landau,* and *Mainz* were declared the property of the Confederation, and garrisoned by its troops. The act of Confederation decreed that constitutional government should be set up in each State, and that the members of all Christian sects should have equal civil and political rights.

16. **German Writers.**—Although Germany was humbled beyond all past experience in her struggle with Buonaparte, her intellectual life was never so rich or comprehensive as at this time. The divisions which split up Germany kept down everything noble in her national history for some time after the peace of Westphalia. In the end they were not altogether unfavourable to literature, for, as politics and

commerce did not afford the same outlet for the energies of the people as existed in free countries, above all in England, the higher class of minds turned aside and devoted themselves wholly to thought and study. In the latter part of the seventeenth and the beginning of the eighteenth century, *Gottfried Wilhelm Freiherr von Leibnitz* had a European reputation as one of the deepest and most original thinkers of his time. It was characteristic of the age that he did not write any of his many works in German. His philosophical system was further developed by *Christian Freiherr von Wolf.* By his "Kritik of Pure Reason," published in 1781, *Immanuel Kant* began a new epoch in philosophy. *Fichte* was also a distinguished philosopher; and *Schelling* and *Hegel* had already made themselves known as thinkers. Fichte was one of the noble band who not only roused the nation to resist the French, but themselves marched against the enemy. Hegel put the last touches to his first great work in his quiet home in Jena as the artillery of the contending armies in the battle of Jena was thundering outside. *Barthold Georg Niebuhr* was one of a number of writers who were at this time writing history according to a wholly new method. Among the scholars who had given a powerful impulse to learning were *Winckelmann* and *Heyne.* In the latter part of the seventeenth century, German poetry held a very low place. The so-called *Second Silesian School* had great fame; but it was altogether without genius. A number of court poets wrote chiefly under French influence. A freer style was brought in at the beginning of the eighteenth century by *Von Hagedow, Von Haller*, a Swiss poet, who was also a man of science and a philosopher, and *Gellert*, whose works were read by all classes. The first of the great classical poets of Germany was *Friedrich Gottlieb Klopstock*, who was far above his immediate predecessors in richness

of imagination and depth of feeling. His chief work is
"The Messiah." *Christoph Martin Wieland* also takes a
high place as a clear and versatile writer. He had the
special merit of arousing some interest in literature among
the higher classes of society. "Oberon," a poem, and
"Agathon" a prose romance, are usually thought the best
of his many writings. A far greater writer than either
Wieland or Klopstock was their contemporary, *Gotthold
Ephraim Lessing.* He was the founder of scientific criticism, and gave to German prose a terseness, clearness, and
strength it had never hitherto possessed. He was also
distinguished as a dramatic poet. Among his works may
be named "Laokoon," "Emilia Galotti," and "Nathan the
Wise." Another famous writer of this time was *Johann
Gottfried von Herder*, who was at once a poet, a critic, and
a philosopher. High above all these rose the illustrious
*Johann Wolfgang von Goethe.* He holds in German
literature the place held by *Shakespeare* in English, and
by *Dante* in Italian literature. Perhaps his greatest work
is "Faust." Specially remarkable for perfect finish of style
are "Torquato Tasso" and "Iphigenie." The poetry of
common life was never more finely brought out than in
"Hermann and Dorothea;" and Goethe's lyrics are probably the most beautiful of any written in modern times.
His chief prose work is "Wilhelm Meister." *Friedrich
von Schiller* is generally supposed to rank next to Goethe
in the list of German poets. He is perhaps even more
popular than Goethe, for it was he who first gave full
expression to the awakening national life of Germany. His
chief writings are dramatic; and of these the best are
"Wallenstein," "Maria Stuart," and "William Tell." His
"Song of the Bell" is the most famous of his shorter pieces.
*Jean Paul Friedrich Richter* wrote an extremely difficult
style; but he is one of the greatest of German humourists.

Of his many romances, "Titan," and "Flower, Fruit and Thorn Pieces," are usually considered among the best. Of the poets who roused the enthusiasm of the nation in the war of freedom, the best known were *Arndt* and *Körner*. The latter died fighting against the French.

17. **Music in Germany.**—Germany has long been distinguished as a music-loving nation. No other country has had so many composers of the highest rank. Of those whom she produced in the eighteenth century the most distinguished were *Sebastian Bach, Händel, Haydn,* and *Mozart.*

# CHAPTER XIX.

### REVOLUTIONARY MOVEMENTS.

*The demand for constitutional government (1)—the desire for unity; murder of Kotzebue; action of the Governments (2)—popular risings in 1830; riot in Frankfurt in 1833 (3)—Lewis I. of Bavaria; the Customs Union (4)—death of Francis I. of Austria; tyranny of King Ernst August of Hanover (5)—death of Frederick William III. of Prussia; high expectations raised by Frederick William IV.; he summons a United Diet (6)— religious movements in Prussia (7)—effect of the French Revolution of 1848 in the smaller States (8)—the Revolution in Austria and Prussia (9)—the Provisional Parliament in Frankfurt; recognised by the Diet; rebellion in Upper Baden (10)—the National Assembly in Frankfurt (11)—action of Christian VIII. of Denmark with regard to Schleswig-Holstein; Frederick VII. adopts the same course; a provisional Government set up in the Duchies; the Frankfurt Assembly supports them; war with Denmark; an armistice concluded by Prussia, and ratified, after some delay, by the Frankfurt Assembly; riot in Frankfurt, and attempted Revolution in Upper Baden (12)—the Prussian Assembly; a new Parliament summoned (13)—the Austrian Diet; Revolutions in Hungary and in Vienna; the Emperor Ferdinand abdicates, and is succeeded by Francis Joseph (14)— dissensions in the Frankfurt Assembly as to the relation of Austria to Germany; the Imperial title offered to the King of Prussia, and refused (15)—the National Assembly removes to Stuttgart, and is dispersed by the King of Würtemberg (16)— disturbances in Saxony, Rhenish Bavaria, and Baden (17)—*

*the Revolution in Hungary; ended by the surrender of Görgey* (18)
—*Constitutional Government set up in Prussia* (19)—*the German Union; Parliament of the Union in Erfurt; Austria tries to reconstitute the Confederation* (20)—*dispute between the Elector of Hessen Cassel and the Chambers; Austria and Prussia interfere; civil war avoided* (21)—*the Frankfurt Diet restored* (22)—*the war with Denmark; Prussia makes peace; defeat of the Schleswig-Holstein army* (23)—*treaty of Commerce between Prussia and Austria* (24).

1. **The demand for free government.**—The Act of Confederation promised that constitutional government should be set up in the various States of Germany. The people had made so many sacrifices in the great struggle with Buonáparte that those who disliked the old despotic system felt they had a right to insist that this promise should be kept. The princes, however, soon forgot what they owed to their subjects. Between 1815 and 1830 constitutions were granted by Sachsen-Weimar, Baden, Bavaria, Würtemberg, Hessen-Darmstadt, and other small States; but in reality very little change was made in the government of these countries. Frederick William III. of Prussia seemed at first inclined to yield to the demand for popular representation; but he contented himself with setting up a number of Provincial Diets. Prince *Metternich*, the ruling spirit of the Austrian Government, was a resolute enemy of the constitutional system.

2. **The desire for Unity.**—The feeling of national life, which had never been very strong after the Great Interregnum, and which almost died out during the Thirty Years' War, had for some time been growing up again. The famous deeds of Frederick the Great had made the people once more proud of the common German name; and this feeling had been strengthened by the war of freedom, and by the achievements of Germans in science,

literature, and art. There was now, therefore, a very general desire that Germany should cease to be a mere collection of States only nominally united. Few were quite satisfied with the Confederation. It left each State practically independent, and every one knew that in a short time it would lose any little power it had ever had. The general discontent showed itself most at the Universities. A large party among the professors and students constantly contrasted the disunion and weakness of Germany in their day with its power and fame when the Empire was at its highest in the Middle Ages; others, knowing that the old state of things could never be brought back, wished for some form of union more suited to the wants of their own time. The Governments of the various States for the most part disliked this movement in favour of unity. *Kotzebue*, a well-known writer of plays, ridiculed those who wasted time in what he thought idle dreams, and was so much disliked that at last, in 1819, a young student murdered him. The Governments believed, or pretended to believe, that this was the result of a widespread conspiracy, and resolved to take severe measures. A conference of ministers was held at Carlsbad to consider the whole matter. Many young men were thrown into prison; various professors—among them, *Arndt*, whose songs had done much to keep up the national enthusiasm in the late war—were deprived of their offices; and strict limits were put to the freedom of the press and the Universities. The Confederate Diet accepted the decisions of the Conference, and appointed a Commission to find out and punish revolutionists. The desire for unity, however, instead of being crushed, became stronger and stronger. The wish for free government also became more common. The great question that arose in many minds was whether the nation should try to obtain unity before freedom, or freedom before unity. All knew that if either were gained the other would soon follow.

3. **Popular risings in 1830. Riot at Frankfurt in 1833.**—The French Revolution in 1830 caused great commotion in Germany. In Prussia and Austria there was little disturbance of the peace; but in several of the smaller States there were popular risings. In *Brunswick* the palace of the Duke, who was greatly disliked, was burned to the ground; and he himself had some difficulty in escaping. His brother, who succeeded him, granted the required constitution. Constitutions more or less liberal were also conceded by the Governments of Saxony, Hessen-Cassel, Sachsen-Altenburg, and Hanover. On April 3, 1833, a riot took place at Frankfurt. A number of armed men, chiefly students and journalists, attacked the town guard, and freed a few political prisoners. They would also have dispersed the Diet; but they were themselves attacked and overcome by the troops. This paltry disturbance was made an excuse for still more harsh measures against the Universities and the press.

4. **Lewis I. of Bavaria. The Customs Union.**—The King of Bavaria at this time was *Lewis I.* He succeeded his father, *Maximilian*, in 1825. Lewis was a man of culture and artistic taste. He brought the University of *Landshut* to *Munich*, and spent large sums in extending and beautifying his capital. He was so liberal a patron of art that artists came from all parts of Germany to Munich. Soon after he became King he made a treaty with Würtemberg, regulating the customs of the two countries. This was the beginning of a movement of great importance to Germany. Prussia united with various North German States, and the Central States united among themselves, for the regulation of the customs. In 1828 the idea of a *Customs Union*, which should take in all German States,

was started; and it soon gained ground. As Prussia was evidently best fitted to form the centre for a movement of this kind, one Government after another concluded with it the necessary treaties. Thus was gradually formed the Customs Union, which was in the end joined by nearly all Germany. It removed many useless restrictions from commerce, and kept alive in the minds of the people the idea of that complete unity which many had so long wished in vain. It also added to the already great influence of Prussia in Germany.

5. **Death of Francis I. of Austria. King Ernst August of Hanover.**—On March 2, 1835, *Francis I.*, the first Emperor of Austria, died. He was succeeded by his son, the weak-minded *Ferdinand*, under whom the policy of Austria continued very much the same, Prince Metternich still taking the leading place in the Government. By the death of *William IV.* of *England*, in 1837, the Kingdom of Hanover passed to *Ernst August*, William's brother. The new King was harsh and violent. He withdrew the constitution granted in 1833, and set up in its place another far less free, which had been conceded at a former time. Seven distinguished professors of Göttingen—amongst them the brothers *Grimm*—who protested against this tyranny, were dismissed from their offices. A revolt which resulted among the students was not put down till some blood had been shed. .

6. **Death of Frederick William III. of Prussia. Frederick William IV.**—Frederick William III. of Prussia, who had seen so many changes of fortune, died on June 7, 1840. Great hopes were raised by his son and successor, *Frederick William IV.* This king began his reign by granting a pardon to all political prisoners, and spoke eloquently of the duties of a sovereign. At the ceremony which took place when the works for completing the cathedral of Köln

were begun, he uttered words full of promise for the future unity of Germany. The expectations formed as to the reign of Frederick William IV. were not fulfilled. He was well-meaning, and certainly did a good deal for his subjects. Under him Berlin became a great centre for German science and learning. But he had no strength of character, and shared far too much those extravagant notions of the authority of Kings which have always hitherto marked the Prussian royal family. His subjects urged him to grant a constitutional system of government, reminding him of the early promises of his father. At last, in 1847, when entreated from all sides, he summoned to Berlin a *United Diet*. This was not a Parliament, but a combination of the several Provincial Diets. It was opened on April 11. The King caused great dissatisfaction by declaring that nothing would induce him to concede a constitution, and thus to change the natural relation between a prince and his subjects.

7. **Religious movements in Prussia.**—Various religious movements took place in the early years of Frederick William's reign. A considerable number, roused at first by the protest of a priest named Ronge against a piece of gross superstition sanctioned by Bishop *Arnoldi* of *Trier*, left the Roman Catholic Church, and formed communities to which they gave the name of *German Catholic Communities*. The Protestant Church, which had been outwardly strengthened under Frederick William III. by the union of the Lutheran and Reformed Churches in 1817, was also deeply moved by the action of a party whose members called themselves the *Friends of Light*. Many of these left the Church, and formed *Free Communities*. Both these and the German Catholic Communities became centres for political agitation.

8. **Effect of the French Revolution of 1848 in the smaller States.**—The year 1848 is a memorable one in German

history. Dissatisfaction was deep and widespread. In all the leading States the people were urgently demanding freer forms of government, and the desire for the unity of Germany had become in many minds almost a passion. When the third French Revolution broke out, its influence was immediately felt in Germany. The popular movement this time was very different from any the Governments had hitherto had to contend with. The people were evidently in earnest, and resolved to obtain, at whatever cost, their chief demands. The princes of the smaller States were alarmed, and most of them, without loss of time, changed their Ministries, the new Ministry in each case frankly adopting a liberal policy. Lewis, King of Bavaria, had to resign his crown in favour of his son *Maximilian;* and the Grand Duke of Hessen Darmstadt associated his son with him in the government.

9. **The Revolution in Austria and Prussia.**—The Revolution was most serious in the two great German States, Prussia and Austria. In Vienna, a rising, headed by the students, was so successful, that on March 13, 1848, Prince Metternich was a fugitive on his way to England. After his departure the greatest confusion reigned in the capital. The revolutionary party everywhere gained the upper hand; and the Emperor was obliged to summon a Diet, to be elected by universal suffrage in all his hereditary lands. He no longer felt safe in Vienna, and went, with the Imperial household, to Innsbruck. In Berlin the Revolution was even more violent. Excited meetings were held; and on March 13 and the following days, there were sharp contests between the people and the soldiers. The King, who was not personally unpopular, hesitated for some time as to the course he should adopt, but on March 17 promised to set up constitutional government. The people were excited, and demanded that the troops should be sent

out of Berlin. On the 18th a crowd gathered before the palace to press the demand. Two shots were suddenly fired, from what quarter no one knew. A cry of treason was raised, and many took up arms. In the afternoon a fierce struggle began. The troops were attacked from behind barricades, and from the roofs and windows of houses. The contest went on till far in the night, and many were killed. Next day the King yielded the point in dispute. He declared that he placed himself "at the head of the movement," and Berlin was put under the protection of armed citizens. The Ministry was dismissed, and, after an electoral law had been passed by the United Diet, orders were issued for the election of a National Assembly.

10. **The Provisional Parliament in Frankfurt.**—Meanwhile, another great movement began elsewhere. It was generally hoped that union as well as freedom was now to be achieved by Germany; but, as Prussia and Austria were in too much disorder to do anything, about 500 Germans from the various States met at Frankfurt, and on March 21 constituted themselves a provisional Parliament. An extreme party wished the Assembly to declare itself permanent; but to this the majority would not agree. It was decided that a National Assembly should be elected forthwith by the German people. The Confederate Diet, knowing that the provisional Parliament was approved by the nation, recognized its authority. Through the Diet the various Governments were communicated with, and all of them agreed to make arrangements for the elections. The discontented party in the provisional Parliament, wishing to establish a Republic, called the people to arms in Upper Baden; but they were put down by the troops of various South German States.

11. **The National Assembly in Frankfurt.**—The National Assembly was opened in Frankfurt on May 18, 1848. It

elected the Archduke *John* of *Austria* as the head of a new provisional central Government. The choice was a happy one. The Archduke was at once acknowledged by the different Governments, and on July 12 the President of the Confederate Diet formally made over to him the authority which had hitherto belonged to the Diet. The Diet then ceased to exist. The Archduke chose from the Assembly seven members, who formed a responsible ministry. The Assembly was divided into two parties, the Right and the Left. These again were broken up into various sections. Much time was lost in useless discussions, and it was soon suspected that the Assembly would not in the end prove equal to the great task it had undertaken.

12. **War with Denmark.**—While the Assembly was sitting, German troops carried on a foreign war. The Duchy of Holstein was subject to the Danish King, but it had always been a part of Germany, and in virtue of it the Danish King was a member of the German Confederation. Schleswig, although a large part of the population was German, did not belong to Germany. The people of Holstein and the Germans of Schleswig, however, maintained that, in virtue of a treaty of 1460, the two Duchies could not be separated, and that, when the male line of the Danish royal family should die out, the connexion of both with Denmark would come to an end. In spite of this, *Christian VIII.*, King of Denmark, made a public declaration in 1846, that the Duchy of Schleswig and the greater part of Holstein must always remain a part of the Danish kingdom. The German party in the two Duchies was alarmed at this step, and the Holstein States appealed to the Confederate Diet. The latter passed a vague resolution, protecting the rights of the Duchies; but the King of Denmark replied that he did not intend to violate these rights. The matter remained in this unsatisfactory state till the death of Christian VIII.

in 1848. *Frederick VII.*, his son, declared himself strongly in favour of the Danish view of the case. The discontent of the German party increased, and a rising took place at the time of the general revolutionary movement throughout Germany. A provisional Government was set up in the Duchies. The King of Denmark sent troops to put down the rebellion; but the Frankfurt Assembly sided with the Duchies, and an army, under the Prussian General *Wrangel*, went to uphold their cause. The Danes were driven out of Schleswig, and compelled to take refuge in their ships. On the other hand, the Danish fleet blockaded the German ports, and did much harm to German trade. The nation never so deeply regretted the want of a navy. Several ships were bought in England and America; but it was soon felt that the war must be carried on under great disadvantages, and on August 27 an armistice for seven months was concluded at *Malmö*. As one of the terms of the armistice was that a temporary Government, made up of two Prussian and two Danish representatives, should take the place of the provisonal Government set up by the Duchies, the National Assembly, which had authorized Prussia to open negotiations with Denmark, at first refused to approve what had been done. Great excitement followed. The Ministry, which approved the armistice, resigned. As no other could be formed, and as all felt that without Prussia the war could not go on, the majority of the Assembly at last, on September 16, agreed to ratify the armistice. The minority, consisting of the extreme Republicans, disapproved of this step, and urged the people to rise against an Assembly which had betrayed the German cause. On the 18th barricades were raised in the streets of Frankfurt. The troops soon dispersed the rioters, but not till the mob had been guilty of a base deed. Two Prussian deputies, belonging to the Right, were recognized as they returned from a ride. Both were seized and murdered. From this time the various parties of the Assembly were greatly embittered, and the time which should have been spent in useful legislation was frittered away in paltry quarrels. A Revolution which was again attempted in Upper Baden had to be put down by force.

13. **The Prussian National Assembly.**—The Assembly which had been summoned to meet in Berlin was opened in that city on May 22, 1848. The Radical party resisted almost all proposals of the Government, and in this they were supported by large classes of the people, who tried to frighten the moderate members into submission by threats. At length, on November 9, the King adjourned the Assembly till the 27th, when it was told to meet in the town of *Brandenburg*, where it might carry on its deliberations in peace. The members of the Right and Centre obeyed; but the Left protested, and continued its sittings in Berlin. It even passed a resolution that Government had no right to levy taxes so long as the Assembly did not fulfil its functions in the capital. It was soon discovered that the Assembly could no more do anything in Brandenburg than in Berlin; and after a few sittings it was broken up. A new Parliament was summoned to meet on February 26, 1849, to consider a constitution, the draft of which the King caused to be published on December 5, 1848.

14. **The Austrian Diet. The Revolution in Hungary and in Vienna. Abdication of the Emperor Ferdinand. Francis Joseph.**—The Austrian Empire was in a state of great confusion. The Diet was opened on July 22 in Vienna, but it was almost powerless. The members, representing many different nationalities, had no common aim; it was with difficulty they could even understand each other. The Emperor came back from Innsbruck to Vienna on August 12; but he had little influence. Of all the dangers which

threatened the Empire, the Hungarian difficulty was the greatest. Headed by the well-known orator *Kossuth*, Hungary demanded complete independence. The Slavonic population joined the Imperial Government in resisting this demand, and *Jellachich*, Ban of *Croatia*, with his wild hordes, tried to quell the Revolution. The Hungarians devoted themselves with much enthusiasm to the national cause. Unfortunately Count *Lamberg*, the Imperial commissary in *Pesth*, was murdered. The Emperor could not forgive this outrage, and on October 6 caused orders to be issued for the instant march of a part of the Vienna garrison against the Magyars. A number of the soldiers, sympathizing with the Revolutionary party, refused to move; and they were supported by many citizens and students. A violent contest took place, in which the loyal troops were beaten. A number of people rushed into the war office, seized *Latour*, the Minister who had directed the troops to proceed against Hungary, and murdered him. The Emperor once more left the capital, and went to *Olmütz*. The Diet continued to sit; but it could do nothing. Vienna was in the hands of the Revolutionists, who proceeded with much activity to prepare against attack. Troops came to the help of the Emperor from all quarters, and on October 21 the city was surrounded. It was not taken till the 30th, and then after a great deal of bloodshed. When at last Vienna was held by the Imperialists, they disarmed the people, and shot those leaders of the Revolution who did not escape by flight. The Diet had already been adjourned, and summoned to meet in *Kremsier* on November 22. The Emperor Ferdinand, who was very delicate, feeling that in so stormy a time the duties of government ought to be undertaken by younger hands, abdicated on December 1, 1848, in favour of his nephew, *Francis Joseph*. The new Emperor was eighteen years of age.

15. **The relation of Austria to Germany. The Imperial title offered to the King of Prussia, and refused.**—A great deal of time was taken up in the Frankfurt Assembly with the discussion of the German land laws. When at last the constitution of the Confederation began to be seriously considered, it was felt that the Assembly was in a much less favourable position than at first, for the Governments had got over their chief difficulties, and were not inclined to adopt any very thorough changes. The chief question that arose was as to the future relation of Austria to Germany. Every one wished Austria proper to form part of Germany; but the Austrian Government insisted that the Empire as a whole should be admitted into the Confederation. A powerful party, therefore, headed by *Baron von Gagern*, president of the Assembly, urged that Austria should be altogether shut out from Germany. This was opposed not only by Austria and the Roman Catholic States which looked to Vienna for guidance, but by the so-called *Great German party*, and by the Democrats, who did not wish Prussia to become the leading German State. Von Gagern tried to win over the latter party by agreeing to universal suffrage and other democratic elements in the new constitution. At last, in March, 1849, the Austrian Government formally demanded that the Empire should form part of the Confederation. It also proposed that a Directory should be appointed, made up of seven persons, the Austrian representative to be permanent president; and that the Parliament elected by the people should be replaced by a States Assembly. Many who had before hesitated now joined Von Gagern's party. On March 27 a majority decided that a President should be appointed, in whose family the honour should be hereditary, and that he should have the title of "Emperor of the Germans." Next day it was resolved to offer the Imperial title to the King of Prussia.

On April 3, a deputation waited on Frederick William to communicate to him the will of the Assembly. His reply was anxiously awaited throughout Germany. He answered that he could not accept the title offered to him without the consent of the German princes, and that the constitution would not give him sufficient power to fulfil the duties of an Emperor.

16. **End of the National Assembly.**—Notwithstanding the disappointment caused by the refusal of the King of Prussia to become Emperor, the Assembly tried to induce the German States to accept the new constitution. Some Governments did so; but the more important States either hesitated or withheld their consent. Austria had already recalled her representatives from the Assembly. Her example was soon followed by Prussia, Hanover, and other States; and on May 20 many of the most distinguished members voluntarily resigned their seats. On May 30 the Assembly changed the place of meeting to Stuttgart. But it had now become contemptible; and on June 18 it was dispersed by the Würtemberg Government. Thus ended an Assembly, the opening of which had seemed to patriotic Germans like the dawning of a new day for their country.

17. **Disturbances in Saxony, Rhenish Bavaria, and Baden.**—Meanwhile there had been disturbances in various parts of Germany. The Saxon Diet, in which the democratic party was strong, had demanded that the Government should accept the Frankfurt constitution. Instead of doing so, the Government dissolved the Diet on May 3. This gave rise to so fierce a struggle between the citizens of Dresden and the troops that the King and his Ministers had to take refuge in the fortress of Königstein. The people made themselves masters of a large part of Dresden; and even when the Prussians came to the help of the Saxon troops order was not restored for several days. There were

still more violent insurrections in Rhenish Bavaria and Baden. Provisional Governments were formed in both these countries; and, like their brother of Saxony, the King of Bavaria and the Grand Duke of Baden had to appeal to Prussia for help. The Prussians soon subdued Rhenish Bavaria; but in Baden they had more difficulty, as the troops of that country almost all joined the Revolutionists. Several engagements took place, in each of which the Prussians were victorious. By the fall of *Rastatt*, on July 23, the struggle was brought to an end, and the Grand Duke, who had been obliged to fly, was able to return to Carlsruhe. The Prussians, however, did not return home for some time.

18. **The Revolution in Hungary.**—Before the close of 1848, the Government of the Emperor Francis Joseph had restored all the German provinces of Austria to order; and in the spring of 1849 the Italian provinces also had to submit. The rising in Hungary was more serious. The Austrian troops under Prince *Windischgratz* were defeated in a series of battles, and driven back with great loss. Buda-Pesth fell into the hands of the insurgents. Many Germans and Poles joined the Hungarians, whose army rose to the number of about 200,000 men. The most prominent generals were *Görgey*, and the Poles *Bem* and *Dembinsky*. The Diet, believing the country to be now perfectly secure, met in *Debreczin*, and formally declared Hungary independent of Austria. A provisional Government, with Kossuth at its head, was formed. The Imperial Government, unable to crush the Revolution, appealed to Russia for help. Russia, afraid that the rebellious spirit might spread into her own provinces, had already concentrated troops on her frontiers, and gladly agreed to help Austria. Towards the end of May, a Russian army entered Hungary. At the same time the Austrian army,

which had been greatly strengthened, invaded the country from the east, while a force, under Jellachich, attacked the Hungarians in the south. The Hungarians still fought bravely; but they could not long hold out against such overwhelming numbers. Buda-Pesth was reconquered by the Austrians, and the Diet was driven even from *Szegedin*, where it had taken refuge. On August 11, a council which Kossuth had summoned at *Arad* appointed Görgey dictator with unlimited power. Two days afterwards he surrendered with his army to the Russian general *Rödiger*. This step was quite unexpected; and Görgey was everywhere accused of treachery. His surrender brought the war to a close. The leaders of the Revolution fled across the Turkish frontier; and most of the fortresses which had not yet been taken at once capitulated. The civil population had suffered fearfully during the war; but what was hardest to bear was the crushing of those hopes which all had cherished, and which had seemed so nearly accomplished.

19. **Constitutional government set up in Prussia.**—The Prussian Parliament, which had been summoned to meet on February 26, 1849, was opened on that date. It consisted of two Chambers. No understanding with the Government could be arrived at, so that on April 27 a dissolution again took place. A Parliament chosen according to a new electoral law met on August 7; and this time the deliberations were more successful. Concessions were made on both sides, and on February 6, 1850, the King took an oath to maintain the new constitution. From that time Prussia must be regarded as, at least nominally, a constitutional State.

20. **The German Union. The Erfurt Parliament. Austria tries to reconstitute the Confederation.**— Meanwhile the King of Prussia had been trying to unite Germany on a new basis. At his invitation the representa-

tives of a number of States met in Berlin in May, 1849. Austria was at this time in the very heat of her great struggle with Hungary. Prussia seized the opportunity to propose that a Confederation of German States should be formed under her leadership, without Austria. On May 26, an alliance was concluded between Prussia, Hanover, and Saxony. This was afterwards called "The Alliance of the Three Kings." The new Confederation was joined by several of the smaller North German States. As the Confederation did not embrace all Germany, it was called "the German Union." A Parliament of the Union was summoned to meet in *Erfurt*, on April 20, 1850. Hanover and Saxony, not approving of this step, refused to send representatives; and the former State withdrew altogether from the alliance. Whilst the Erfurt Parliament sat, a Congress of the princes of the Union was opened in Berlin, on May 10. Austria had by this time begun to recover from the shock caused by the Hungarian Revolution. Alarmed by the attempt of Prussia to seize the place in Germany which she looked on as lawfully hers, and resolved to overturn the so-called Union, she had already, in conjunction with Bavaria and Würtemberg, called on all German States to send representatives to Frankfurt in order to reconstitute the Confederation. The summons was favourably responded to by Hanover, Saxony, the two Hessens, and various other minor States. On the very day on which the Congress of princes who accepted the leadership of Prussia met in Berlin, the representatives of Austria and of the States which grouped themselves around her assembled in Frankfurt. Germany was thus openly divided into two hostile factions.

21. **Civil War threatened.**—The prevailing bitterness of feeling was greatly increased by a miserable quarrel, which as nearly as possible plunged the country into a

civil war. The Elector of *Hessen Cassel*, with the help of his very unpopular minister *Hassenpflug*, tried to obtain supplies without giving the Chambers time to deliberate on the budget. When the Chambers protested, they were dissolved on September 2; and an order was issued for the levying of all taxes as usual. This caused so great a commotion that the Elector was obliged to leave Cassel. The Frankfurt Diet, to which he appealed, sided with him; and on November 1 Austrian and Bavarian troops entered his territory in order to enforce the Diet's decision. Prussia was prepared for this step; and on November 2 the towns of *Cassel* and *Fulda* were held by her army. There was a powerful peace party in Berlin; and its counsels so far prevailed that General *Radowitz*, the Minister of Foreign Affairs, had to resign his portfolio in favour of *Von Manteuffel*. But when Austria demanded that the Prussian troops should be withdrawn from Hessen-Cassel, the Prussian Government prepared for war. The question whether Prussia or Austria was to occupy the first place in Germany had been steadily becoming the leading question in German politics; it appeared as if the moment had now come for its decision. But as all saw the frightful evils which a civil war caused by such a question would bring upon the country, a last attempt was made to settle the present difficulty; and it was successful. Prince *Schwartzenberg*, the Austrian Minister, and *Von Manteuffel*, the Prussian representative, met at *Olmütz* on November 28. They agreed that "free conferences" of all German princes should be held forthwith in order to arrange the constitution of Germany; and that Prussia and Austria should together settle the affairs of Hessen-Cassel and those of Schleswig-Holstein.

22. **The Frankfurt Diet restored.**—The so-called "free conferences" were opened in Dresden on December 23.

They led to nothing. But Prussia herself began to feel that, however unsatisfactory it might be in some respects, the constitution of 1815 would be better than the present confusion. She therefore formally recognized the Diet which Austria had assembled at Frankfurt, and her example was followed by the other members of the Union. From June 12, 1851, the Diet continued to sit as it had done before 1848. So far as appearances went, the Revolution had effected no change in the affairs of Germany. But this was not really the case. It had brought into prominence the great question as to the relative position of Austria and Prussia in Germany; and it made obvious to those who could look beneath the surface in favour of which side that question must in the end be settled.

23. **The War with Denmark.**—On the expiry of the armistice of Malmö in March, 1849, the war with Denmark had begun again. The Germans were at first successful. Two Danish ships of war, the "Christian VIII." and the "Gefion," being unable to leave the harbour of *Eckernfjorde*, were so vigorously fired upon from the shore that the former was blown up and the latter surrendered. The *Düppel* entrenchments were stormed by the Bavarians and Saxons; and the Schleswig-Holstein corps, under the Prussian General *Bonin*, took *Kolding*, and pushed on to the fortress of *Fridericia*. Here, on July 5 and 6, the troops of Schleswig-Holstein suffered a decided defeat. On July 10 an armistice was signed, in which Schleswig was provisionally separated from Holstein. An understanding could not be arrived at; but, as Denmark was supported by the Great Powers, the circumstances of Germany made it impossible for her to carry on the war. On July 2, 1850, Prussia concluded peace; and the other German Governments were obliged to acquiesce. The people of Schleswig-Holstein refused to submit to the demands of Denmark, and

continued the war; but on July 25 their army was completely routed by the Danes at *Idstedt*, and compelled to return to the frontiers of Holstein. By the interference of Austrian troops, Prussia consenting, in 1851, peace was restored, the government of Schleswig-Holstein being resumed by the King of Denmark. By a protocol signed in London in 1852 by the Great Powers, the King of Denmark was guaranteed in his possession of the Duchies; and the succession for them as well as for the Danish kingdom was settled on the *Glücksburg* line. But neither the States of the Duchies nor the Diet accepted the London protocol, so that the settlement remained incomplete.

24. **Treaty of commerce between Prussia and Austria.**—In 1851 it appeared as if the Customs Union were about to fall to pieces, in which case the Southern States would have united themselves in commercial matters to Austria, and the Northern for the most part to Prussia. This difficulty was got over by a treaty of commerce concluded between Prussia and Austria on February 18, 1853.

# CHAPTER XX.

### RECENT EVENTS.

*The war of Austria with Sardinia and France; the partial union of Italy makes Germans desire the unity of Germany (1)—death of Frederick William IV. of Prussia; William I.; dispute of the Prussian Government with the House of Representatives as to the army; Von Bismarck made Prime Minister (2)—unsatisfactory relations of Austria and Prussia (3)—disputes with respect to Schleswig-Holstein (4)—Prussia and Austria make war on Denmark; Denmark gives up the Duchies (5)—the Duchies give rise to misunderstandings between Prussia and Austria; the Convention of Gastein (6)—further disputes between Prussia and Austria; the two Powers prepare for war; Prussia concludes an alliance with Italy (7)—Count Bismarck proposes to reconstitute the Confederation (8)—the Prussian people opposed to war; attempt of the neutral Powers to maintain peace (9)—outbreak of war (10)—real causes of the war; advantages of Prussia (11)—the Prussians overrun Hessen-Cassel, Saxony, and Hanover (12)—the Prussians cross the Bohemian frontier (13)—battle of Königgrätz (14)—Prussian successes (15)—the Peace of Prague; Austria shut out from Germany; secret alliance between Prussia and the South German States (16)—annexations to Prussian territory; King William and Parliament reconciled (17)—formation of the North German Confederation (18)—France shows jealousy of Prussia; attempts to buy Luxemburg; Prussia protests; war prevented by a Conference (19)—constitution of the Confederation; the Customs Parliament; obstacles to the full union of Germany (20)—Leopold, prince of Hohenzollern, becomes* a candidate for the Spanish crown; opposition of France; declaration of war against Germany (21)—the South German States remain true to Prussia; real causes of the war (22)—first victories of the Germans (23)—Further victories; battle of Sedan; surrender of Napoleon (24)—siege of Paris (25)—surrender of Strassburg and Metz; further French disasters (26)—The North German Confederation becomes a German Confederation; King William of Prussia is made Emperor in Germany (27)—Peace of Frankfurt (28)—feeling of the Germans as to the war (29)—constitution of the Empire (30)—variety of national life in Germany (31)—scientific and literary writers in Germany (32)—German artists (33).

1. **The Italian War of 1856. Effect of the partial union of Italy upon Germany.**—The years which followed the revolutionary period begun in 1848 were on the whole prosperous. Commerce flourished, and much was done to promote popular education. In 1859 a war broke out between *Austria* on the one hand, and *Sardinia* and *France* on the other. Austria tried to drag the Confederation into the struggle; and many of the smaller States would willingly have supported her. But Prussia, though she mobilized parts of her army, adhered to the principle that the Confederation had no right to enter upon any war which did not directly bear upon German interests. By this war Austria lost Lombardy. The partial union of Italy under *Victor Emmanuel* gave a fresh impulse in many German minds to the desire for unity. Those who wished the different States to be joined more closely were still divided into two parties. The *National Union* thought Prussia should be placed at the head of the Fatherland, the Austrian Empire being altogether shut out from Germany. The *Great German* party insisted that no arrangement could be satisfactory which did not include among the Confederate States Austria and the sister Duchies.

2. **King William I. of Prussia. Otto von Bismarck-Schönhausen.**—King Frederick William IV. of Prussia died on January 2, 1861. He was succeeded by his brother, *Frederick William Lewis*, who had already, since October 8, 1858, during the continued illness of the King, acted as *Prince Regent*. The new King ascended the throne as *William I*. He was crowned at Königsberg on October 18, 1861, with great pomp. He was an enthusiastic soldier, and had long wished to see the Prussian army reorganized. His efforts to achieve this end led to disputes between the Government and the Representative Assembly. The latter refused to sanction the expenditure necessary for the required additions to the standing army, and even demanded that the time for the military training of the male population should be reduced from three to two years. The deputies accurately represented the wish of the nation, as was proved by the result of two general elections in 1862 and 1863. On October 8, 1862, the King appointed *Otto von Bismarck-Schönhausen* prime minister and minister of foreign affairs. Bismarck first appeared in public life as a member of the Prussian United Diet in 1847. In 1851 he was made Prussian representative at the Frankfurt Diet. There he carefully studied the Austrian policy, and maintained firmly the rights of his country in the direction of German affairs. He was afterwards Prussian ambassador at the courts of St. Petersburg and Paris. In his new position Bismarck displayed great energy of character, with tendencies as despotic as possible, and an utter indifference to public opinion. With his aid, and in direct violation of the constitution, the King carried out his scheme of army reform.

3. **Relations of Austria and Prussia.**—Meanwhile the relations of Prussia to Austria and the German Confederation were not satisfactory. Bismarck openly declared

in the Prussian Parliament that the German problem could be solved only by "blood and iron." In August, 1863, the Emperor Francis Joseph surprised Germany by summoning a Congress of princes to Frankfurt, with the view of forming a new German constitution. The scheme failed, on account of the refusal of Prussia to have anything to do with it. Prussia herself proposed that a Representative Assembly should work side by side with the Frankfurt Diet; but Austria would not listen to this suggestion.

4. **The Schleswig-Holstein question.**—The jealousies of the two rival States boded no good to Germany; but for a time they were forgotten in a question of absorbing interest to the whole country. On March 30, 1863, *Frederick VII.* of Denmark raised anew the old subject of dispute, by issuing a decree that Schleswig should be separated from Holstein and Lauenburg, and fully incorporated with Denmark. This was contrary to the fundamental law of the Duchies of 1460, and excited deep indignation throughout Germany. On October 1 the Confederate Diet resolved on federal execution against the King of Denmark; but, before it could be carried out, he unexpectedly died on November 16, 1863. His successor, *Christian IX.*, confirmed the decree of March 30. On the other hand, with the death of Frederick VII. the male line of the Danish royal family had died out; and it was maintained in Germany that Christian IX. had no right whatever to the Duchies of Holstein and Lauenburg. It was further maintained that these Duchies were inseparable from Schleswig and that all three, therefore, must now pass to the nearest heir. The nearest heir was the Duke of *Augustenburg;* but in 1852 he had formally resigned his right to the Duchies. His son Frederick, however, had in 1859 protested against this step; and he now, with the assent of the Duke, come forward and asserted his claims. Other

German princes put forth claims to the Duchy of Lauenburg.

**5. Prussia and Austria make war on Denmark. Denmark gives up the Duchies.**—The Confederate Diet had not signed the London protocol, and was therefore at liberty to declare the Duchies vacant. On December 8, 1863, it resolved that they should be occupied by Confederate troops till the question of inheritance should be settled. Shortly afterwards an army of 12,000 men, consisting of Saxons and Hanoverians, entered Holstein. Meanwhile Austria and Prussia were unable to agree with the Diet as to the policy which ought to be pursued towards Schleswig, and announced their intention to carry on the war with Denmark as independent Powers, altogether apart from the Confederation. This decision met with great opposition from the German people. Both in Prussia and Austria the Chambers refused to grant supplies for the purpose of carrying on a war which was the affair of the Confederation alone. Nevertheless the two Governments persisted in their determination. The Austrian army was placed under General *von Gablenz;* that of Prussia was commanded by Prince *Frederick Charles*, King William's nephew; while over both, as commander-in-chief, was the aged Field Marshal *Wrangel.* On February 1, 1864, the united armies crossed the Eider, and attacked the *Danewirk*, which the Danes deserted on the morning of February 6, falling back behind the strong *Düppel* entrenchments. After a siege which lasted three week, these were at last stormed with great bravery by the Prussian troops on April 18. The fortress of *Fridericia*, which was besieged by the Austrians, was soon afterwards unexpectedly deserted by the Danes. An armistice till June 26 was then concluded; and attempts were made, at a Conference held in London, to bring about peace. But the Danes refused to concede anything, and on the expiry of the armistice the war was resumed. It was obvious, however, that Denmark, unsupported by any of the Great Powers, could not long continue a war against Austria and Prussia. Discouraged by several fresh reverses, she made proposals for peace ; and, on October 30, 1864, a treaty was signed, by which the King of Denmark resigned all his rights in the Duchies of Schleswig, Holstein, and Lauenburg, in favour of the Emperor of Austria and the King of Prussia.

6. **Disputes between Austria and Prussia. The Convention of Gastein.**—The two Powers compelled the troops of the Confederation to withdraw from Holstein, and placed the Duchies in the meantime under civil commissioners appointed by both Governments. It soon became plain that their interests with respect to the Duchies violently conflicted. Prussia, guided by Bismarck, evidently wished in the end to annex the Duchies to her own territory. Austria desired no increase of territory from the Duchies ; but she was resolved that Prussia should obtain none, and favoured the claims of the Prince of Augustenburg, whose pretensions were of course decidedly opposed by Prussia. The dispute between the two Powers ran so high that in the summer of 1865 an interruption of their good relations, if not the outbreak of war, appeared almost unavoidable. The evil day was put off for a time by the *Gastein Convention*, a treaty concluded on August 14 by Count von Blome, the Austrian plenipotentiary, and the Prussian Minister, Bismarck ; and signed a few days afterwards by the Emperor Francis Joseph and King William. By this treaty the Austrian Emperor, in return for a money compensation, resigned all his rights in the Duchy of Lauenburg in favour of the King of Prussia ; and it was decided that, till the question of inheritance should be settled, Schleswig should be placed under Prussian, and Holstein under Austrian

administration. The port of *Kiel* was in the meantime to be occupied by Prussia, though open to the fleets of both Powers.

7. **Further disputes between Prussia and Austria. Preparations for War. Alliance between Prussia and Italy.**—The Prussians took possession of the Duchy of Lauenburg on September 1. At the same time, the Government which had been set up by the two Powers in common was dissolved; and General von Gablenz entered Kiel as the Austrian viceroy in Holstein, while Herr von Manteuffel began his duties in Flensburg as Prussian representative in Schleswig. But the difficulties between the two rival Powers were not lessened by this arrangement. It would not have suited the designs of the Prussian Government if they had been. Whether or not Herr (now Count) von Bismarck, in inducing Austria to join Prussia in carrying on the Danish war apart from the Confederation, had foreseen the difficulties likely to arise on the conclusion of peace, and resolved to bring to an issue the question as to the position to be held in future in Germany by Prussia and Austria; there can be no doubt he had now made up his mind to involve the two Powers in a great and decisive struggle. An occasion of quarrel soon arose. Herr von Manteuffel strictly forbade all agitation in Schleswig in favour of Prince Augustenburg. On the other hand, Austria, which was no more willing now than formerly that the Duchies should come into the possession of Prussia, allowed the Prince's friends to promote his cause in Holstein as much as they chose. On January 26, 1866, Count Bismarck addressed a formal protest to the Austrian Government against its policy in Holstein. The Austrian Minister, Count Mensdorff, replied, on February 7, by asserting that the Austrian policy must be maintained. It was now very evident that war could not long be deferred. The fortresses in the Saxon and Silesian provinces of Prussia were put in

a state of readiness, while Austria gave orders for the concentration of troops in Bohemia. The minor States also began to arm. In March, Prussia greatly strengthened her position by entering into an alliance with Italy, in consequence of which the latter Power agreed to join Prussia in declaring war against Austria, while Prussia undertook not to conclude the war until the province of Venice had been conquered.

8. **Count Bismarck proposes to reconstitute the Confederation.**—In the midst of these preparations, and while Austria was doing her utmost to excite the Confederation against Prussia, Count Bismarck came forward with a proposal for the reconstitution of the Confederation. His plan was that North Germany should, in military matters, become subject to Prussia, while Austria and Bavaria took the lead in South Germany. At the same time he proposed that there should be a Representative Assembly elected by the whole German people. The scheme came to nothing; but by the latter suggestion Bismarck conciliated many Liberals.

9. **Attempts to avert war.**—The war which every day seemed to render more certain was far from being popular in Prussia. It was regarded as "a war of brothers;" and many petitions were addressed to the King urging him even at the last moment to preserve peace. But the Prussian Government was not lightly to be turned from its purpose. In the beginning of May orders were issued for the mobilization of the entire army. Austria, on her side, brought up troops from all parts of the Empire, and concentrated them in Bohemia and Moravia. For a moment there were hopes that the storm might even yet be turned aside, for the neutral Powers proposed that a Conference should be called in order to settle the questions which threatened the peace of Europe. But the proposal fell to the ground through the

obstinacy of Austria. Nothing then remained but the conflict for which all Germany was prepared.

10. **Outbreak of war.**—The first open act of hostility took place in the Duchies which had nominally given rise to the dispute. On June 7, Herr von Manteuffel, the governor of Schleswig, entered Holstein, and compelled General von Gablenz to withdraw with his troops from the Duchy. Austria was indignant at this insult, and urged that it was the duty of the Confederation to resist with all its forces a Power which had thus violated an essential principle of the Confederate constitution. Most of the minor States supported Austria, and on June 14 it was decided to mobilize the army of the Confederation, exclusive of the Prussian contingent. The Prussian plenipotentiary in the Diet, by command of his Government, at once declared that Prussia no longer recognized the Diet as existing, and, having announced the scheme of a new constitution by which Austria was excluded from Germany, withdrew from the Assembly.

11. **Real causes of the war.**—It cannot be too carefully remembered that the war now about to begin, and which proved one of the most rapid and decisive in history, had in reality very little to do with the petty question with which it was nominally associated. The dispute with respect to the Duchies was the occasion, it was not the cause, of the war. The causes which really led to it had been in operation at least since the time of Frederick the Great. For centuries Austria had led Germany. From the moment when Prussia became strong enough to be regarded as a rival of Austria, a struggle to settle the question as to which Power was permanently to guide the destinies of the Fatherland became inevitable. As we have seen, this question acquired great prominence during the brief revolutionary period of 1848-49. The time for

settling it had now come. Those who wished Germany to become great and progressive, even if they could not approve of the violence with which Bismarck had hurried on the war, could not but desire that Prussia should be successful. No one acquainted with the condition of the two States doubted on which side victory would declare itself. Prussia was comparatively small; but her population was very loyal, and united by a greater number of common aims than that of Austria; and her army was perhaps the most intelligent and highly organized in Europe. The needle-gun also gave the Prussian troops a great advantage over those of Austria. The Prussian plan of campaign was drawn up by *Von Moltke*, the chief of the General Staff, and one of the greatest and most scientific generals of the present century.

12. **Hessen-Cassel, Saxony, and Hanover overrun by the Prussians.**—Of the smaller North German States, Saxony, Hanover, Hessen-Cassel, and Nassau had declared for Austria. On June 16 General *von Beyer* entered Hessen-Cassel, and without opposition seized the capital, the Elector himself being taken prisoner. On the same day Prince *Frederick Charles* and General *Herwarth von Bittenfeld* crossed the Saxon frontier, and in a few days made themselves masters of the whole of Saxony, with the unimportant exception of the fortress of Königstein. The Saxon troops, accompanied by the King, and commanded by the Crown Prince, had gone to join the Austrians in Bohemia. Meanwhile, General *von Manteuffel* had with his troops left Holstein, and joined General *von Falkenstein* near *Harburg* in Hanover. King *George* hastily left his capital, and placed himself at the head of his army near *Göttingen*. He wished to join the Bavarians; but as Hessen-Cassel was in possession of the Prussians, and as by marching to the south-east he would have to fight his way through Prussian

troops and the army of *Coburg-Gotha*, this was no easy task. The Prussian lines were drawn gradually closer and closer around the Hanoverians. On June 27 a body of Prussians were defeated at *Langensalza*. But this success was of no real service to King George. He was surrounded on all sides; and the help which he expected from the Bavarians did not come. On June 29 he capitulated with his whole army.

13. **The Prussians cross the Bohemian frontier.**—The northern army of Austria—so called to distinguish it from the army which carried on the war against Italy—occupied the country from the east of Austrian Silesia westwards to the neighbourhood of Prague. It was commanded by Field-Marshal *Benedek*, and numbered, taking in the Saxon army, about 280,000 men. The Prussian forces were divided into three armies. The first, made up of about 100,000 men, was stationed, under Prince Frederick Charles, in Lower Silesia. The Crown Prince commanded the second, which numbered about 116,000 men, and occupied Upper Silesia. The third, amounting to about 40,000 men, acted as the right wing of the first. It was under General von Bittenfeld, and was in possession of Saxony. When the way had been cleared by the occupation of Saxony, the three armies were ordered to cross the Bohemian frontier, and to unite near *Gitschin*. This was done in the course of a few days. Prince Frederick Charles won an important victory near *Gitschin*; and the left wing of the Crown Prince's army, under General *von Steinmetz*, defeated the Austrians at *Nachod* and *Skalitz*.

14. **Battle of Königgrätz.**—The united army was joined on July 2 by King William, who assumed the supreme command. Next day the great battle of *Königgrätz* was fought. Benedek had taken up a good position, protected in front by the *Elbe* and the *Bistritz*, on the right by the fortress of

*Josephstadt*, and on the left by that of *Königgrätz*. His head-quarters were on the heights overlooking the village of *Sadowa*. The battle began about seven o'clock in the morning. Prince Frederick Charles hoped to be supported by the Crown Prince; but the army of the latter was stationed at some distance, and as rain had fallen heavily during the night, was hindered in its march by the state of the roads. The battle raged with great fury for some hours. Many glances were cast in the direction from which the Crown Prince was expected. At length his troops were seen in the distance; and early in the afternoon his army was in the heat of the battle. The Austrians could not long resist the enemy thus reinforced. The Crown Prince broke through their right wing, General von Bittenfeld through their left; and the centre retreated before Prince Frederick Charles. The retreat of the Austrians was at first orderly; but, as they were vigorously pursued, their ranks were broken, and each saved himself by flight or as he best could. In this great battle, one of the most important in modern history, the Prussians lost about 10,000 men; but the Austrians lost about 20,000, besides 18,000 prisoners.

15. **Prussian successes.**—After the battle of Königgrätz the Prussian arms were everywhere successful. On July 15 another victory was gained at *Tobitschau*, to the south of *Olmütz*. The Austrian army escaped into Hungary, pursued by Prince Frederick Charles; while the second and third Prussian armies pushed on towards Vienna. In central Germany the success of the Prussians was equally decided. Setting out from *Eisenach* on July 1, and marching towards the Main, General von Falkenstein drove the Confederate troops before him, and triumphantly entered Frankfurt on July 16. Two days before, the remnant of the Confederate Diet, feeling Frankfurt unsafe, had taken refuge in Augsburg. General von Falkenstein was ap-

pointed Governor-General of Bohemia; but his successor, General von Manteuffel, conducted the campaign with equal skill and energy.

16. **The Peace of Prague.**—Austria, feeling that the struggle had been practically decided at Königgrätz, had for some time been trying to obtain an armistice. The negotiations were at first unsuccessful; but on July 26 the preliminaries of peace were agreed upon between the two countries, and the smaller States also hastened to come to terms. The *Peace of Prague* was signed on August 23. By this treaty Austria was for ever excluded from Germany. She undertook to pay forty millons of thalers as an indemnity for the expenses of the war, in return for half of which sum she resigned all her rights in Schleswig-Holstein in favour of Prussia. Peace was also concluded with Bavaria, Würtemberg, and Baden before the end of August; with Hessen-Darmstadt in September; and with Saxony in October. Bavaria had to cede certain small strips of territory; and Hessen-Darmstadt, besides giving up the Landgraviate of *Hessen-Homburg*, had to yield the right of garrisoning Mainz. But, what was far more important, the two latter countries, together with Würtemberg and Baden, entered into a secret alliance with Prussia for the defence of Germany, by which they engaged to give the Prussian King the supreme command of their troops in time of war.

17. **Annexations to Prussian territory. King William and Parliament.**—Meanwhile, Prussia had annexed to her own territory *Hanover, Hessen-Cassel, Nassau,* and *Frankfurt.* King William returned to Berlin, amid the enthusiasm of his subjects, on August 4. The newly-elected House of Representatives, dazzled by the successes of the army, willingly forgave the Government for the unconstitutional acts by which it had carried out its scheme of

military reform; and a reconciliation took place which nothing has since seriously disturbed.

18. **The North German Confederation.**—The South German States remained independent; but all States to the north of the Main, including the northern half of Hessen-Darmstadt, united to form a North German Confederation under the leadership of Prussia, the whole military system of the Confederation being placed under the control of that country. On February 24, 1867, the first Diet of the Confederation met at Berlin, and began its deliberations on the constitution.

19. **France and Prussia.**—Germany had scarcely emerged from its great national struggle when it was threatened by a new danger. France had been violently excited by the Prussian successes. Even before the preliminaries of peace were settled, she gave Prussia to understand that she would have to be "compensated" for the political changes to which these successes must give rise; and early in August, 1866, the French ambassador at Berlin formally demanded the cession of the left bank of the Rhine. But Prussia was firm, and even at the risk of a second war refused to yield to this demand. The Emperor Napoleon, anxious not to be wholly baffled, entered into negotiations with the King of Holland for the purchase of *Luxemburg*, which had formerly belonged to the German Confederation. Prussia protested; and for a time the quarrel seemed likely to end in war. While the dispute was going on, Count Bismarck suddenly surprised Europe by the publication, in March, 1867, of the secret treaty between Prussia and the South German States. The danger was warded off for a time by a Conference held in London, through which Luxemburg was definitely separated from Germany, and formed into a neutral State, its neutrality being guaranteed by the Great Powers.

20. **Constitution of the Confederation. Customs Parliament. Obstacles to full union.**—The constitution of the North German Confederation was quickly settled, and came into force on July 1, 1867. The affairs of the Confederation were to be regulated by a Diet elected by the North German people, and by a Federal Council made up of the representatives of the North German Governments. The King of Prussia was to be president of the Confederation. Although this constitution was a great advance on the old state of things, none looked on it as final. A great party— the so-called *National-Liberal* party—had already been formed, whose leading aim was the union of South Germany with the Confederation. This party warmly supported Count Bismarck both in the Confederate Diet and in the Prussian Parliament. A Customs Parliament, elected by the whole of Germany, met in Berlin in May, 1868; and Baden and Hessen-Darmstadt signed a convention by which their military system was placed upon the same footing as that of the Confederation. Baden would willingly have become a member of the Confederation; but the other South German States were opposed to union. In Würtemberg the Democratic party, in Bavaria the so-called Ultramontane party, were the chief foes of the National Liberals. The Democrats hated Prussia for its despotic tendencies, the Ultramontanes for its Protestantism. The opposition of these parties was so bitter that it seemed very doubtful whether the complete union of Germany could be achieved during the present generation. Suddenly an event happened by which, amid the applause of the whole Fatherland, the long wished-for goal was reached.

21. **France declares war against Prussia.**—Early in July, 1870, *Leopold*, the hereditary Prince of *Hohenzollern*, at the request of the Spanish Government, and with the permis-

sion of King William of Prussia as head of the Hohenzollern family, became a candidate for the Spanish throne. The Emperor Napoleon, who had never heartily accepted the reconstitution of Germany, and who was anxious for an opportunity to establish his waning popularity in France, resolved to make Leopold's candidature the pretext for a war with Germany. A cry was raised in the French Legislative Assembly that a foreign Power was about to place one of its princes on the throne of Charles V. A section of the French people took up the cry, and called loudly for the submission of Germany to the wish of France. To take away all cause of dispute, the Prince of Hohenzollern formally resigned his candidature on July 12. Not content with this triumph, Napoleon insisted that the King of Prussia should give an assurance to France that the candidature of the Prince of Hohenzollern would not be renewed. M. Benedetti, the French ambassador, came on the 13th to *Ems*, where the King was staying, and on a public promenade urged this demand. King William not only refused to grant it, but declined to listen further to M. Benedetti on the subject. An official telegram from Ems informed the German Governments of this fact next day. War had now become certain; and the King hurried towards Berlin. On the 15th he was met at the Brandenburg station by the Crown Prince, Counts von Bismarck, von Moltke, and von Roon, and informed of what had taken place that day in the French Legislative Assembly. All that was now wanting was the formal declaration of war. While still in Brandenburg, therefore, the King of Prussia gave orders for the mobilization of the North German army. Next day the Federal Council met, and expressed its hearty concurrence with the views of the Government; and on the 19th the Confederate Diet was opened by the King with a speech of great dignity and moderation. On the same day, the

French declaration of war was received and communicated to the Assembly.

**22. The South German States remain true to Prussia. Real causes of the War.**—Napoleon, misinformed as to the real state of Germany, had hoped that the South Germans, if they did not actually join France, would at least remain neutral. But, though in Bavaria and Würtemberg there were strong parties in favour of such a course, they were true to their engagements. On the 16th the King of Bavaria and the Grand Duke of Baden ordered the mobilization of their troops; and next day the King of Würtemberg followed their example. On the 20th the South German princes formally announced to the King of Prussia that their forces were at his disposal; and the Prussian Crown Prince at once left Berlin to take the command of the united army. Throughout all Germany the prospect of the war excited much enthusiasm. It must not be supposed that the miserable Hohenzollern dispute had really anything to do with the war. It was of even less importance than the Schleswig-Holstein quarrel had been in the Austro-Prussian war. In a few days the world almost forgot that the Prince of Hohenzollern had been a candidate for the Spanish throne. What France was really about to fight for was the maintenance of her supposed supremacy in Europe. Germany had taken up arms in her own defence, and perhaps she was not unwilling to engage in a struggle by which she might thoroughly humble a Power that had for centuries lost no opportunity of adding to her divisions, robbing her of her territory, and depriving her of her just place among the nations.

**23. First victories of the Germans.**—The German army, including the forces both of North and South Germany, numbered more than a million men. This vast force was under the supreme command of the King of Prussia, whose chief adviser was again General von Moltke, head of the General Staff. It was divided into three armies, some part of each of which remained behind for the protection of the country. The first, under General *von Steinmetz*, was placed near *Trier* as the right wing; the second, under Prince *Frederick Charles*, assembled in *Rhenish Bavaria;* the third, consisting of the South German army and of three Prussian corps, and commanded by the Prussian *Crown Prince*, occupied the right bank of the Rhine from *Mannheim* to *Rastatt*. By the end of July these three armies were ready for action, and some skirmishing took place. But real fighting did not begin till next month. On August 4 the third army began its march towards the Lauter, and the first battle was fought at *Weissenburg*. The French were defeated, and the whole of the third army encamped on French soil. On the 6th a great victory was won by the same army at *Wörth* over Marshal *MacMahon*. The loss on both sides was heavy; but the defeat of the French was complete. They fled in such wild disorder that MacMahon's corps was for some time hopelessly scattered. The Crown Prince at once began his march across the Vosges mountains, leaving the Baden division to besiege Strassburg. On the day of the battle of Wörth a part of the first and second armies gained a brilliant victory near *Saarbrücken*. The bravery with which the heights of *Spicheren* were stormed has rarely been equalled. After this battle the whole German army entered France.

24. **Further victories. Battle of Sedan. Surrender of Napoleon.**—The three German armies now pressed on towards the Moselle. The scene of the great battles which were next fought, and which rapidly followed one another, was the country immediately in front of *Metz*. Marshal *Bazaine*, who had now assumed the supreme command of the French army, and who apparently wished to join Mac-

Mahon, began his march from Metz on the 14th; but he was attacked by a portion of the first German army at *Courcelles*, and driven back. Next day he again set out towards *Verdun*. On the 16th the battle of *Mars-la-Tour* or *Vionville* was fought. It continued from morning till night, and portions both of the first and second armies took part in it. The result was unfavourable to the French; but on the 18th they were still more decidedly defeated at *Gravelotte*, and obliged to take refuge in Metz. That fortress was instantly surrounded by the first and second armies, the supreme command of both of which was given to Prince Frederick Charles. The Prussian Crown Prince had awaited at *Nancy* the issue of the battles before Metz. His orders now were to proceed against Marshal Mac-Mahon, who had reorganised and greatly strengthened his army at Châlons. To aid the Crown Prince in this difficult undertaking, a fourth army was formed from corps which had hitherto belonged to the second army. It was in the end placed under the Crown Prince of Saxony, and called the army of the Maes. The King of Prussia himself assumed the supreme command of the armies of the two Crown Princes. Both were in full march westwards, and the Prussian Crown Prince had fixed his head-quarters at *Ligny*, when the news came that Marshal MacMahon had left Châlons. It was soon discovered that he had been in *Rheims*, and was marching towards *Rethel*. It was therefore concluded that he was making for Metz, with the intention of operating with Marshal Bazaine against Prince Frederick Charles. The Germans at once turned to the right, and marched in pursuit of the enemy. MacMahon had concentrated his troops near *Vouziers*. On August 28 he advanced towards the Maes in the direction of *Beaumont*. Two days afterwards an important battle was fought near the latter place, the result of which was that the

French were driven towards *Sedan*, while the road leading to Metz was occupied by the Germans. MacMahon's great scheme was thus already baffled. The decisive battle of the campaign was fought on September 1. After severe fighting the French were driven from all sides into Sedan, which the Germans surrounded, and into which they were prepared to pour a destructive fire. Nothing remained for the French but to surrender. The Emperor Napoleon, who had for some time freely exposed himself on the battle-field, yielded his sword to King William; and next day the two monarchs had an interview. The conditions of the capitulation were agreed upon by Count von Moltke and General Wimpffen, the latter having assumed the command of the French early on the previous day, when Marshal MacMahon was disabled by a severe wound. All the troops in Sedan, amounting to 84,000 men, together with 50 generals and 5,000 other officers, yielded themselves prisoners of war, while the entire war material of the army became the property of the Germans. Those officers who passed their word of honour to take no future part in the war were set free. The Emperor Napoleon received as his residence the Castle of *Wilhelmshöhe*, near *Cassel*.

25. **Paris besieged.**—The tidings of the French Emperor's surrender caused much excitement in Germany. Many hoped that the war would now cease; but this hope was soon shown to be groundless. The German people had made up their minds that the cession of *Elsass* and German *Lorraine* should be a condition of peace. The French Government of the National Defence, which displaced the Empire, at once declared that France would give Germany any sum of money, but would not yield an inch of its territory or a stone of its fortresses. Germany, therefore, all but unanimously approved of the continuance of the war. Almost immediately after the battle of Sedan, the armies

of the two Crown Princes began their march towards Paris. On September 5 King William entered Rheims, and in a fortnight afterwards the Germans were before Paris, the third army occupying the country to the south and south-east, the army of the Maes that to the north and north-east. The Prussian Crown Prince fixed his head quarters in Versailles, where those of King William were also placed on October 5. Meanwhile two distinct efforts to break through the German lines had been made, one by General *Ducrot* on September 19, another by General *Vinoy* on September 30; but both times the French were driven back. On October 13 and October 21 similar attempts were made, but with a like result. The French were somewhat more successful on October 28, when they took possession of the village of Le Bourget, and began to mass troops there. Two days afterwards, after a brave defence, they had to retreat.

26. **Surrender of Metz. Further French disasters.—** Meanwhile, a new French army, called the army of the Loire, had been raised and had begun to operate with a view to the relief of Paris; and General *Faidherbe* had also formed an army in the north. But fresh disasters had befallen France. Strassburg had surrendered on September 27; and on October 27 Marshal Bazaine, after having several times tried to escape from Metz, capitulated with his whole army, which consisted of 173,000 men, with 3 marshals and 6000 officers. Metz itself was surrendered to the Germans. The troops which had so long surrounded Metz were then free to prosecute the war which had anew broken out on the field. The first army was placed under General von Manteuffel, and, with the exception of the troops left behind for the occupation of Metz and Lorraine, proceeded in a north-west direction, against Faidherbe. The greater part of the second army marched towards the

south, where Prince Frederick Charles was to assume the supreme command. On October 12 General *von der Tann* had taken possession of *Orleans;* but on November 8, his troops being enormously outnumbered by the army of the Loire, he retreated. Next day he was hotly attacked, and on the 10th fell back upon *Tours*. He was joined by the Grand Duke of Mecklenburg, who was sent with troops from Paris to hold the French in check until the second army should come up. The Grand Duke gained some advantages before the arrival of Prince Frederick Charles; but when the latter appeared, the army of the Loire, which had begun its march towards Paris, was driven back at all points, and on December 4, after severe fighting, Orleans was once more occupied by the Germans. The army of the Loire was then broken up into two great divisions, one under General *Chanzy*, the other commanded by General *Bourbaki*. The former army was repeatedly defeated, and at length altogether scattered, by Prince Frederick Charles; the latter marched towards the east, with a view to effect a diversion by the invasion of South Germany. In the north Faidherbe displayed great energy; but he was twice defeated in the neighbourhood of *Amiens;* he was overcome also at *Bapaume* and *St. Quentin*. A new German army, called the south army, was formed to oppose Bourbaki in the east, and placed under General von Manteuffel, who was succeeded in the north by General von Goeben. For a moment South Germany appeared in real danger from the advance of Bourbaki, for although he was pursued by General von Manteuffel, the latter was far in the rear. The danger was averted by the courage of General *von Werder*, who, with the Baden division, had for some time been holding Generals *Cambriel* and *Garibaldi* in check, and who now resolved, at whatever cost, to prevent the further advance of Bourbaki's army. For three days Bourbaki strove, with his large army, at *Hericourt*, to drive back Werder's small force; but the Baden troops fought with such bravery that the French, on January 17, 1871, were themselves obliged to retreat in disorder. Bourbaki was displaced by General *Clinchant;* but the latter succeeded no better. Harassed on every side by General von Manteuffel, Clinchant crossed the Swiss frontier with his whole army, consisting of 84,000 men, on February 1.

27. **Union of Germany. King William declared Emperor.**—During the progress of the war the South Germans, proud of the common German name, began to feel how small are the points of difference between themselves and their northern kinsfolk compared with those great interests by which all Germans are united. This feeling gave rise to a desire for a closer union with the Northern Confederation; and in the middle of October, 1870, plenipotentiaries were sent from all the Southern States to Versailles for the purpose of bringing about the desired change. The result of the negotiations was that treaties were signed with Hessen and Baden on November 15; with Bavaria on November 23; and with Würtemberg on November 25. By these treaties, which afterwards received the approval of the North German Diet and the South German Parliaments, the Northern Confederation was changed into a *German Confederation*. This change was accompanied by another of great importance. On December 4 King *Lewis II.* of Bavaria proposed to the other German sovereigns, and to the Senates of the three free towns, that the President of the Confederation should receive the title of *German Emperor*. The proposal being agreed to, King William was, on January 18, 1871, in the hall of Mirrors in the palace of Versailles, in presence of a brilliant company of German princes and representatives of the army, solemnly proclaimed Emperor in Germany.

28. **Peace of Frankfurt.**—On the following day—the very day on which Faidherbe was defeated at St. Quentin—the French made a last attempt to escape from Paris; but their plans were ill arranged, and they were driven back with heavy loss. The Government of the National Defence, feeling that further resistance was now impossible, opened negotiations with a view to peace. On January 28, Paris formally surrendered; and an armistice for three weeks was concluded, which, however, did not apply to the military operations in the eastern provinces. The preliminaries of peace were signed on February 26 by Count Bismarck and the South German plenipotentiaries on the one hand, and by MM. *Thiers* and *Favre* on the other. According to these, France ceded to the German Empire the province of Elsass (excluding *Belfort*) and German Lorraine (including *Metz* and *Thionville*); and undertook to pay 5,000 millions of francs as an indemnity for the expenses of the war. On March 1 a portion of the German troops entered Paris and occupied a small part of it; but two days afterwards they left it, the National Assembly at Bordeaux having already ratified the preliminaries of peace. The German and French plenipotentiaries, who met at *Brussels* on March 27 for the purpose of concluding a treaty, could not come to an agreement on various points. The delay caused by the misunderstandings, and the troubled state of France, gave rise to an uneasy feeling in Germany. Count Bismarck, therefore, himself interfered, and on May 6 met M. Favre at *Frankfurt*. Here a treaty was formally signed on the 10th; and it was afterwards ratified by the German and French Governments. The treaty of Frankfurt differed only in details from the preliminaries which had before been concluded. The district round Belfort was yielded to the French; but in return the latter ceded some additional territory in Lorraine.

**29. Feeling of the Germans as to the War.**—The German people were displeased that France was allowed to keep Belfort; but on the whole they regarded the results of the war with pride and pleasure. The ancient military fame of Germany had been more than maintained; the Fatherland had been united; and the national sentiment was gratified by the conquest of the long-lost provinces of Elsass and Lorraine, which would henceforth form a defence against French attacks. The Austro-Prussian war had raised Prussia to the first place in Germany; the present war raised Germany to the first place in Europe.

**30. Constitution of the Empire.**—The Emperor had left Versailles on March 7. Ten days afterwards he entered Berlin; and on March 21 the first Diet of the new Empire was opened. The first object of the Diet was to adapt the constitution to the altered circumstances of Germany. In less than a month this task was completed. Except that it is more extended in its application, the new constitution is essentially the same as that of the North German Confederation. Including the three free towns, the Empire consists of twenty-five States. Each of these regulates its own affairs in so far as they do not affect those of other States, and is allowed to send and receive diplomatic representatives. What concerns the whole country is left to the Imperial Government. In joining the Confederation, Bavaria and Würtemberg retained many important rights; but the whole tendency of future events must be to limit the action of individual Governments, and to place greater power in the hands of the Imperial authorities. The duties of legislation rest with the Federal Council and the Diet; the executive power is wielded by the Emperor. He has the right to declare war and to make peace, to form alliances and to conclude treaties. He is represented by the *Imperial Chancellor*, whom he appoints, and who presides in the Federal Council and guides the course of public business. The Imperial Chancellor is also the Minister for Foreign Affairs.

31. **Condition of Germany.**—The German Empire must not be confounded with the Empire which ceased to exist in 1806. It is the restoration of the old German Kingdom rather than of the Holy Roman Empire. Some fear lest Prussia should become too powerful, and the various German States be moulded too much after one pattern. But influences remain to prevent such a result. All the States are united under one head for great national ends; but each has a certain individuality of its own, whose roots are in some cases to be found in the distant past. Bavaria, Würtemberg, Baden, Saxony, and the other minor States have each a history as distinct, although not so important, as that of Prussia. Unity, which patriots so long strove to win, has been obtained; but it will always be unity in variety.

32. **Scientific and Literary Writers.**—During the present century Germany has maintained the high place in science, literature, and art which she had previously won for herself. No other country has an intellectual life so rich and many-sided. It would be impossible to give here the names of even the chief writers of recent times. In theology and Biblical criticism we find, among many other names, those of *Schleiermacher, De Wette, Neander, Ewald, Baur, Zeller,* and *Strauss. Hegel* is generally regarded as the most illustrious German philosopher after Kant. He founded a powerful school, which is now split up into different parties. *Schopenhauer, Herbart,* and *Beneke* also wrote well-known philosophical works. Every department of physical science has received new developments during the present century in Germany. In his "Kosmos," *Alexander von Humboldt* presented a connected view of

the great forces of nature which, for width of knowledge and clearness of exposition, has never been surpassed. *Ritter* stands at the head of German geographers. Among the astronomers of Germany may be named *Zach, Enke,* and *Gauss. Oken* made great discoveries in natural history. *Müller, Liebig, Helmholtz, Mayer, Bunsen, Kirchhoff, Haeckel,* are only a few out of many whose names are associated with scientific work of the highest order. The world may be said to owe the science of language to Germany. Among the greatest cultivators of this science may be named the brothers *Grimm, Bopp,* and *Pott. Wolf, K. O. Müller, Hermann, Böckh,* and *Bekker* are well known for their services to classical scholarship. *Ranke, Schlosser, Leo, Gervinus, Dahlmann, Häusser, von Sybel, Mommsen, Curtius, Waitz,* are among the most distinguished German historians. In imaginative literature, the *Romantic School* long held a leading place. Its greatest representatives were the brothers *Schlegel, Tieck,* and *Hardenberg (Novalis).* It conferred great benefits on Germany by opening to it the treasures of its own ancient literature. Somewhat different from the older members of the Romantic School, but cultivating a similar spirit, were the well known writers, *Chamisso, de la Motte Fouqué, von Arnim, Clemens Brentano,* and *Immermann. Platen* was a classicist. *Rückert* began his career as a national poet during the war of liberation; but he afterwards chose a wide variety of subjects. *Uhland* devoted himself chiefly to ballad and romantic poetry. Probably the most brilliant poet since Goethe was *Heinrich Heine,* the liveliest, wittiest, most sarcastic, and most unscrupulous of all German writers. Around him a school was formed, called *Young Germany,* represented, amongst others, by *Laube* and *Gutzkow. Anastasius Grün, Herwegh,* and *Freiligrath* are poets more or less in sympathy with this school. In German as in English literature, novels have taken a very prominent place during the present century. *Gutzkow, Auerbach, Freytag, Hackländer, Spielhagen,* and *Heyse* are among the most successful recent novelists.

33. **German Artists.**—German art is scarcely less rich in great names than German literature and science. In architecture the name of *Schinkel* is well known; in sculpture, those of *Rauch* and *Rietschel;* in painting, those of *Overbeck, Cornelius* and *Kaulbach.* The chief musical composers during the present century have been *Beethoven, Weber, Meyerbeer, Schubert, Mendelssohn-Bartholdy,* and *Schumann.*

# INDEX.

## A.

Aachen, the favourite city of Charles the Great, 36; coronations to take place at, 105; treaties concluded at, 163, 177.
Abderrhaman, 34.
Aetius, 18, 19.
Adalbert, Archbishop of Bremen, 63.
Adelheid, Otto I. marries, 50.
Adolf, King, 97.
Ædui, the, 11.
Agilolfings, the, 24.
Agnes, the regency of, 62.
Albert I., 98.
Albert II., 113.
Albert the Bear, 73.
Albert the Degenerate, 97.
Alemanni, the, 17, 22, 23, 41.
Alfonso, of Castile, elected King of the Romans, 94.
Anastasius, 22.
Anastasius Grün, 209.
Ancient Germany, character of, 3; tribes in, 3; groups of tribes in, 4; classes of men in, 5; villages and Hundreds in, 7; chiefs in, 7; the Comitatus in, 7; meetings of the people in, 8; the army in, 9; religion in, 9.
Anhalt, Bernard of, 77; Christian of, 153.
Arabs, defeat of the, by Charles Martel, 29.
Archduke, the title of, confirmed to the House of Austria, 114.
Ariovistus, 11.
Aristocracy, rise of a new Frankish, 27.
Arminius 13, 14.
Army, the, in ancient Germany, 9; Germans in the Roman, 11; the Prussian, reorganized, 210, 211, 245.

Arndt, 221, 225.
Arnulf, Bishop of Metz, 23.
Arnulf, King, 41; crowned Emperor, 41.
Astrology, believed in, 161.
Attila, 19.
Auerbach, 270.
Auerstadt, battle of, 205.
Augsburg, the Diet of, in 1530, 138; confession, the, 138; the religious peace of, 143.
Augustus II., King of Poland, 167.
Augustus III., King of Poland, 171, 173.
Aulic Council, the, 120, 160.
Aurelius, Marcus, 15.
Ausbürger, 90.
Austerlitz, battle of, 201.
Austrasia, 24.
Austria, the Mark of, 35; given to Leopold I., 54; made a duchy, 75; Styria united to, 87; falls to the house of Habsburg, 96; wars of, with France, 163-171; wars of, with Prussia, 175-188, 194-218; gain of, by first partition of Poland, 190; gain of, by second and third partitions of Poland, 196; the relation of, to Germany, 235; the Revolution in, 1848-9, 229, 233, 234; disputes between, and Prussia, 248; prepares for war with Prussia, 249; war with Prussia, 251.
Axel Oxenstiern, 156, 157.

## B.

Babenberg, the house of, 54, 87.
Bach, 222.
Baden, Peace of, 170; the Margrave of, made an Elector, 200; insurrection in, 237.

Baner, General, 157.
Basel, the council of, 113; treaty of, 196.
Batavians, the, 4, 14.
Baur, 268.
Bavaria, 18, 23, 24, 34, 37, 46, 48; taken from Henry the Lion, 77; made a kingdom, 201; becomes part of German Empire, 265.
Bavarian succession, war of the, 121.
Beethoven, 270.
Bekker, 269.
Benedek, Marshal, 253.
Benedict XII., 100.
Benefices, 25.
Berengar, 50.
Berlichingen, Götz von, 135.
Berlin, first mentioned, 73; Buonaparte in, 206.
Bernadotte, 212, 214.
Bernard, Duke of Weimar, 157.
Bertha, Henry IV.'s queen, 63.
Bible, Luther's translation of, 134, 145.
Bismarck-Schönhausen, 245, 248, 249, 250, 257, 258, 266.
Blenheim, battle of, 169.
Blücher, 206, 211, 213, 216, 217, 218.
Böckh, 269.
Boehm, Jacob, 160.
Bohemia, wars of Charles the Great with, 36; the Duke of, made King, 75; falls to the house of Luxemburg, 98; the doctrines of Wycliffe in, 109; war in, 110; Sigmund receives the crown of, 110; disturbances in, 151; Frederick V. of the Palatinate chosen King of, 152; severely punished by Ferdinand II., 152.
Boleslaw Chrobry, 54.
Boniface, Saint, 30.
Bopp, 269.
Bora, Catherine of, 134.
Boso, Duke, 40.
Brandenburg, given to Frederick, Count of Hohenzollern, 111.
Breitenfeld, battle of, 156.
Bremen, the seat of an archbishoprick, 40.
Bructeri, the, 3.
Bull, the Golden, 105.
Bunsen, 269.
Büren, Frederick of, 67.
Burgrave, the, 56.
Burgundians, the, 4, 16, 17.
Burgundy, 24, 59, 61, 75, 84, 105, 117.

## C

Cæsar, Caius Julius, 11.
Cambray, the League of, 120; Peace of, 133.
Campo Formio, Peace of, 198.
Canossa, humiliation of Henry IV. at, 67.
Carinthia, 35; falls to the house of Austria, 106.
Carlman, 29, 30.
Casimir IV., King of Poland, 118.
Castles, the building of, 55.
Catherine II., of Russia, 187.
Cerealis, 15.
Chamisso, 209.
Charles the Great, conquers the Saxons, 33; conquers the Lombards, 33; conquers part of Spain, 34; deposes the Duke of Bavaria, 34; conquers the Avars, 34; his government, 35; is crowned Roman Emperor, 36; the extent of his Empire, 36; his death, 37.
Charles the Bald, 37, 38, 39, 40.
Charles the Fat, the great Empire of, 40; deposed, 40.
Charles IV., elected King, 102: crowned Emperor, 105; crowned King of Burgundy, 105; grants the Golden Bull, 105; adds to his hereditary lands, 106; founds the University of Prague, 106; his death, 106.
Charles V., elected King of the Romans, 127; decides to uphold the Reformation, 131; holds the Diet of Worms, 1521, 132; his wars with Francis I. of France, 133; holds the Diet of Augsburg, 1530, 138; condemns the Lutheran heresy, 138; grants the Religious Peace of Nürnberg, 139; his expeditions against Hayraddin Barbarossa, 139; renewed wars with Francis I. of France, 139; defeats the Schmalkaldic League, 141; proclaims the Interim, 141; has to fly from Maurice of Saxony, 143; signs the Treaty of Passau, 143; makes war on Henry II. of France, 143; abdicates, 144; his death, 144.
Charles VI., ascends the throne, 170; his Pragmatic Sanction, 171; gives up Lorraine, 171.
Charles VII., 176, 177.
Charles the Bold, 116, 117.
Charles, of Lorraine, 165, 176, 180.

# INDEX.

Chatti, the, 3; defeat of, by Drusus, 12.
Cherusci, the, 3.
Chiefs in ancient Germany, 7.
Childeric, King, 20.
Childeric III., dethroned, 30.
Chlodio, King, 19.
Chlodwig, King, 20; conquers Gaul, 21; causes of success of, 21; unites all Frankish tribes, 22; lands seized by, 22; successors of, 23.
Christian IV., of Denmark, 153, 154.
Church, power of the, 43, 56.
Circles, Germany divided into, 122.
Civilis Claudius, 14.
Clemens Brentano, 269.
Closterseven, convention of, 181.
Clothair I., 23.
Code, the Salic, 17.
Comitatus, the 7, 20.
Condé, General, 157.
Confederation, the Swabian, 118; the German, 219, 231, 241, 246, .250; the North German, 256, 257.
Confederation of the Rhine, the, 202.
Conrad I., 45.
Conrad II., elected King, 59; his wise government, 59; becomes King of Burgundy, 59; his wars, 60; his Edict, 61; his death, 61.
Conrad III., elected King, 73; war with Henry the Proud, 73; joins the second Crusade, 74.
Conrad IV., 81, 82.
Conrad, son-in-law of Otto I., 49, 50.
Constance, wife of Henry VI., 78.
Constantine, 18.
Constanz, the council of, 108.
Cornelius, 270.
Corvinus, Matthias, 115, 117.
Counts, 20, 24.
Crefeld, battle of, 182.
Crespy, the peace of, 139.
Crusade, the second, 74; the third, 77.
Cumberland, the Duke of, 181.
Curtius, 269.
Customs Union, the, 226.
Customs Parliament, the, 257.
Czaslau, battle of, 176.

## D.

Dahlmann, 269.
Daun, Marshal, 180, 183, 186.
Denmark, Charles the Great and, 36; Henry I. and, 47; Otto I. and, 49; Otto II. and, 53; Frederick I. and, 75; becomes independent of German Kings, 84; wars with, 231, 241, 247.
De la Motte Fouqué, 269.
Dettingen, battle of, 177.
Dessau, Leopold of, 170.
De Wette, 268.
Diet, the, 44; made up of three colleges, 125; made a permanent body, 160; its powerlessness, 160.
Diets, provincial, 124.
Donauwerth, battle of, 169.
Donar, 9.
Dresden, peace of, 177.
Drusus, 12.
Duchies, fall of the, 85.
Dukes, 24; position of, as feudal lords, 42.
Dürer, Albert, 145.
Dutch, origin of word, 2; High and Low, 2.

## E.

Eadgyth, or Edith, wife of Otto I., 48.
East Pomerania, ceded to the Elector of Brandenburg, 159.
Ebroin, 28.
Ecclesiastical Reservation, the, 144.
Eidgenossen, the, 102, 109, 116, 121.
Electors, the seven, 84.
Electoral League, the first, 101.
Elizabeth, St., of Hungary, 86.
Elizabeth, of Russia, 187.
Empire, connexion of Germany with the, 51, 83, 85; fall of the, 202.
"Emperor Elect," title of, taken by Maximilian I., 122.
"Emperor of Austria," 203.
England, alliance of Prussia with, 179; alliance of, with Austria and Russia, 198, 200.
Enke, 269.
Eormenric, 16.
Erfurt Parliament, the, 239.
Ernst August, of Hanover, 227.
Ernst, Duke, 60.
Eugene, Prince, 168, 169, 170, 171.
Ewald, 268.

## F.

Family, the, in ancient Germany, 6.
Favre, M., 266.

# INDEX.

Fehrbellin, battle of, 164.
Femgerichte, the, 91.
Ferdinand I., founder of the Austrian branch of the House of Habsburg, 133; becomes King of Bohemia and Hungary, 136; elected King of the Romans, 138; takes title of Emperor without being crowned by the Pope, 147.
Ferdinand II., becomes coadjutor to Matthias, 150; his policy, 150, 151; crowned Emperor, 152; obtains the support of the Catholic League, 152; treats Bohemia with unexampled severity, 152; accepts the aid of Wallenstein, 154; issues the Edict of Restitution, 154; dismisses Wallenstein, 155; appeals to him for help, 155; rewards his murderers, 157; death of Ferdinand, 157.
Ferdinand III., 157.
Ferdinand, Emperor of Austria, 227, 234.
Ferdinand, Duke of Brunswick, 194, 205.
Feudalism in Germany, 25, 42.
Fink, surrender of, 185.
Flemming, Paul, 161.
Fleurus, battle of, 195.
Fontenay, the battle of, 38.
France, Burgundy and, 84, 117; Charles V. and, 133, 139, 143; gains by the Peace of Westphalia, 158; wars with, 163-171, 176-177, 179-188, 194-218, 257-266.
Francia, East, 41.
Francis I., 129, 133, 177.
Francis II., 194; resigns the Imperial crown, 202.
Francis I. of Austria, 227.
Francis Joseph, Emperor of Austria, 234; summons Congress of princes, 246.
Frankfurt, election of Emperors at, 105; riot at, in 1833, 226; the provisional Parliament in, 230; the National Assembly in, 230, 232, 233, 235, 236; the Peace of, 266.
Franks, the, 17, 18-24; Dukes of the, 29; separation of East and West, 41.
Franz von Sickingen, 134.
Frederick I. (Barbarossa), elected King, 75; his expeditions to Italy, 75; makes his vassal Kings do homage, 75; becomes King of Burgundy, 75; his home government, 76; takes Bavaria from Henry the Lion, 76; divides Saxony, 77;
joins the third Crusade, 77; his death, 77; legend regarding, 77.
Frederick II., crowned King, 80; his character, 80; absence of, from Germany, 80; rebellion of his son Henry, 80; marries Isabella, 81; sets up an Imperial Tribunal, 81; his struggle with the Papacy, 81; his death, 82.
Frederick the Fair, 99.
Frederick III., sides with the Pope against the Council of Basel and the princes, 113; concludes the Concordat of Vienna, 114; confirms to the house of Austria the title of Archduke, 114; fails to obtain the Bohemian and Hungarian crowns, 115; difficulties with his Austrian subjects, 116; his relations to Charles the Bold, 117; driven from Austria by Matthias Corvinus, 117; his death, 118.
Frederick I., of Prussia, 167, 173.
Frederick II., of Prussia, youth of, 174; enters on the First Silesian war, 175; carries on the Second Silesian war, 177; acknowledges Francis I., 177; his life during years of peace, 178; concludes an alliance with England, 178; begins the Seven Years' War, 179; his victories and defeats, 179-188; his alliance with the Russians, 187; concludes the peace of Hubertusburg, 189; his home government, 189; takes part in the first partition of Poland, 190; sides against Joseph II., 190; forms a League to preserve the Imperial constitution, 191; his death, 191.
Frederick William I., of Prussia, 174.
Frederick William II., of Prussia, 191, 194, 204.
Frederick William III., of Prussia, ascends the throne, 204; his army defeated at Jena, 205; appeals to the youth of Prussia, 211; concludes an alliance with the Emperor of Russia, 211; enters Leipzig, 215; sets up provincial Diets, 224; his death, 227.
Frederick William IV., of Prussia, high expectations with regard to, 228; summons a united Diet, 228; his conduct in the disturbances at Berlin, 230; refuses the title of Emperor, 256; sets up constitutional government, 238; forms the

"German Union," 239; agrees to the restoration of the Diet, 241; his death, 245.
Frederick V., of the Palatinate, becomes King of Bohemia, 152; his army defeated, 152; his flight, 152.
Frederick of the Rhenish Palatinate, war against, 115.
Frederick, Elector of Saxony, 133.
Freemen, in ancient Germany, 5; decrease of numbers of, 42.
Free towns, decay of, 163.
Freiligrath, 269.
French Revolution, the, 193.
Freytag, 270.
Friends of Light, 228.
Frisians, the, 17, 29, 30.

## G.

Gastein, Convention of, 248.
Gaus, 7.
Gauss, 269.
Gefolge, the, 7, 20, 26.
Gellert, 220.
George I., of England, 167.
George II., of England, 177.
Gerbert, 54.
Gerhardt, Paul, 161.
German, origin of word, 2.
Germans, relations of, to surrounding peoples, 2; High and Low, 2; character of, in ancient times, 5; classes of ancient, 5; conversion of, 30.
German Catholics, 228.
German Empire, constitution of the, 267.
Germanicus, 13.
Gilds, 57, 89, 125.
Ghibelins, 74.
Gneisenau, 210.
Goethe, 221.
Görgey, General, 237, 238.
Goths, the, 4, 16, 18; the East, 16; the West, 16.
Gothic architecture, 92.
Granson, battle of, 116.
Graudenz, Courbière in, 206.
Great German party, the, 235, 244.
Great Elector, the, 163, 164.
Gregory VII., 65, 66.
Grimm, the brothers, 227, 269.
Gudrun, 93.
Gustavus Adolphus, comes to the aid of the Protestants, 155; defeats Tilly at Breitenfeld, 156; enters Munich in triumph, 156; tries to force Wallenstein to an engagement, 156; is killed, 156.
Gutzkow, 269, 270.

## H.

Habsburg, the Counts of, 87; the house of, receives Austria, 96; receives Carinthia, 106; receives Tyrol, 106; Austrian and Spanish branches of the house of. 133; extinction of the male line of the house of, 171.
Hackländer, 270.
Haeckel, 269.
Hamburg, burned by the Northmen, 40.
Händel, 222.
Hanno, Archbishop of Köln, 62.
Hanover, seized by Buonaparte, 200; overrun by the Prussians, 252; annexed to Prussia, 255.
Hansa, the, 89, 125, 158.
Hans Sachs, 145.
Harold Blue Tooth, 49.
Haugwitz, 210.
Häusser, 269.
Haydn, 222.
Hayraddin Barbarossa, 139.
Hegel, 220, 268.
Heidelberg, castle of, destroyed, 166.
Heine, Heinrich, 269.
Heliand, the, 44.
Helmholtz, 269.
Henry I., elected King, 46; defeats the Hungarians, 46; seizes Lotharingia, 47; builds towns, 47.
Henry II., 54; his war with Boleslaw Chrobry, 54; his kindness to the Church, 55.
Henry III., increases the royal power, 61; proclaims a General Peace, 61; defeats the Hungarians, 62; deposes and creates Popes, 62; his death, 62.
Henry IV., his youth, 63; offends the Saxons, 63; his war with the Saxons, 64; his quarrel with Gregory VII., 65; humbled by Gregory VII., 66; his war with Rudolf of Swabia, 67; the Saxons submit to him, 68; rebellion of his sons, 68; his death, 68.
Henry V., struggle of, with the Papacy, 69; concludes the Concordat of Worms, 69; his difficulties in Germany, 69.

Henry VI., his efforts to conquer Sicily, 78; Richard I. of England and, 78; tries to make the crown hereditary, 79.
Henry VII., elected King, 98; secures Bohemia for his son, 98; becomes Emperor, 99; his death, 99.
Henry the Wrangler, 52.
Henry the Proud, 70, 73.
Henry the Lion, 73, 74, 76, 77.
Henry Raspe, 82.
Henry, Prince of Prussia, 187, 188.
Henry II., of France, 142, 143.
Henry VIII., of England, 120, 129.
Herder, 221.
Hermann Billung, 49.
Hermann, 269.
Herminones, the, 4, 18.
Herstall, Pippin of, 28.
Herwegh, 269.
Herzog, the, 9.
Hessen-Cassel, the Landgrave of, made an Elector, 200; dispute between Elector of, and Chambers, 240; overrun by the Prussians, 252; annexed to Prussia, 255.
Heyse, 270.
Hoche, General, 195.
Hochkirchen, battle of, 182.
Hofer, 209.
Hohenlinden, battle of, 199.
Hohenzollern, the Counts of, 87; the house of, receives Brandenburg, 111.
Holbein, Hans, 145.
Holy League, the, 120.
Horn, General, 157.
Hroswitha, 57.
Hubertusburg, Peace of, 188.
Humanists, the, 126, 130.
Humboldt, Wilhelm von, 210.
Humboldt, Alexander von, 268.
Hundreds, 7.
Hungarians, wars of the, with Lewis the Child, 41; defeated by Henry I., 47; defeated by Otto I., 50; defeated by Henry III., 61.
Hungary, shakes off allegiance to the German Kings, 84; Ferdinand I. becomes King of, 136; rebellion of, against Leopold I., 165; crown of, made hereditary, 166; revolt of, against Joseph II., 192; Revolution in, 1848-9, 234, 237, 238.
Huniades, John, 115.
Huns, the, 16.
Huss, John, 109, 110.
Hussite War, the, 110.

I.

Immermann, 269.
Imperial Chamber, the, 119.
Ingaevones, the, 4, 18.
Inheritance, laws of, 87.
Innocent III., 79.
Innocent IV., 81.
Innocent X., 158.
International Law, 160.
Interim, the, 141.
Interregnum, the, 94.
Irminsul, destroyed, 33.
Isabella, sister of Henry III. of England, 81.
Istaevones, the, 4, 18.
Italy, partial union of, 244; alliance between Prussia and, 250.

J.

James I., of England, 152, 153.
Jemmappes, battle of, 194.
Jena, battle of, 205.
Jellachich, of Croatia, 25.
Jerome, of Prague, 110.
Jesuits, the, 147.
Jews, persecution of the, 105.
Joanna, the Infanta, 119.
John XXII., 100.
John XXIII., 108, 109.
John, King of Bohemia, 98.
John, Elector of Saxony, 134, 138.
John, Waiwode of Transsilvania, 136.
John Frederick, Elector of Saxony, 141.
John, of Austria, elected head of the Provincial Central Government, 231.
Joseph I., 169, 170.
Joseph II., elected Emperor, 189; his government of his hereditary dominions, 190, 191; failure of his schemes, 192; his death, 192.
Jourdan, General, 195, 197, 198.
Julian, 18, 19.
Jülich-Cleve, 149, 163.

K.

Kaiserslautern, 195, 196.
Kant, 220.
Karolingia, 38.
Karolingian Empire, extent of the, under Charles the Great, 36; broken up, 40.

# INDEX. 277

Katzbach, battle of the, 213.
Kaulbach, 270.
Keith, Marshal, 182.
Kelper, John, 160.
"King of the Romans," 55, 78, 94.
"King of Germany," title of, taken by Maximilian I., 122.
Kings, in ancient Germany, 7; position of the feudal German, 43; revenue of the German, 44; loss of power by the German, 70, 83, 145; the German, and their hereditary lands, 102; position of the German, in consequence of great hereditary possessions, 124.
Kirchhoff, 269.
Klopstock, 220.
Knighthood, 88.
Köln, cathedral of, 92, 227.
Königgrätz, battle of, 253, 254.
Königsberg, founded, 83.
Körner, 221.
Kosciuszko, 196.
Kotzebue, 225.
Kranach, Lucas, 145.
Kunersdorf, battle of, 184.

## L.

Ladislaus, son of Albert II., 115.
Landsturm, the, 211.
Landwehr, the Prussian, 211; the Austrian, 207.
Landen, Pippin of, 28.
Laube, 269.
League, the Rhenish, 89; the Hanseatic, 89, 125, 158; the old, of High Germany, 103; the Swabian, 107; the Catholic, 149.
Learning, under the Ottos, 57; revival of, 126.
Leibnitz, 220.
Leipzig, battle of, 213.
Leo, 269.
Leo X., 129; his Bull burned, 131.
Leoben, preliminaries of Peace signed at, 198.
Leopold I., wars of, with Lewis XIV., 164, 166, 168, 169; consents to recognise Frederick I. as King of Prussia, 167.
Leopold II., 192, 194.
Lessing, 221.
Leszczynski, 171.
Letter of Majesty, the, 149.
Leuthen, battle of, 182.
Lewis the German, 37, 38, 39, 40.

Lewis the Pious, crowned during his father's lifetime, 37; afterwards crowned by Pope Stephen III., 37; rebellions of his sons, 37.
Lewis the Child, 41; pays tribute to the Hungarians, 42.
Lewis IV., war of, with Frederick the Fair, 99; quarrel with Pope John XXII., 100; becomes sole King, and is crowned Emperor, 100; is supported by his subjects against the Popes, 100; offends the princes, 101; his death, 102.
Lewis I., of Bavaria, 226.
Lewis II., of Bavaria, 265.
Lewis XIV., of France, makes war on the United Provinces, 163; wars of, with Leopold I., 164, 166, 168, 169 seizes Strassburg, 164; stirs up the Hungarians and Turks against Leopold I., 165.
Liebig, 269.
Liegnitz, battle of, 186.
Liti, the, 5.
Lodi, battle of, 197.
Lombard cities, Frederick I. and the, 75; Frederick II. and the, 80.
Lombards, 4, 17; conquest of, by Charles the Great, 33; Charles the Great becomes King of the, 34; Otto I. becomes King of the, 50.
Lorraine, district in, seized by Henry II. of France, 142; given up by Charles VI., 171.
Lothar, the Emperor, 37, 38, 70.
Lotharingia, 38; seized by Henry I., 47; divided into two-Duchies, 58.
Loudon, Marshal, 183, 186, 187.
Lowositz, battle of, 179.
Lunéville, peace of, 199.
Luther, Martin, opposes Tetzel, 129; his thesis, 129; is excommunicated, 131; burns the Pope's Bull, 131; appears before the Diet of Worms, 132; his stay at the Wartburg, 133; his marriage, 134; his controversy with Zwingli, 137; his death, 141.
Lützen, the battle of, 156.
Luxemburg, Emperors of the house of, 98, 104-111; France desires to purchase, 256.

## M.

Mack, surrender, of, 201.
Magdeburg, archbishoprick of, 49; the sack of, 155.

Mainz, the see of, 30, 43, 56, 200; given to Lewis the German, 38; the French in, 195.
Malplaquet, battle of, 170.
Mannus, 5.
Mansfeld, Count, 151, 153, 154.
Marcomanni, the, 4, 12, 15, 18.
Marcomannic War, the, 15.
Marchfield, the, 24.
Margaret Maultasch, 101, 106.
Margraves, 35.
Margraves' War, the, 115.
Marengo, battle of, 199.
Maria Theresa, pragmatic sanction in favour of, 171; claims of, to the Austrian inheritance, disputed, 173; appeals to Hungary, 176; concludes peace with Frederick II., 176, 177; her regret for the loss of Silesia, 178; conduct of her troops during the Seven Years' War, 179-188; her death, 190.
Marlborough, the Duke of, 169, 170.
Maroboduus, 14.
Marsi, the, 3; defeated by Germanicus, 13.
Martel, Charles, 29.
Martin, cousin of Pippin of Herstall, 28.
Mary, daughter of Charles the Bold, 117.
Matricula, the, 133.
Matthias, acknowledged as head of the house of Austria, 148; crowned Emperor, 150; his feeble government, 150.
Maurice, Duke of Saxony, 140, 142, 143.
Maximilian I., marriage of, with Mary, 117; power of, 118; obtains Joanna as a wife for his son Philip, 119; holds a Diet at Worms, 1495, 119; sets up the Imperial Chamber, 119; joins the League of Cambray, 120; helps the Holy League, 120; serves under Henry VIII. at Terouenne, 120; makes war on the Swiss League, 121; carries on the war of the Bavarian succession, 121; takes the titles of "Emperor Elect" and "King of Germany," 122; divides Germany into Circles, 122; sets up the Aulic Council, 122; his death, 123.
Maximilian II., 147.
Maximilian, Duke of Bavaria, 149, 153.
Maximilian, Emmanuel, Elector of Bavaria, 169.

Mayer, 269.
Mendelssohn-Bartholdy, 270.
Melanchthon, 134, 138.
Merowig, King, 20.
Merowingians, character of the, 24; household of the, 25; dethroned, 30.
Metternich, Prince, 212, 224.
Metz, seized by Henry II. of France, 142; surrender of, 263.
Meyerbeer, 270.
Middle Ages, end of the, 123.
Minden, battles of, 14, 183.
Minnesänger, the, 92.
Missi Dominici, 35.
Moguls, the, 81.
Moltke, Von, 252, 260, 262.
Molwitz, battle of, 175.
Mommsen, 269.
Montecuculi, General, 164.
Morat, the battle of, 116.
Moreau, 197.
Morgarten Pass, battle of, 103.
Mozart, 222.
Mühlberg, battle of, 141.
Müller, 269.
Müller, K. O., 269.
Munich, founded by Henry the Lion, 76; Gustavus Adolphus at, 156.
Murat, Joachim, 202.
Music, in Germany, 222, 270.

N.

Näfels, battle of, 107.
Napoleon Buonaparte, first victories of, 197; forces Austria to accept the peace of Campo Formio, 198; his campaign in Italy, 1800, 199; his contemptuous treatment of Germany, 200; defeats the allies, 1805, 201; forms the confederation of the Rhine, 202; his war with Prussia, 204-207; his war with Austria, 1809, 208; his war with Prussia, Russia, Austria, and Sweden, 211-216; his escape from Elba, 217; his final defeat, 218.
Napoleon III., declares war with Prussia, 258; surrenders to the King of Prussia, 262.
National Union, the, 244.
National Liberal party, the, 257.
Neander, 268.
Neerwinden, battle of, 195.
Nero, 14.
Netherlands, the house of Austria

## INDEX.

receives the, 117; Charles V. resigns the, to Philp, 144; Austria receives the Spanish, 170; revolt of the, against Joseph II., 192; Austria cedes the, to France, 198, 199.
Neustria, 24.
Nibelungenlied, the, 93.
Nicholas V., 100.
Niebuhr, 220.
Nobles, in ancient Germany, 5; feudal, 42; the lower class of, 70; increase of immediate, 85.
Noble houses, leading, 86.
Northmen, depredations by the, 38; burn Hamburg, 40; defeated by Arnulf, 41.
North German Confederation, the, 256, 257.
Novalis, 269.
Nürnberg, the Religious peace of, 139.

### O.

Oken, 269.
Opitz, Martin, 160.
Otto I., civil wars under, 48, 50; increases his power, 49; his wars, 49; first visit to Italy, 50; marries Queen Adelheid, 50; becomes King of the Lombards, 50; second visit to Italy, 51; is crowned Emperor, 51; his death, 52.
Otto II., crowned Emperor, 52; marries Theophanô, 52; marches to Paris, 53; goes to Italy, 53; his death, 53.
Otto III., 54.
Otto IV., 79.
Otto of Nordheim, 64, 65.
Ottocar, King of Bohemia, 83, 87, 95.
Oudenarde, battle of, 170.
Overbeck, 270.

### P.

Palace, Mayors of the, 26, 28.
Palatinate, overrun by French troops, 166.
Palsgraves, 26, 35; provincial, 52.
Papacy, Henry III. and the, 62; Henry IV. and the, 65, 66, 67, 68; Henry V. and the, 69; Lothar and the, 70; Frederick I. and the, 75, 76; Kings Philip and Otto and the, 79; Frederick II. and the, 80, 81; Lewis IV. and the, 100, 101.

Paris, attacked by the Northmen, 39; Peace of, 188; first Peace of, 216; second Peace of, 218; besieged, 53, 263.
Partition of Poland, the first, 189; the second, 196; the third, 196.
Paschal II., 69.
Passarowitz, Peace of, 171.
Passau, Treaty of, 143.
Patricians, the, 56, 125.
Pavia, battle of, 133.
Peace, General, proclaimed by Henry III., 61; proclaimed by the Diet, 118, 119.
Peasantry, the, 43, 125; war of the, 135.
People, Literature of the, 126.
Peter III., of Russia, 187.
Pfahlbürger, 90.
Philip, King, 79.
Philip, son of Maximilian I., 119.
Philip, Charles V.'s son, 142, 144.
Philip, Landgrave of Hessen, 134, 135, 141.
Pichegru, General, 195.
Pippin, of Landen, 28; of Herstall, 28.
Pippin the Short, 29; becomes King of the Franks, 30; defeats the Lombards, 32; is made Patrician, 32.
Pisa, the Council of, 108.
Pius VI., 191.
Plague, the, 105.
Platen, 269.
Podiebrad, George, 115, 116.
Poland, submission of, to German Kings, 49, 55, 60, 75; throws off allegiance to the German Kings, 84; the Teutonic Order and, 118; Prussia independent of, 163: partitions of, 189, 196.
Pope, the German Kings and the, 85.
"Potato War," the, 190.
Pott, 269.
Pragmatic Sanction, in favour of Maria Theresa, 171.
Prague, the University of, 106, 109: Peace of, 255.
Pressburg, Peace of, 201.
Princes, secular, 55; spiritual, 56; independence of the, 55, 70, 83, 114, 124, 144, 159, 163.
Private War, 43, 56.
Protestants, the Lutherans are called, 137.
Prussia, conquest of, 83: western part of, ceded to Casimir IV., 118:

Albert of Brandenburg becomes Duke of, 136; Duchy of, joined to Electorate of Brandenburg, 149; the Elector of Brandenburg becomes King of, 167; effect of Seven Years' War on the position of, 188, 189; gain of, by first partition of Poland, 190; gain of, by second and third partitions of Poland, 196; joins Austria against France, 194; humiliated by France, 205-207; war with France, 210-218; religious movements in, 228; the Revolution in, 1848-9, 229, 230, 233, 238; the National Assembly of, 233; constitutional government in, 238; relations of, to Austria and the German Confederation, 245; disputes between Austria and, 248; prepares for war with Austria, 249; war with Austria, 251; annexations to, 1866, 255; France declares war against, 258.

### Q.

Quadi, the, 4.
Quatre Bras, battle of, 217.

### R.

Ranke, 269.
Rastatt, Peace of, 170; congress opened at, 198.
Rauch, 270.
Reformation, beginnings of the, 129; causes of the, 130; Charles V. and the, 131; progress of the, 133; in Switzerland, 137; political effects of the, 144.
Renaissance Architecture, 145.
Restitution, the Edict of, 154.
Revolution, in 1830, 226; in 1848-9, 228-241.
Rhenish Bavaria, insurrection in, 237.
Richard, Earl of Cornwall, elected King of the Romans, 94.
Richard I. of England, and Henry VI., 78.
Richelieu, Cardinal, 157.
Richter, 221.
Rietschel, 270.
Ripuarians, the, 18.
Ritter, 269.
Roman law, in Germany, 125.
Romantic School, the, 269.

Romanesque, architecture, 57.
Rossbach, battle of, 181.
Rückert, 269.
Rüdiger, Count, 165.
Rudolf, of Swabia, 67.
Rudolf, of Habsburg, elected King, 95; his war with Ottocar, King of Bohemia, 95; secures Austria and the sister Duchies for his family, 96; his government, 96; his death, 97.
Rudolf II., 148, 149, 150.
Rudolf III., of Burgundy, 59.
Rugii, the, 4.
Rupert, King, 107.
Ryswick, peace of, 166.

### S.

Sachsen-Wittemberg, given to the Margrave of Meissen, 111.
Sachsenspiegel, the, 90.
Sackville, Lord George, 183.
Salians, the, 17.
Salic Code, the, 19.
Salzburg, the bishoprick of, made an archbishoprick, 34.
Sans Souci, 177.
Saxons, the, 17; conquered by Charles the Great, 33; Henry IV. offends the, 63; wars of, with Henry IV., 64, 67; submission of the, to Henry IV., 68.
Saxony, 41; taken from Henry the Lion, 77; made a kingdom, 201; disturbances in, 236; overrun by the Prussians, 252.
Saxe, Marshal, 177.
Scharnhorst, 210.
Schelling, 220.
Schiller, 221.
Schinkel, 270.
Schlegel, 269.
Schleiermacher, 268.
Schleswig-Holstein, 231, 241, 242, 246, 248.
Schlosser, 269.
Schmalkaldic League, formed, 138; defeated, 141.
Schönbrunn, battle of, 208.
Schubert, 270.
Schumann, 270.
Schwabenspiegel, the, 90.
Schwartzenberg, Prince, 212.
Schwerin, Marshal, 176, 180.
Schwyz, 102.
Sedan, battle of, 262.

Seidlitz, General, 181.
Semnones, the, 4.
Sempach, battle of, 107.
Sequani, the, 11.
Serfs, 43; the freeing of, 90.
Seven Years' War, the, 179-188.
Sicambri, the, 3.
Sicily, Henry VI. and the kingdom of, 78.
Sigmund, elected King, 108; at the Council of Constanz, 108; war with Bohemia, 110; receives the crown of Bohemia, 111; his death, 111.
Silesian School, the first, 161; the second, 220.
Silesian War, the first, 175; the second, 177.
Slaves, in ancient Germany, 5.
Slavonic lands, conquest of, 83.
Sobieski, John, 165.
Spanish Succession, war of the, 168.
Spielhagen, 270.
Stein, 210.
Strassburg, seized by Lewis XIV., 164.
Strauss, 268.
Suevi, the, 4.
Suleyman, the Sultan, 136, 139.
Swabia, 41, 48.
Sweden, concessions to, by Peace of Westphalia, 159.
Swiss League, the, and Maximilian I., 121.
Switzerland, the Reformation in, 137; independence of, acknowledged, 159.
Sword, the Knights of the, 83.

T.

Taborites, the, 111.
Tencteri, the, 3.
Testri, battle of, 28.
Tetzel, John, 129.
Teutonic Kingdom, the, 38.
Teutonic Order, the, conquers Prussia 83; defeated by Jagellon, 118; cedes to Casimir IV. the western part of Prussia, and does homage for the rest, 118; comes to an end as a sovereign power, 136.
Thassilo, 34.
Theudebert, 23.
Theodoric, the Great, 17, 18.
Theodoric, son of Chlodwig, 23.
Theophanô, 52, 53, 57.
Thiers, M., 266.

Thorn, Peace of, 118.
Thuisto, 5.
Thuringia, 18, 41, 64, 86.
Thurn, Count, 151.
Thusnelda, 13.
Tiberius, 12.
Tieck, 269.
Tilly, Count, 152, 153, 154, 155, 156.
Tilsit, peace of, 207.
Torgau, battle of, 186.
Torstenson, General, 157.
Towns, the building of, in time of Henry I., 47; growth of, 56; Free Imperial, 89, 125; Leagues of, 89.
Trent, Council of, 147.
Tribes, ancient, 3; groups of, 4, 17; wanderings of, 16.
Tribur, Assembly held at, 40.
Truce of God, the, 71.
Tyrol, falls to the house of Austria, 106.
Tyrolese, loyalty of the, 209.
Turenne, 157, 164.
Turks, threaten Germany, 114; driven back by the Hungarians, 115; the, in Maximilian I.'s time, 121; invasion of Austria by the, 165.

U.

Ubii, the, 4.
Uhland, 269.
Ulrich, Duke of Würtemberg, 140.
Ulrich von Hutten, 126, 130, 135.
Universities of Germany, 126.
United Diet, at Berlin, 228.
Union, the Protestant, 149; the German, 238.
United Provinces, independence of the, acknowledged, 159; war of the, with Lewis XIV., 163.
Usipetes, the, 3.
Utraquists, the, 111.

V.

Vandals, the, 4, 16.
Varus, Quinctilius, 12, 13.
Velleda, 14.
Verdun, the treaty of, 38.
Vienna, declared the capital, 98; the Concordat of, 114; Congress of, 216.
Villages, in ancient Germany, 7.
Voltaire, 178.
Von Arnim, 269.
Von Sybel, 269.

## W.

Wagram, battle of, 208.
Waiblings, 74.
Waitz, 269.
Wallenstein, Albert von, raises an army, 154; defeats the Protestant armies, 154; receives a check at Stralsund, 154; is dismissed, 155; is again summoned to the Emperor's aid, and raises a second army, 156; is defeated at Lützen, 156; is murdered, 157.
Wartburg, Luther at the, 133.
Wattignies, battle of, 195.
Waterloo, battle of, 217.
Weber, 270.
Wedel, General, 184.
Weinsberg, the women of, 73.
Weissenburg, battle of, 260.
Welau, treaty of, 163.
Welf, made Duke of Bavaria, 64.
Welfs, the, 74.
Wenceslaus, 106, 107.
Wergeld, the, 6, 20.
Westphalia, the Peace of, 158.
Widukind, resistance of, to Charles the Great, 33.
Wieland, 221.
William of Holland, 82, 94.
William I., of Prussia, mounts the throne, 245; his quarrel with Parliament, 245; signs the Gastein Convention, 248; assumes supreme command in the war with Austria, 253; is reconciled to Parliament, 256; his action with respect to French demands, 258; assumes supreme command in the war with France, 259; Napoleon surrenders to, 262; is declared Emperor, 265.
William III., of England, 166.
William IV., of England, 227.
Willibrord, 30.
Willigis, 53.
Wilfrith, 30.
Winfrith, 30.
Witchcraft, believed in, 161.
Wittelsbach, Otto of, 77.
Wladislaus, King of Bohemia and Hungary, 117.
Wodan, 9.
Wolf, Christian Freiherr von, 220.
Wolf, 269.
Worms, the Concordat of, 69; the Diet of, 1495, 119; the Diet of, 1521, 132.
Wörth, battle of, 260.
Wrangel, General, 157, 232.
Wurmser, Marshal, 195, 197.
Würtemberg, the Duke of, made an Elector, 200.
Wycliffe, the doctrines of, in Bohemia, 109.

## Z.

Zach, 269.
Zacharias, Pope, 30.
Zähringen, the house of, 87.
Zeller, 268.
Ziethen, General, 186.
Zisca, John, 110.
Zorndorf, battle of, 182.
Zwingli, Ulrich, 137.


THE END.

www.ingramcontent.com/pod-product-compliance
Lightning Source LLC
Chambersburg PA
CBHW032122230426
43672CB00009B/1828